Professional Development of International Teaching Assistants

Edited by Dorit Kaufman and
Barbara Brownworth

Case Studies in TESOL Practice Series

Jill Burton, Series Editor

Teachers of English to Speakers of Other Languages, Inc.

Typeset in Berkeley and Belwe
by Capitol Communication Systems, Inc., Crofton, Maryland USA
Printed by United Graphics, Inc., Mattoon, Illinois USA
Indexed by Coughlin Indexing, Annapolis, Maryland USA

Teachers of English to Speakers of Other Languages, Inc.
700 South Washington Street, Suite 200
Alexandria, Virginia 22314 USA
Tel. 703-836-0774 • Fax 703-836-6447 • E-mail info@tesol.org • http://www.tesol.org/

Managing Editor: Marilyn Kupetz
Copy Editor: Kelly Graham
Additional Reader: Sarah J. Duffy
Cover Design: Capitol Communication Systems, Inc.

ISBN 1931185271

Library of Congress Control Number 2005908945

Table of Contents

**PART 3: COLLABORATIVE PRACTICES AND
PARTNERSHIPS ACROSS DISCIPLINES**

Acknowledgments

Special thanks to our colleagues Jill Burton, Kelly Graham, and Marilyn Kupetz whose expertise and wisdom have enhanced this volume of ITA case studies. We thank them for their generosity of time and attention to detail. We dedicate this volume to our families and especially to Arie Kaufman and Thom Brownworth for their love and encouragement.

Dorit Kaufman and Barbara Brownworth

Series Editor's Preface

The Case Studies in TESOL Practice series offers innovative and effective examples of practice from the point of view of the practitioner. The series brings together from around the world communities of practitioners who have reflected and written on particular aspects of their teaching. Each volume in the series covers one specialized teaching focus.

◈ CASE STUDIES

Why a TESOL series focusing on case studies of teaching practice?

Much has been written about case studies and where they fit in a mainstream research tradition (e.g., Nunan, 1992; Stake, 1995; Yin, 1994). Perhaps more importantly, case studies also constitute a public recognition of the value of teachers' reflection on their practice and constitute a new form of teacher research—or teacher valuing. Case studies support teachers in valuing the uniqueness of their classes, learning from them, and showing how their experience and knowledge can be made accessible to other practitioners in simple, but disciplined ways. They are particularly suited to practitioners who want to understand and solve teaching problems in their own contexts.

These case studies are written by practitioners who are able to portray real experience by providing detailed descriptions of teaching practice. These qualities invest the cases with teacher credibility, and make them convincing and professionally interesting. The cases also represent multiple views and offer immediate solutions, thus providing perspective on the issues and examples of useful approaches. Informative by nature, they can provide an initial database for further, sustained research. Accessible to wider audiences than many traditional research reports, however, case studies have democratic appeal.

◈ HOW THIS SERIES CAN BE USED

The case studies lend themselves to pre- and in-service teacher education. Because the context of each case is described in detail, it is easy for readers to compare the cases with and evaluate them against their own circumstances. To respond to the wide range of language environments in which TESOL functions, cases have been selected from EFL, ESL, and bilingual education settings around the world.

The 12 or so case studies in each volume are easy to follow. Teacher writers describe their teaching context and analyze its distinctive features: the particular demands of their context, the issues they have encountered, how they have effectively addressed the issues, what they have learned. Each case study also offers readers practical suggestions—developed from teaching experience—to adapt and apply to their own teaching.

Already published or in preparation are volumes on

- academic writing programs
- action research
- assessment practices
- bilingual education
- community partnerships
- content-based language instruction
- distance learning
- English for specific purposes
- gender
- grammar teaching in teacher education
- intensive English programs
- interaction and language learning
- international teaching assistants
- journal writing
- literature in language learning
- mainstreaming
- teacher education
- teaching EFL in primary schools
- teaching English from a global perspective
- teaching literature
- technology in the classroom

◈ THIS VOLUME

Although of particular relevance to North America, this volume has much of interest for any educators in academic communication in English. *Professional Development of International Teaching Assistants* charts the development of international teaching assistant (ITA) programs, the support needs of ITAs, and the roles that students and other teaching staff can play in making university study productive at all levels.

Jill Burton
University of South Australia, Adelaide

CHAPTER 1

Collaborative Paradigms and Future Directions in International Teaching Assistant Professional Development

Dorit Kaufman and Barbara Brownworth

◈ INTRODUCTION

The influx of international students has greatly enriched the intellectual, sociolinguistic, and cultural diversity of English-speaking university campuses in recent years. These dramatic demographic shifts in universities in Australia, Britain, Canada, and the United States have also introduced challenges that have affected all aspects of the academic environment. In the United States, in particular, a significant percentage of all graduate students, including international students, serve as teaching assistants in undergraduate classes. They participate in a variety of activities that include teaching in lecture classes, leading small-group discussions and laboratory sessions, and advising students during office hours. The international teaching assistant (ITA) paradigm, so prevalent in the United States, is rare in universities in other parts of the world. This paradigm has enriched educational experiences on university campuses across the country, but it has also presented particular sociocultural, linguistic, and pedagogical challenges that have led to the emergence of a wide range of linguistic and professional development programs for ITAs in recent years.

The concept of the teaching assistant is not new in university education in the United States. Storr (1953, pp. 130–131) traces its roots to the 1850s. In 1876, Johns Hopkins University President Daniel C. Graham offered financial fellowships for outstanding scholars and initiated a trend that has significantly increased the population of graduate students in the United States. Several initiatives have also led to a significant increase in the undergraduate student population. These have included post-World War II incentives, an increase in student grant and loan programs in response to the launch of Sputnik, and passage of the Higher Education Act of 1965. The increased numbers of undergraduate students have undoubtedly provided a strong impetus for further promoting the ITA paradigm. Indeed, generous fellowships for graduate study have attracted a large number of international students and have led to an unprecedented growth in the number of international graduate students in U.S. universities. In 1976, the percentage of international students in U.S. universities was 5.5%. Within two decades, this percentage had almost doubled to 10.5% in 1996. In the 1999–2000 academic year, more than a third (38.2%) of all doctorates, and nearly half (48.9%) in the field of engineering, were awarded to international students (Borjas, 2005). The steady growth in the number of international students at U.S. colleges and universities peaked by the 2002–2003 academic year, with 586,323 (4.6%) students who came primarily from India, China, and Korea (IIE Open Doors, 2004).

◈ ITA DEVELOPMENT: A PROFESSIONAL COMMITMENT AND UNIVERSITY-WIDE ENDEAVOR

In the mid-1980s, the ITA model in U.S. universities encountered escalating opposition and dissatisfaction. It was perceived as a major problem by parents, administrators, and undergraduates. Demands for quality and accountability and growing ethnocentrism on the part of undergraduates had led to mounting discontent with the ITA paradigm and to calls for locally viable solutions to the "foreign TA problem" (Bailey, 1984, p. 3). The National Association for Foreign Student Affairs (NAFSA) publication by Bailey, Pialorsi, and Zukowski-Faust (1984), *Foreign Teaching Assistants in U.S. Universities,* was among the first of several volumes to include a collection of articles that focused on this issue and its effect on U.S. universities. The articles raised awareness of the ITAs' difficulty in adapting to the new country and to the U.S. academic culture and discussed the influence of their instruction on undergraduate students. The articles also described the early development of curricula as well as the emergence of initiatives to prepare ITAs and to improve their linguistic and classroom performance.

Over the past two decades, the so-called problem has evolved to become the ITA challenge. Since the mid-1980s, the ongoing influx of international students and the continued growth in the undergraduate student population have further exacerbated the situation and required the attention of university administrators at the highest levels. Mounting pressure from stakeholders, including parents and undergraduate students, combined with advocacy efforts by language educators have prompted universities to institute new mandates that place restrictions on ITAs' eligibility to assume teaching roles. These new policies have included assessment of language proficiency, preparation of teaching assistants before assigning them for teaching roles, and mentoring ITAs during their formative period as teaching assistants. Appointment of ITAs as teaching assistants has become increasingly contingent on their English language proficiency and on appropriate participation in programs designed to prepare them to teach undergraduate courses. On-campus assessment of ITAs using, for the most part, the Speaking Proficiency English Assessment Kit (SPEAK) test became mandatory when students had not taken the Test of Spoken English (TSE) prior to their arrival. A minimum passing score requirement on language proficiency tests became a primary condition before assigning teaching responsibilities to international students. Specially designed programs for ITA professional preparation, including courses for the development of language and communication skills, cross-cultural awareness, and mentoring, were established to provide the necessary support for international students.

Diversification in the demographics of undergraduate students, due to growth in immigration trends, and the increase in the number of nonnative English speakers focused attention on the need for improving cross-cultural awareness among all faculty, teaching assistants, and students on university campuses. Preparation of all teaching assistants has become a university-wide concern and challenge. Growing heterogeneity at universities has raised awareness of the need for greater openness to negotiating divergent discourses and cultural differences. Consequently, new programs for preparing native-English-speaking (NES) and nonnative-English-speaking (NNES) teaching assistants have emerged. Great strides have also been made in increasing understanding of the issues involved in ITA assessment and linguistic and pedagogical preparation. Noteworthy growth has also occurred in university administrative commitment and resource allocation for establishing and maintaining programs to increase ITAs' English language and communication skills and to prepare them for their instructional tasks.

An important step in professionalizing the ITA domain took place in 1993, when TESOL's ITA Interest Section was granted full status after it was first established with interim status at the 1992 TESOL convention. The ITA Interest Section serves as the primary professional networking group for TESOL members who work with ITAs as researchers, teachers, and program administrators and who focus on issues related to ITAs' acculturation and professional development. The establishment of this interest section has given greater visibility to the issues related to ITA professional development and has recognized the professional contribution of ITA specialists and the unique perspective that they bring to TESOL. The interest group has provided a forum for networking and channels for communication and peer support not only at the annual convention but also through electronic media and professional literature. Furthermore, it has sponsored a range of activities that include research presentations, academic sessions, and discussion groups at the annual international convention and preconvention institutes and has brought to the forefront research, instructional, and administrative issues on the preparation of ITAs for instructional roles and other responsibilities in university settings. A newsletter and a discussion list, as well as resources and links to ITA programs in the United States and Canada, are available on the ITA Interest Section Web site (http://ita-is.org/). The group's visibility has increased in recent years, and the topics introduced at the annual convention and in publications have significantly diversified to include assessment, research-based course design, materials development, standards for spoken English discourse, and the communication culture of academic classrooms.

The support of the TESOL organization and its recognition of the importance of this interest section and ITA professional development were further underscored when funding was granted to establish the *Discourse Within the Disciplines* (1999) project. The project provides access to videotaped examples and transcripts of university classroom discourse of NNES teaching assistants and focuses on discipline-specific language and discourse (Papajohn, 2000). The project's Web site presents authentic classroom data from university courses taught by teaching assistants in areas such as chemistry, economics, engineering mechanics, hydraulics, and mathematics. The project invites the contribution and participation of researchers and language professionals who are interested in discipline-specific discourse. The transcripts can be used in courses and programs for ITA development to demonstrate a range of linguistic and pedagogical skills, successful communication strategies, and instances of communication breakdown and repair. The project bridges research in applied linguistics with the practice of ITA professional development.

◈ GLOBAL LINGUISTIC AND PEDAGOGICAL DEVELOPMENTS: EFFECT ON ITA PROGRAM DESIGN

Despite the momentous advances in the area of ITA professional development in recent years, the field is still in its infancy, and much remains to be accomplished in developing research-based programs and curricula to enhance ITAs' acculturation to the social and academic climate and their professional preparation as instructors. As was discussed earlier, the field of ITA preparation has been influenced by demographic shifts in undergraduate and graduate student populations at universities across the United States and by enhanced cross-cultural awareness and increased commitment and resources to this endeavor. Other areas that are likely to have a growing effect on ITA program design include the globalization of English and the emergence of professional standards across disciplines.

Globalization of English

Global mobility and increased linguistic diversity in U.S. universities at both the undergraduate and graduate levels have occurred concurrently with the growing prestige and expanding role of English in the academic, cultural, and political landscape of more and more universities worldwide (Crystal, 1995, 1997; Fishman, Cooper, & Conrad, 1977; B. Kachru, 1992; McArthur, 1998, 2002; Thumboo, 2001). The number of people who use English for communication is currently far higher in countries where English is not the native language than in countries where it is the official language (Seidlhofer, 2004). English serves as a communication bridge for speakers of different languages. It is increasingly being used, for example, as an official language and the language for communication among groups of nonnative English speakers in East and Southeast Asia (Kirkpatrick, 2002). In a growing number of countries, English is fast becoming a dominant second language (B. Kachru, 1985). In these countries, exposure to English begins in the early school grades, and the media, tourism, travel, and the Internet contribute to increased proficiency in the language. Furthermore, English is becoming the second language of academia at more universities around the world, and proficiency is required for course work and presentation at international conferences.

The internationalization of English has led to its diversification. Internationalization has also redefined the notion of native and nonnative English language proficiency, thereby stimulating research into mapping diasporic, nonnative, and national varieties of world Englishes (B. Kachru, 1992; Sridhar & Sridhar, 1986; Thumboo, 2001). As a language of wider communication, English has become pluricentric, and many localized varieties are spoken throughout the world. Its emergent role and status as a lingua franca (Y. Kachru, 2001; Pakir, 2001) have already affected the fields of second language acquisition research and language teaching and have contributed to reforming curricula and pedagogical approaches in ESL and EFL contexts worldwide (Y. Kachru, 2001; Pennycook, 1994; Seidlhofer, 2004). The growing impact of this phenomenon will substantially contribute to improved English proficiency skills among international students arriving at universities in English-speaking countries. Increased research on nonnative varieties of English will raise awareness of the need to design programs that are tailored to students from countries where English has become the nativized and official language or is a dominant second language. Improved English proficiency skills among ITAs will contribute to shifting the focus of their professional development from improving communication skills to enhancing acculturation strategies and advancing pedagogical content and professional skills.

Professional Standards Across Disciplines

Global increase in the use of English in social and academic domains, internationalization of educational institutions, and the growing emphasis on the need for language instruction across the curriculum (AAAS, 2001) have significantly advanced the visibility of language educators and language teaching in all educational contexts. Furthermore, standards-based practices that have been infused into educational reform in recent years have strengthened language education and the preparation of qualified educators. The new standards, developed across disciplines, have increased accountability, incorporated an emphasis on strong foundational knowledge of the discipline, and enhanced clinical practice opportunities and effective pedagogy (Darling-Hammond, 2001). The standards have affected pedagogical content directions (Shulman, 1986, 1987), program goals, and assessment of teacher candidates' knowledge, skills, and dispositions (INTASC, 1992, 2002). Professional standards were articulated for practicing teachers (NBPTS, 2001), educational units (NCATE, 2001), and programs across the disciplines (e.g., ACTFL, 2002; NCTM, 2000; TESOL, 2002). These have defined the body of knowledge, skills, and dispositions that qualified educators should acquire as part of their professional development. The standards have underscored accountability and have articulated the integration of conceptual frameworks and assessment in program design and educational practice. Implementation of the standards has guided reformulation of conceptual frameworks, review of programs and organizational structures, revision of curricular content, and integration of enhanced clinical experiences in teacher education (Darling-Hammond & Bransford, 2005). Standards-driven practices across disciplines have promulgated assessment for program and unit improvement and accountability. The development of standards and benchmarks across educational contexts continues worldwide.

The shifting epistemological stance and the incorporation of standards-based practices in language education have engaged language educators in rethinking the knowledge base and the pedagogical practices in language teacher education programs. Research in pedagogical approaches has increased in recent years and, combined with standards-based curriculum development, assessment, accountability, and accreditation, has affected program development and learning experiences. In the past two decades, language pedagogy has integrated a rich palette of instructional paradigms that emphasize the centrality and the diversity of learners and their active engagement in authentic and meaningful activities. These notions have been integrated in curriculum design, assessment, and classroom practices and have led to the emergence of paradigms that include cooperative learning (D. W. Johnson & R. T. Johnson, 1984; Kessler, 1992); models that foster learners' autonomy, action research, reflective practices, and partnerships (Nunan, 1988); assessments that are embedded in their sociocultural educational contexts; opportunities for experiential learning; self and peer observation and evaluation; and construction of knowledge through inquiry and reflective practice (Benson, 2001;

Brown, 2004; Burns, 1999; Edge, 1996, 2002; Freeman & Richards, 1996; Gebhard & Oprandy, 1999; Graves, 1996; K. E. Johnson, 1999; Kaufman, 2000, 2004; Murphy & Byrd, 2001; Nunan & Lamb, 1996; Richard-Amato, 2003; Shohamy, 2001; Zamel & Spack, 2002). The advent of content-based instruction (CBI) as a paradigm in language education across all educational levels underscored the growing importance of developing language proficiency in all academic areas (Brinton, Snow, & Wesche, 1989; Crandall, 1993; Crandall & Kaufman, 2002; Kaufman & Crandall, 2005; Mohan, 1986; Mohan, Leung, & Davison, 2001; Short, 1993; Snow & Brinton, 1997; Stoller, 2004). CBI has also motivated collaborative practices among language educators and their colleagues across disciplines. These practices have included development of linked courses, coteaching of courses, and greater awareness by all educators of the challenges of learners' acculturation and language acquisition in a host environment.

Research into pedagogy and teacher development has also promulgated notions about the centrality of sociocultural processes in preparing professionals (Freeman & Johnson, 1998; Hall, 2002; K. E. Johnson, 2000; Murrell, 2001; Prabhu, 1996), increased attention to teachers' prior beliefs about teaching and learning and how these shape their teaching practice (K. E. Johnson, 1992; Pennington, 1995), sustained reflection that promotes reformulation of existing notions (Evans, 2002; Goodlad, 1990; Kaufman, 2000; Pennington, 1995), teachers' self-image as emerging professionals, and the effect of classroom discourse and modes of communication on creating contexts that encourage or inhibit learning (Bailey & Nunan, 1995; Casanave & Schecter, 1997; Edge, 2002; Stigler & Hiebert, 1999). These educational concepts have enhanced insights into the construction of ideas about teaching and learning and have fostered greater understanding of the acquisition of teaching skills and the development of professional dispositions (NCATE, 2001).

Developments in pedagogy have had an effect on a variety of language education endeavors, including ITA development. One example is the increased participation of undergraduate students in the professional preparation of ITAs. This has occurred in alignment with a shift away from teacher-centered transmission models toward knowledge-centered and learner-centered approaches in language education. Undergraduates' input into the teaching and learning process has emerged as an important component of ITA preparation in a growing number of programs. It has given voice and ownership to undergraduates, enhanced their sensitivity to linguistic and cultural diversity, and raised their awareness of their role as learners and mentors (Plakans, 1997). At the same time, undergraduates' participation has raised ITAs' awareness of the importance of the learners' voice in academic classrooms, the blurring of boundaries between teaching and learning, and the relevance of learning from learners in the process of teaching.

Emerging standards across the professional spectrum have affected teacher education programs and the teacher candidates who graduate from these programs. Despite the proliferation of ITA programs, however, standards have yet to be developed in this area. The ITA programs that have emerged in universities across the United States were molded by variables that included local needs, advocacy efforts by language educators, awareness of the need for these programs by university administrators, resource allocation, and collaborative initiatives of departments across the disciplines. As a result, multiple paradigms have appeared, ranging from a few workshops, to a series of courses, to a comprehensive instructional and formative mentoring program that supports ITAs in their first year of teaching.

TESOL's commitment to the articulation of professional standards to promote excellence in the teaching of English globally (as set forth in its *Forward Plan*, 2001) was emphasized with the establishment of the TESOL Standards Committee in 2002. The members of the committee represent a cross-section of educational levels and international settings. The committee's charge is to explore existing standards projects and to consider future projects and priority areas for standards development, as proposed by the TESOL membership. With increased awareness of the importance of professionalizing ITA preparation, this should become a high-priority area for standards development and will undoubtedly contribute to enhancing the image of ITA language educators in the academic community.

◈ PARTNERSHIPS IN PROFESSIONAL DEVELOPMENT

Partnerships among units throughout a university greatly enhance ITA preparation and benefit all involved. Establishment of a university-wide center facilitates interdepartmental collaboration and underscores a university-wide commitment and ownership of ITA preparation. An example is Stony Brook University's (SBU) interdepartmental collaborative initiative that has greatly enhanced ITA preparation and enriched the educational experiences of undergraduate students, teacher candidates, and other participants whose activities at the university have been integrated into ITA professional development.

SBU is a Research I university within the State University of New York (SUNY). The university, like other tertiary academic institutions across the United States, has experienced a steady growth in the number of international students. In the fall of 2004, SBU had 2,055 international students from 100 countries (647 undergraduate and 1,408 graduate students). Mirroring national trends, the top countries of origin for international students are China, Korea, and India. International students at SBU have increasingly participated in instructional responsibilities in diverse undergraduate classes. At SBU, ITAs are involved in instructional activities such as teaching a subsection or a whole class, conducting recitation sections or laboratories, and grading tests. The varying levels of English language proficiency among ITAs, the diversity in their pedagogical background experience, and their unfamiliarity with the sociocultural aspects of the host country and the academic context of the university have challenged the university to develop a paradigm for preparing ITAs that is tailored to the local context. The linguistic and ethnic diversification in the undergraduate population, combined with a high number of teaching assistants whose native language is other than English, have underscored the need for designing programs for the professional development of all teaching assistants—NES and international—to prepare them for their role as instructors. The university established a unit called the Center for Excellence in Learning and Teaching (CELT), which is dedicated to the professional development of all teaching assistants and new faculty across the university. In addition to the full-time director and staff support, CELT has engaged senior distinguished teaching professors (who have earned the title for their exemplary teaching over the years) and other faculty who contribute their time and expertise to this endeavor. The center conducts orientation workshops just before the academic year and organizes professional development sessions throughout the academic year. Preparation of teaching assistants has included a focus on linguistic and sociocultural issues, pedagogical content, instructional design, and implementation.

In addition to offering programs at CELT, SBU prepares ITAs through course work in the ESL program that is charged with the linguistic and professional development of ITAs, supplemented by workshops and mentoring within the home department conducted by faculty who are specialists in the discipline. The ESL program is based in the Department of Linguistics and includes six full-time faculty members serving more than 200 international students per academic year. It is dedicated to developing international students' communication skills, accent improvement, and cross-cultural awareness, classroom presentation skills, and pedagogy. Its home within a department that includes programs in linguistics and TESOL teacher education at the undergraduate, graduate, and doctoral levels has presented opportunities for interfacing theory and practice, sites for fieldwork and clinical practice, and collaborative activities for language development, mentoring, and professional development both within the department and with units outside the department (Kaufman & Brooks, 1996; Kaufman & Brownworth, 2002). For example, collaborative initiatives involving ITA preparation have included the CELT, the ESL program, and the graduate TESOL teacher education program. As part of their teacher education course work, graduate teacher candidates are required to design and present workshops for practicing ITAs. These workshops are integrated into the CELT workshop program and the topics focus on linguistic, pedagogical, and cross-cultural issues. They vary from one semester to the next and are enhanced by the creativity and initiative of the graduate students who design them. Titles of past workshops have included "The Impact of Nonverbal Communication," "Fielding Questions," and "Cross-Cultural Issues in the Classroom." The workshop design and implementation process have encouraged teacher candidates to reflect on the elements that constitute effective pedagogy, such as design and adaptation of learning experiences, verbal and nonverbal modes of instruction, individual and group learning, and the importance of considering learners' background and prior experience. Input and participation during workshops, combined with a review of the teaching assistants' written evaluations, have provided TESOL candidates with important insights and feedback about the relevance and contribution of the workshops for the professional development of teaching assistants. At the same time, TESOL candidates have gained important insights into their own development as professionals.

An ESL tutoring center, which was established with funding from an SBU Presidential Mini Grant for Departmental Diversity Initiatives, has become an integral component of the ESL program in recent years. The center has served as one of the field experience sites for TESOL teacher candidates and has engaged them in tutoring sessions for ITAs. To enhance continuity and to provide depth to these sessions, each teacher candidate spends 3 hours a week tutoring three students for the duration of the semester. Through this longitudinal process, teacher candidates gain valuable insight on the linguistic, cultural, and pedagogical needs of participating ITAs. The knowledge gained also guides the design and implementation of the workshops described earlier. Graduate teacher candidates also participate in assessing ITAs' microteaching, an assignment that is one of the exit requirements from the

ESL program. Evaluation is conducted jointly with other ESL faculty and a guest faculty member from the ITAs' home department. Evaluations focus on the students' proficiency and pedagogical skills.

Another partnership initiative that has contributed to the affective, social, and linguistic preparation of ITAs has paired individual ITAs with senior citizens who participate in SBU's Round Table program for continuing education. The group includes retired professors, teachers, and business professionals who serve as conversation partners for ITAs and who meet with their assigned ITA partner weekly throughout the semester. The program has been most rewarding for both groups. The Round Table members have welcomed the opportunity to befriend international students who have, in turn, benefited by increasing their communication and social skills. In many cases, the partnerships grow into long-term friendships that continue after the semester ends. In addition, students have been invited to the senior citizens' homes for the holidays and visits during periods of illness and celebration. The SBU paradigm also includes a university-wide host program sponsored by the international programs unit. Hosting families from the community welcome ITAs into their homes for the academic year. The ITAs sign up for the program and meet with designated host families for the first time at a university-sponsored dinner. This marks the beginning of a relationship that often continues beyond the academic year. The combined collaborative initiatives at SBU have greatly enriched the ITAs' experience in linguistic, academic, social, and affective domains.

❖ BEGINNINGS, CHALLENGES, AND GROWTH: MODELS FOR ITA DEVELOPMENT

The nature of linguistic and pedagogic preparation that would constitute a minimum threshold for ITAs' success and the types of screening procedures used to determine language proficiency and pedagogical skills have been major topics for deliberation (Ard, 1989; Halleck & Moder, 1995). In addition to acculturation and the acquisition of a new speech genre (Bakhtin, 1986), emerging research has pointed to specific areas that warrant attention, for example, the role of discourse in ITAs' assessment and instruction (Madden & Myers, 1994; Young & He, 1998) and the multiple layers of meanings conveyed through nonverbal and paralinguistic behaviors (Jenkins & Parra, 2003). Pickering (2001) found that hesitation and repairs are common features of nonfluent ITAs' speech and result in disengagement and withdrawal. Pickering also discussed how choice of tone contributes to communication failure between ITAs and undergraduate students by obfuscating information and presenting the ITAs as unsympathetic and uninvolved.

Borjas (2005) investigated whether ITA course instructors adversely affected undergraduate students' scholastic achievement and found that, with adequate professional preparation, ITAs' classroom performance had no adverse effect on undergraduate students' performance, even when the ITAs' communication skills did not match those of their NES counterparts. Furthermore, NNES undergraduate students were even less affected than NES undergraduate students. Although the study did not define what was meant by *adequate preparation*, it underscored the importance of preparing ITAs to become effective classroom instructors.

Much deliberation has taken place at universities across the United States, in recent years, on what constitutes the best preparation for ITAs, where programs should reside, and how to obtain resources to support them. Over the years, three major paradigms for ITA professional development have emerged. First, a centralized unit conducts orientations, workshops, and other activities for the professional development of all teaching assistants—NES and international. Second, a university's ESL program serves as the locus for preparing ITAs for their roles through course work. The program works independently or collaborates with an academic department (e.g., linguistics) or an administrative unit (e.g., the office of undergraduate studies, the graduate school, the office of international programs). Third, workshops and seminars are held within the respective academic departments and include informal individual mentoring, supervision, and assessment from faculty in these departments. Such formal and informal preparation is tailored to the specific needs of each department and to individual teaching assignments. In most universities, variations on the first two paradigms have been the most prevalent and have often been supplemented by programs in the ITAs' home departments.

◈ CASE STUDIES ON ITA DEVELOPMENT

Case studies of ITA programs capture the evolution of units within their local contexts and provide insights into the interaction among myriad pedagogical, administrative, and fiscal perspectives that play a role in establishing and maintaining ITA programs. The case studies selected for this volume present a kaleidoscope of ITA preparation models ranging from brief orientation sessions to comprehensive series of courses and extensive mentoring models. The case studies underscore the social, political, administrative, linguistic, and academic challenges involved in establishing programs and designing the curriculum to prepare ITAs for their professional roles within the boundaries of the local context and available resources.

The volume is enriched by the contributors' narratives recounting their experiences, challenges, and successful accomplishments in establishing new programs and building on existing ones. Some programs are still in their initial stages, others have evolved over many years; some include short-term components such as a presemester orientation, others have become full-fledged university-wide centers created to provide professional development for all teaching assistants, including ITAs. Resources allocated for ITA professional development also vary widely across institutions. ITA programs range from a single-handed effort to broad-based commitment from faculty and administrators. The case studies bring to the fore the voices of undergraduate students, ITAs, language educators, and administrators and the respective roles they play in the conceptualization, development, and support of ITA programs.

The case studies are set against the backdrop of U.S. academic institutions. However, the issues that they raise are relevant to programs and institutions worldwide. Change, progress, and commitment are themes that are interwoven through all the case studies. The chapters in this volume highlight the internationalization of U.S. universities and the historical and administrative forces that have shaped ITA programs and provided opportunities for curriculum reform, research in linguistics and pedagogy, interdepartmental partnerships, and enrichment of undergraduate education. Many of the programs began through the efforts of a few dedicated individuals who have raised awareness of the seriousness of the issue and have crafted solutions that planted the seeds for full-fledged programs. The evolutionary process in the development of the ITA programs described in this volume highlights multiple issues including (a) the emergence of mandates and policies at universities, (b) screening procedures and assessment instruments, (c) shifting responsibility for ITA development from a single faculty member or program to a centralized unit at the university designated for the professional development of all teaching assistants, and (d) increasing departmental responsibility for those who supervise teaching assistants in their departments.

Collaboration with departments across the university has benefited ITA programs, raised awareness of cross-cultural issues campus-wide, encouraged interdisciplinary paradigms, and resulted in efficient use of resources. The university-wide concern about the quality of undergraduate education, coupled with the need for adequate preparation of teaching assistants, has motivated the involvement of departments across the academic spectrum. A theater department's expertise, for instance, has contributed to highlighting the importance of nonverbal communication and expressive modes that affect the learner's academic success (Papajohn, chapter 10). Similarly, collaboration in departments of speech and hearing (Petro, chapter 11), communication sciences (Ross, chapter 7), and occupational therapy (Miller & Matsuda, chapter 4) has enriched the professional development of ITAs and opened new interdisciplinary avenues and research opportunities. University-wide commitment is underscored by the establishment of a centralized unit that offers scaffolding through mentoring activities for ITAs not only prior to their assuming instructional responsibilities, but also while they are teaching (Jacobson, Lawrence, & Freisem, chapter 3).

Computer, video, and wireless technologies have enhanced exposure to English around the world and contributed to increasing the English language skills of ITAs prior to their arrival at U.S. universities. These technologies have also expanded the notion of a community of learners and presented new possibilities for classroom learning, assessment, and professional development (Beatty, 2003; Bransford, Brown, & Cocking, 2000; Perkins, Schwartz, West, & Wiske, 1995). ITA programs have used technology for administrative and instructional purposes, assessment, and self and peer review. Examples in this volume include videotaped microteaching for mentoring and use of WebCT (Cotsonas, chapter 8), using authentic voice as reflected in videotapes of ITAs (Schroeder & Kohler, chapter 9), and videoconferencing as a screening process (Piñeiro, chapter 6). Kidder and Tapper (chapter 2) describe the increased use of technology to handle routine procedures such as registration, enrollment for courses and tests, Web-based instructional materials, e-mailed journals, multimedia computers in language laboratories, and computerized speech displays. They also discuss using technology for digital data collection and using online archives of digital video for research into ITAs' discourse and cross-cultural communication, and they underscore the contribution of this research to strengthening their program's profile at the university.

A broad range of ITA program models exists in U.S. universities. There is variation in the location of the program within the university's organizational structure, the number of academic faculty involved, and the availability of resources and support by university administration. Collaboration with administrative and academic units across the university contributes to the visibility of ITA preparation programs. The level of engagement of other units ranges from participation on advisory boards to partnering in assessment of ITAs' proficiency and pedagogical skills. Involvement of the graduate school, for example, enforces compliance and attendance at noncredit courses offered by ITA programs. Ross (chapter 7) describes how concerns about undergraduate perceptions of ITAs, along with growing visibility of the ITA program at the university, have led to the integration of modules on ITA issues into the First Year Experience curriculum for entering undergraduate students. The ITA program plays a prominent role in providing professional development for instructors who teach these modules. Involvement of undergraduate students in mentoring and assessment activities (Gorsuch, chapter 5; Heidish, chapter 12) has empowered participants and contributed to increased cross-cultural awareness and greater understanding of linguistic and cultural diversity among those participants.

◈ CONCLUSION

Universities have been greatly enriched by the infusion of linguistic and cultural diversity introduced by undergraduate and graduate international students and faculty. The recent demographic shifts have brought challenges that cross disciplinary boundaries and affect all aspects of the academic environment. Global changes, expanding technologies, and the spread of English, as well as developments in pedagogy, professional practice, and standards have converged as key elements for program development and curricular changes across the educational spectrum. ITA professional development has evolved in recent decades and has challenged universities and educators. The diversity of contexts and the lack of a codified knowledge base and standards for professional practice for ITA preparation have led to myriad models tailored to local contexts. Visibility of these programs, allocation of resources, and administrative support at universities vary widely across campuses. The establishment of TESOL's ITA Interest Section and the formulation of standards in teacher education, along with emerging research in this area, have greatly empowered language educators in their efforts to raise awareness on their campuses and to develop collaborative paradigms in the professional preparation of ITAs. Development of standards in this area will further advance the articulation of the knowledge base and professional practices and will promote greater uniformity in the quality of programs without compromising creativity and diversity.

Increased research in this area and its dissemination will add credibility and greater visibility to ITA programs and language educators. Limited resources in all areas of the academic spectrum present opportunities for building on existing resources to design innovative programs that are worthy of emulation. Resources can be found in academic departments, technology support units, and administrative offices across the university. In designing collaborative paradigms with academic and administrative units, language educators can reflect on their own expertise in cross-cultural communication and pedagogy—important assets to colleagues and university administrators at times of changing demographics—and design initiatives that underscore the expertise and knowledge that they bring to this collaboration. Increased commitment and resources to ITA preparation in recent years have led to the proliferation of programs and the increased experience and expertise in the area of ITA development. Building on growing expertise in this area, as well as a broader research initiative and systematic approach to researching language use in the various classes taught by ITAs, will further inform and strengthen the profession, introduce curricular changes, and promulgate the best practices for ITA professional development.

◈ CONTRIBUTORS

Dorit Kaufman is the director of the Professional Education Program and the TESOL Teacher Education Program at Stony Brook University, State University of New York (SUNY). Her research interests include children's first language attrition and narrative development, teacher education, content-based instruction, and standards-based assessment. She is the recipient of the R. Neil Appleby Outstanding Teacher Educator Award and the SUNY President's and Chancellor's Awards for Excellence in Teaching.

Barbara Brownworth is the aural/oral ESL coordinator and SPEAK Test director at Stony Brook University, State University of New York (SUNY). She also oversees the program for ITAs. Her doctoral work focused on prosodic features of English for second language learners. She has presented at several international TESOL conferences and is a member of the ITA Interest Section. Her current interest is in curriculum design and evaluation as well as the role of dictation in ITA development.

PART 1

Grounding Practice in Research and Researching Practice

CHAPTER 2

A Research-Informed Approach to International Teaching Assistant Preparation

Gordon J. Tapper and Kathryn L. Kidder

◈ INTRODUCTION

The Academic Spoken English (ASE) program at the University of Florida (UF) was conceived in 1986 in response to strident public protest that undergraduates could not understand their international teaching assistants (ITAs). With comprehensibility concerns there also came such student complaints as "My ITA sounds harsh." This underscored the fact that challenges for ITAs in the U.S. classroom extended beyond mere linguistic competence to the many aspects of cross-cultural communicative transfer. It also became apparent that their diverse cultural backgrounds brought international teachers and U.S. students to the classroom with different expectations.

Confronted with these challenges, the UF administration asked sociolinguist Andrea Tyler to develop a curriculum that could efficiently produce comprehensible instruction while respecting the many demands on international graduate teaching assistants at a major research university. As the foundation of what would become the ASE program, she adopted a discourse analytical approach based on microexamination of language data collected by video- and audiotaping the ITAs in real-time situations. This approach was informed by a Gumperzian notion of the multiple microsources of miscommunication between interlocutors (Gumperz, 1982). Throughout the years, this notion has been developed through further scholarship on the various contextualization cues (rhythm, intonation, lexicon) that contribute to miscommunication between speakers from different cultures.

For ITAs at UF this research approach, illuminating communication through data collection and analysis, is also the key to stimulating self-critical awareness of the behaviors that contribute to miscommunication in their classrooms. In the one-on-one conferencing component of advanced ASE courses, the instructor guides an ITA in analysis of actual linguistic, cultural, and pedagogical behaviors, using data collected either in the ITA's classroom or in a structured activity with a native-English-speaking (NES) undergraduate assistant.

Extensive connections with various institutional entities at UF have aided ASE in gaining and maintaining support for its ITA professional development and research missions while ensuring that ASE's goals harmonize with those of the many departments whose ITAs are supervised. ASE is administratively accountable to both the College of Liberal Arts and Sciences (CLAS), home to the majority of the ITAs, and to the Office of Research and Graduate Programs (RGP).

This chapter details how four key elements have contributed to UF's approach to ITA professional development:

- a historical and continuing linguistics-based research approach to the collection and analysis of real data

- a pedagogical approach focused on stimulating learner self-critical awareness

- the incorporation of NES undergraduate cross-cultural informants

- institutional connections that ensure relevance within a changing academic community

◈ CONTEXT

Institutional Framework

UF is a growing, public, Research I university. The oldest and largest of 11 state universities, its current enrollment of 44,000 includes some 10,000 graduate students. International enrollment has increased steadily over the past few decades, and a current initiative to raise the proportion of graduate students to 25% has notably augmented the numbers. Just over 2,000 international graduate students were registered in the fall of 2004.

Although academic departments bear ultimate responsibility for instruction, the key roles in institutional support of ITAs continue to be played by ASE's originators—the graduate school (now part of RGP) and the linguistics department that share the funding for personnel, purchasing, and other administrative services, as well as the research agenda including the director, equipment, space, and stipends (see Figure 1). Graduate faculty members who belong to the Graduate Council make policy decisions affecting ITAs. The graduate school enforces oral proficiency policies, identifies potential ITAs for testing, and ensures that they meet Florida's statutory qualifications for teaching.

The interdisciplinary linguistics department, with theoretical as well as applied interests, is ASE's academic home. Association with linguistics anchors ASE in language learning theory and informs its methodology. Linguistics graduate students constitute much of the ASE instructional staff. The current curriculum is based on the concepts and research of its linguistics-based founder, with input and development over the years from program participants.

Students

ASE students reflect the general graduate enrollment at UF. There are more males than females (although the number of women is increasing rapidly), more Asians than people from other international regions (despite significant admissions from Eastern Europe and Latin America), and most are studying hard sciences and engineering, which have large undergraduate service courses. However, ASE has served graduate students from all UF colleges and a broad variety of fields, from pharmacy and veterinary medicine to anthropology, music, and architecture. Figure 2 shows recent ITA enrollment by departments.

Although ASE was developed to serve current and potential ITAs, three of its

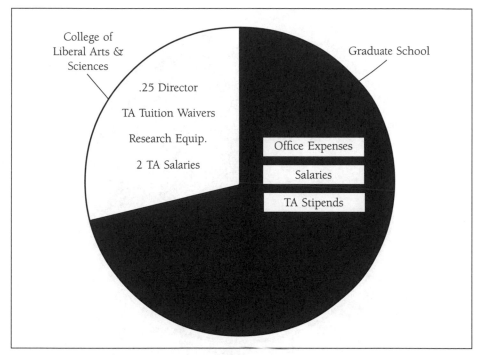

FIGURE 1. ASE Funding Sources

four courses are open to any international graduate student with a need for improved oral skills. The total annual enrollment figure therefore includes new ITAs actually in the classroom, students preparing to teach, and students who do not expect to teach at UF. Some learners voluntarily enroll in ASE courses, but ITAs with limited oral proficiency are required to attend.

Staff

The head of ASE is a full-time lecturer-coordinator whose duties include teaching as well as administration. Since 1999, ASE has employed an additional lecturer. The permanent staff mentor and supervise the linguistics graduate students and part-time adjuncts who constitute the approximately eight additional teaching staff. All have native or near-native English proficiency and previous teaching experience.

As many as 10 paid undergraduate assistants, selected for their interest in cross-cultural communication, serve multiple roles in ASE. Some videotape ITAs' classes and labs. Others serve as language and culture informants who work with small groups of international students on speaking tasks assigned by the instructor and provide feedback on communicative ability. Unpaid conversation partners are also welcomed. The linguistics connection provides a mutually useful pairing when ASE instructors match their students with undergraduates taking classes in second language acquisition or teaching methods.

Several new positions have recently been authorized in response to program growth. The current ASE director has a doctorate and is charged with strengthening

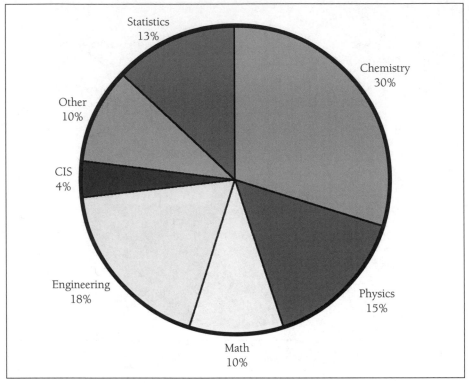

FIGURE 2. Demographics of Students in the ITA Course by Department, Fall 2002–Fall 2004

research activities. Because of increased computerization, the second lecturer's duties have been redefined to include programming and technical support. A half-time office assistant has assumed clerical and fiscal responsibilities. Each fall semester, several incoming linguistics graduate students are employed as assistants to the instructional staff while preparing to teach ASE classes the following year.

◈ DESCRIPTION

ASE at UF provides two related services to the university community. It administers and grades a monthly test to screen potential ITAs for oral English proficiency, and it provides language courses for a growing population of international graduate students. Four courses are currently offered: one for ITAs in their first semester of teaching and the remainder for students preparing to teach or simply wishing to improve their oral English skills. All are taught in UF's standard 15-week semester (12 weeks in summer) and graded on a pass/fail basis. They are credit-bearing and eligible for graduate assistant tuition waivers but do not count toward a graduate degree.

Placement in ASE courses is determined by students' scores on the Test of Spoken English (TSE) or its locally administered version, the Speaking Proficiency English Assessment Kit (SPEAK) test, as required by Florida statute. The test developer prescribes a score range from 20 to 60, with results reported in intervals of

5. The UF Graduate Council established a two-tier SPEAK/TSE pass system (see Table 1). Examinees with scores of 55 or 60 are exempt from an English requirement, while those with 45 or 50 must enroll in the ITA support course, "English for Academic Purposes" (EAP) 5836, during their first semester of teaching. Students with scores of 40 or below are not allowed to teach or tutor more than two students and are encouraged to enroll in EAP 5835 to prepare for future assignments. EAP 5837 is available for students with higher proficiency or those who need an extra semester to attain a score of 45. EAP 5937, a sampler of oral skills for international graduate students, is offered in summer terms.

Overview of ASE Courses

Table 2 outlines the four ASE courses. EAP 5836 is the ITA professional development class. Topics for the weekly 2-hour seminar are listed in Appendix A. Central to its methodology are regular, videotaped observations of the participants' actual teaching, with subsequent analysis and individual feedback in biweekly conferences with the instructor. Therefore, enrollment is limited to six students per section. Currently, eight sections are offered in fall terms, four in spring, and two in summer.

Assessment of Student Achievement

Student progress in ASE courses is subject to multiple assessments. As in all UF courses, instructors base their pass/fail grades on attendance and fulfillment of course requirements. Language production data are plentiful because class work is regularly taped and evaluated by students and instructors. Feedback from student assistants is also considered. Each course has a major oral project requirement so that pre- and postcourse communication ability can be holistically compared.

EAP 5836 includes additional assessment measures. After 6 weeks of instruction, ITAs solicit formative evaluation of their language and teaching by administering early feedback forms to their students. Firsthand comments from their students about the ITAs' comprehensibility supplement the instructor's feedback and provide motivating reinforcement.

EAP 5836 students undergo a formal exit evaluation at the end of the semester instead of repeating the SPEAK/TSE. The ASE instructor and a faculty member from the student's academic department meet to review the ITA's videotaped teaching. Using an evaluation form based on the ITA Test (Smith, Meyers, & Burkhalter, 1992), they assess the degree to which the ITA meets standards of intelligibility, fluency, and pedagogy. The ITA is then either cleared for future teaching under normal departmental supervision or referred for further ASE support. This process

TABLE 1. ORAL PROFICIENCY SCORES AND ASE COURSE PLACEMENT

SPEAK Test Score	Course	For Whom
40 or under	EAP 5835	Students preparing for teaching
45–50	EAP 5836	ITAs in their first semester of teaching (REQUIRED)
45–60	EAP 5837	Graders and tutors
55–60	No requirement	

TABLE 2. ASE COURSE DESCRIPTION

EAP 5835 ASE 1	EAP 5836 ASE 2	EAP 5837 ASE Tutorial	EAP 5937 ASE Summer Course
General academic language for graduate students and potential teaching assistants. 4 credits, 9 class hours per week. Students in EAP 5835 work on • Practical language: conversation strategies, active listening, questioning, requests, explanations, persuasion, expressing opinions, giving and getting advice • Pronunciation, including supervised language lab with audio, video, and multimedia practice • Videotaped academic presentations with linguistic and pedagogical critique • Discussions: leading and participating • Intercultural skills	REQUIRED during the first semester of teaching for ITAs with SPEAK scores of 45–50. Please note this is a 3-credit course. EAP 5836 includes • Seminar (2 hours weekly) on language, culture, and pedagogy • Videotaped teaching biweekly • Conferences for individual coaching on language and teaching biweekly • Exit Evaluation: ASE and academic department review videotapes to verify ITA's competence	For advanced learners. Appropriate for graders and tutors. 3 credits, 3 hours each week + videotaped tutoring. Student-teacher conferences biweekly. EAP 5837 includes • Interpersonal communication skills for the academic setting • Regular interaction with English-speaking students • Individual feedback on language, teaching, and intercultural skills	For intermediate-advanced learners. EAP 5937 offers • Presentation, discussion and interpersonal communication skills for the academic setting • Regular interaction with English-speaking students • Digital pronunciation lab

fulfills the state oral proficiency mandate by supplementing SPEAK screening with assessment of actual classroom performance.

Institutional Relations

Informing the university community about ASE is an ongoing effort. The size of the institution and the realities of personnel turnover make it important to continually seek ways to disseminate information about the issues and requirements that come into play when international students are appointed to teach.

ASE's key interface with the university community is through the graduate school, which has a well-developed information and enforcement system. ITA oral proficiency requirements and appointment procedures are explained during orientation for new graduate coordinators in the UF Graduate School's *Graduate Catalogue* (2005), in mailings, and during on-campus orientations for new students. The graduate school also works directly with academic departments to ensure that only qualified individuals are permitted to teach.

ASE's principal information mechanism is its Web site (http://ase.ufl.edu). One section is targeted to faculty and staff and the remainder addresses student concerns. Readers can consult the Web site for an additional appendix related to this case study. SPEAK test registration is fully handled online. ASE distributes a brochure on courses and testing and maintains regular office hours for telephone and walk-in consultation. Additional sources of information are the UF Graduate School's course catalogue and *Teaching at the University of Florida* (2005), both online.

ASE regularly collaborates with other UF teaching support services. The Office of Instructional Resources provides orientation for all new teaching assistants at the beginning of the fall term, and departments follow up with discipline-specific preparation. The University Center for Excellence in Teaching offers developmental activities for faculty and graduate assistants. ASE staff members have been guest presenters in both programs and regularly attend their activities. ASE has also assisted academic departments with concerns such as teaching assistant admissions and language problems of faculty and postdoctoral associates.

A recent outreach effort has been geared toward more direct contact with undergraduates. ASE staff have hosted "Success With Your ITA," a forum in which undergraduates in university residence halls can voice their concerns about cross-cultural and language issues in the classroom. At the same time, students are informed that the university has procedures in place to screen and supervise ITAs.

Challenges in Development

It would be misleading if this description of the UF ITA program made ASE appear to be a static entity. In fact, its history has been one of evolution in response to challenges of staffing, growth, and a changing environment. A review of some of these issues may provide a more balanced view.

The public clamor for a solution to a so-called ITA problem seems to have given program developers strong institutional support to do whatever was needed in the initial years. Fortunately this allowed expeditious expansion from one to three courses as experience revealed that the needs of international graduate students were varied and not always rapidly or simply met. A decade later, administrators supported additional development when demand for summer courses became insistent. Such flexibility in responding to actual needs has been a strong asset.

Other concerns have been more difficult to resolve. One example relates to the demands that the complexity of some ASE courses place on teaching staff. In addition to teaching a seminar, instructors in EAP 5836 are required to observe ITAs who are located throughout the 2,000-acre campus during the 15 hours a day when classes are taught. Added time is also required to review videotapes and hold individual conferences. Linguistics graduate students chosen to teach in ASE have generally considered that the benefits of this experience for future employability outweigh the extra work. However, concerns for equity eventually prevailed and, in 1999, a higher pay rate was established not only for instructing the two courses that require conferencing but also for mentoring new staff.

External factors have caused some of the greatest challenges. Enrollment increases due to the admission of greater numbers of international graduate students and the undergraduates they teach have prompted major ASE growth in the past decade (see Figure 3).

Beginning with a single ITA course for 8–10 students per semester in 1986, ASE grew to a fairly stable total of 48 students per term after two additional courses were initiated. A jump in enrollment occurred in 1997 and began to seem routine in succeeding years. New staff had to be hired at the last minute and mentored on the job. Video equipment and conferencing space were inadequate. SPEAK testing also increased exponentially. By the 2002 school year, ITA course enrollment had increased by 500% from what it had been in the early 1990s. The dramatic increase in needs for staff development and supervision, fiscal management, test registration and reporting, office hours, and outreach came close to threatening program stability and quality before remedies were applied. Strains on the program were eventually relieved by increased funding for teaching staff, student assistants, and electronic equipment as well as the assignment of additional space. However, the importance of timely administrative attention to external issues affecting ITA programs and a proactive stance in confronting them cannot be overstated.

The stress of growth had the positive result of accelerating the computerization of program functions. To save staff time, a system of online SPEAK registration was

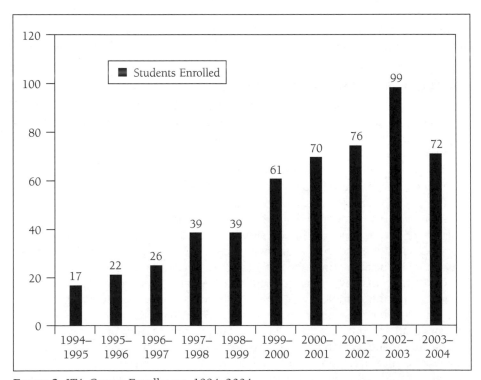

FIGURE 3. ITA Course Enrollment, 1994–2004

developed, with automated response to examinees and electronic score reporting. The ASE Web page was expanded to make course information and instructional texts directly available to users. Utilities such as schedule forms and recordkeeping systems followed. Recently, the switch to digital camcorders and audio recorders has enriched the quality of the data collected. This technological complexity has increased the learning curve for ASE staff, but it is hoped that the research benefits as well as the opportunity for instructors to acquire competence in a variety of computerized language applications will persuade staff that the trade-off is worthwhile.

Another ambiguous result of growth has been the gradual standardization of curriculum and materials in response to a larger, sometimes less experienced staff with more turnover. Lesson plans are now provided for most of the courses instead of a more flexible framework for instruction (see Appendix B for a sample). Staff members teaching a given course meet weekly for orientation to the content and methods of the coming lessons. In EAP 5836, a team-teaching approach has been adopted. Two course sections are combined for the seminar, with a new instructor serving as apprentice to a veteran. Although they promote quality standards for instruction, these measures may limit the staff creativity that has enriched the program.

Also affecting ASE in recent years are the geopolitical factors that have resulted in changes in the countries of origin of new ITAs at UF (see Figure 4). A decrease in students from China and an increase in those from India have occasioned changes in

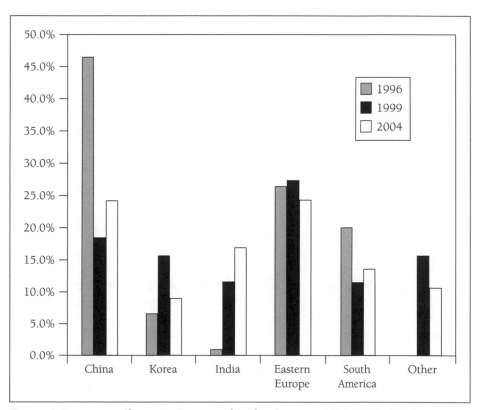

FIGURE 4. Percentage Change in Demographics by Country: 1996, 1999, 2004

instructional needs. Indian students, whose previous education has been in English, albeit often in dialects difficult for U.S. undergraduates, have different needs from students who arrive with little practical experience in English. Furthermore, improved world communications mean that some Eastern European and Chinese students now come to the United States with much greater previous exposure to English. All of these factors necessitate adjustments to increase the relevance of the ITA course and feedback methods for a more diverse population.

◈ DISTINGUISHING FEATURES

Four key elements distinguish UF's approach to ITA professional development: the collection and analysis of natural language data, the utilization of NES undergraduates, a sociolinguistic research orientation, and the use of periodic program self-assessments.

Data Collection and Analysis

Although ASE uses an ITA course textbook (Smith, Meyers, & Burkhalter, 1992), the primary instructional resource is, as indicated earlier, the natural language data obtained by videotaping an ITA teaching an undergraduate class or lab. Once collected, the video and audio data are evaluated according to a variety of discourse analytical criteria for their effect on comprehensible instruction and cross-cultural communicative competence. This process of collecting and analyzing real language data is the heart of the ASE method.

ITAs and their instructors use the process to develop ITAs' self-critical awareness of their communication in English. Instructors model methods of critical analysis early in the course and guide students toward gradually assuming that role for themselves. Filling out questionnaires as they self-critique presentations (also a method of data collection) prepares learners for independent awareness of their performance and for continued language development after the course is over.

Another benefit of the data collection approach relates to program relevance. Rapid changes in undergraduate expectations (e.g., current student preferences for richly multimedia-supported instruction and their directness in offering input on course design) and shifts in ITA demographics point to the need for regular data collection to keep language feedback pertinent.

Utilization of NES Undergraduates

Feedback from NES undergraduate employees is another source of data about ITA communicative competence. Often video- or audiotaped for microanalysis, interactions with undergraduates provide international students with immediate and compelling feedback about their performance in English and generate data for instructor evaluation and for research.

Undergraduates are employed as

- Camera operators who videotape ITAs teaching their classes. This vantage point allows them to contribute valuable, immediate feedback about the communicative and teaching effectiveness of an ITA from an undergraduate perspective.

- Panelists and role-players in the ITA course. To help ITAs better understand their students, undergraduate volunteers are invited to answer ITAs' questions about topics ranging from undergraduate educational backgrounds and extracurricular activities to their social lives and perceptions of internationals. In other seminars, undergraduates are employed as role-players to help tease out U.S. attitudes toward grading, academic honesty, gender, and sexual harassment and to allow ITAs to experiment with ways of dealing with such issues.

- Classroom aides. Undergraduate students employed to assist daily in the EAP 5837 and 5937 courses provide invaluable feedback about students' communicative and interpersonal strengths and weaknesses. Working in small groups and simulating specific language tasks needed in the international students' daily lives, they can indicate when communication breaks down, suggest NES alternatives, and even note their emotional response to communication styles.

Sociolinguistic Research Orientation

Grounded in a sociolinguistic understanding of the sources of cross-cultural miscommunication, ASE has recently regained the financial ability and departmental authorization to engage in an explicit research program. What follows is a brief history of the development of research on ITA communication at UF and its effect on the ASE program.

In one of the earliest studies of ITA discourse, ASE's founding director Andrea Tyler and graduate student John Bro (1993) studied the sources of miscommunication in 10-minute prelab chemistry lectures. They found that missing or misused discourse markers in ITA speech more significantly added to NES processing effort than did misordering the sequence of information. Tyler (1995) followed up this study by noting the potentially negative consequences for ITA-student frame alignment caused by the cultural variability of discourse management strategies (specifically, Asian versus U.S.), creating the possibility of conflicting participant frames in U.S. classrooms and labs.

Tyler's work at UF moved the analysis of cross-cultural miscommunication from a focus on the ITA alone to a more realistic discussion of the bidirectionality of co-constructed miscommunication, implicating NES students in instances of interlocutor awkwardness. By applying Goffman's (1974) notions of cross-cultural differences in *face*, *frame*, and *footing* to the analysis of ITA discourse, Tyler forcefully indicated the need for further data collection efforts to catalogue the cross-cultural varieties in frame alignment, as well as student-teacher schemas, amid a growing multicultural educational landscape. This approach, combining data collection from real encounters between culturally different interlocutors with a linguistic theory of interaction rituals in face-to-face behavior, greatly illuminated the emerging field of ITA discourse and contributed to the broader area of cross-cultural communication.

Inspired by these beginnings, ASE has continued to incorporate a research imperative into its approach to ITA development. This is manifested not only in an ITA seminar rich in theoretically informed concepts of student-teacher alignment and the contextualization cues that contribute to cross-cultural miscommunication, but also in the tradition of preparing students and staff in the deployment of these concepts in analyzing videotaped real language data.

Although labor intensive, staff development in data collection and analysis methods has proven beneficial not only to ASE but also to the linguistics graduate assistants who teach in the program. For instance, Lucy Pickering's work in ASE led to her coauthoring a study (Pickering & Wiltshire, 2000) of the pitch drop character of Indian English intonation. The conclusion that this feature adds to the discourse processing effort for speakers of U.S. English has contributed to an understanding of the prosodic challenges confronting this population.

Most recently, institutional changes have offered enhanced resources to ASE's research into cross-cultural miscommunication, allowing faculty and graduate student investigations of topics such as the native and nonnative English speaker use of sarcasm for classroom rapport, employment of paraphrasing, prosodic differences (primarily intonation), and phatic communication in teacher-student relations. With the move to exclusively digital data collection and with the inception of a growing online archive of digital video, ASE is orienting itself to develop a major resource for future research into ITA discourse and cross-cultural communication. This research is expected to enhance ASE's effectiveness as well as increase the pedagogical resources available to other ITA programs.

Periodic Program Self-Assessments

ASE uses the process of data collection and analysis not only to prepare ITAs, but also to determine the program's effectiveness. On four occasions in the past 6 years, ASE has solicited substantial external feedback to supplement its ongoing internal scrutiny.

In 1997, the graduate school requested a comprehensive assessment of ASE, including a program description, internal measures (summaries of student and staff evaluations), and external measures (comparisons of the student evaluations of ITAs taking EAP 5836 with those of NES counterparts and an analysis of ITA exit evaluations). A survey in 2000 solicited faculty and administrative perceptions of the needs of international students. In 2001, ASE requested an external assessment under the aegis of the University Center for Excellence in Teaching. Surveys of stakeholder views on ASE services were complemented by qualitative data from follow-up focus groups (see Greene & Shehan, 2001; UF ASE, 2000).

These external evaluations have confirmed the results of regular internal reviews such as the formative course evaluations that ASE students complete at midterm and the official university course evaluations administered at the end of each semester. Input from ASE staff is also solicited at regular meetings and in a postterm evaluation session. These efforts ensure a fit between ASE methods and the changing expectations of its clientele, and they inform future course planning.

A Final Note on Program Features

The four program features described in this chapter have typified ASE since its inception and have been central to its support of ITAs. A research-based strategy of recording discipline-specific language in an actual classroom or with the input of undergraduate assistants followed by subsequent linguistic analysis has promoted

ITAs' teaching success while they are in the process of language change. Continuous assessment has promoted program relevance.

Technology makes the method possible: camcorders, videotapes, VCRs, and DVD players in classes and conferences, wordlists exchanged on audiotape or as electronic files, Web-based instructional materials, e-mailed journals, multimedia computers in the language laboratory, and computerized visual display of speech. Ultimately, however, people make the program: university administrators who provide funding, policy decisions, and enforcement of ITA standards; a qualified, caring, innovative staff sharing their talents in a collaborative environment; and staff developers who work regularly with instructors to facilitate their continued development.

❖ PRACTICAL IDEAS

Expand Institutional Relations

An ITA program that functions well and avoids public complaints can be largely invisible on campus. Ironically, however, invisibility in an academic institution, particularly during periods of budget cuts, can have negative consequences for long-term budgetary health and curricular relevance. Therefore, ASE has continually tried to expand its connections with a variety of institutional entities, including the following:

- Departmental course supervisors. Regular face-to-face and electronic interaction with faculty responsible for undergraduate instruction keep the academic departments aware of the ITA program and clarify for ASE their changing expectations for teaching assistants.

- Undergraduate faculty. UF and other universities are implementing diversity awareness requirements. Consequently, faculty often welcome opportunities to pair students in credit-bearing undergraduate courses with international students in language classes for mutually beneficial collaborative assignments.

- Graduate school research units. Incorporating a research element into an ITA program can increase the program's status in an academic community where research is central.

- Department chairs and graduate coordinators. Periodic program assessment initiatives that solicit feedback on administrators' opinions of the ITA program can provide useful information about desired changes and promote positive visibility.

- Undergraduates. Offering informational programs such as ASE's residence halls effort can initiate dialogue with undergraduates about the reciprocal responsibilities and opportunities of students and ITAs in the U.S. classroom.

Cultivate a Research Mentality

Although research into ITA communication is not expected of all ITA professionals, the collection and analysis of real language data in teaching observations and classroom simulations can closely resemble the procedures of a research project. This is particularly true if efforts are made to systematize the collection and analysis process through measures such as development of protocols, staff development, and use of digital technologies. Approaching ITA professional development from a research stance can stimulate new insights into the immediate communication issues for a particular ITA. Additionally, an open, curious, and structured approach to data can illuminate broader issues of changing trends and patterns, information that is needed to guarantee the continuing relevance of ITA development. Finally, as previously noted, a research program can increase respect for an ITA program at a research university.

Expand the Role of Undergraduate Culture Informants

Even if they are not preparing to be ESL teachers, undergraduate assistants can be more fully utilized if they are viewed as participants in such a program. This means treating them as professionals rather than naïve informants, explaining to them the rationale for procedures, valuing their input, encouraging their contribution of teaching ideas, and occasionally even designing lessons to explicitly develop their teaching and cross-cultural communication potential. As undergraduate assistants become more competent and confident in their roles as cross-cultural teacher-communicators, they also become a richer resource for the ITAs and the instructors.

◈ CONCLUSION

Born in controversy, ASE has developed into a recognized force for improving instruction at UF. Undergraduates benefit from the improved language and cultural skills of their ITAs. ITAs hone their communication skills to become more successful as graduate students and professionals. ASE has made these accomplishments by combining a sociolinguistic research impetus with the utilization of NES undergraduates prepared for this task, strong institutional relations, and periodic program self-assessments to guarantee the relevance and effectiveness of this approach to ITA development.

The future is certain to include more adaptation to ever-changing realities. Graduate student numbers are expected to continue to grow, exacerbating needs for funding, staff, space, and equipment. Proactive, positive visibility in the university community may be required to survive competition for resources. ASE may need to make more efforts to help undergraduates understand the value and strategies of intercultural communication. Technologies will change, requiring staff to constantly upgrade their skills. ASE will be challenged to develop curriculum and instructional materials to efficiently and effectively target the communication needs of a population of international graduate students who arrive with stronger English skills and more cultural savvy than their predecessors.

Informed growth and change will retain the essence of successful program features while being open to new challenges. Thus, ASE at UF expects to intensify its instructional and research efforts to illuminate and facilitate cultural encounters between U.S. undergraduates and scholars from around the world.

◈ CONTRIBUTORS

Gordon J. Tapper is coordinator of Academic Spoken English at the University of Florida and has been employed in the program since 1989. His current research interest focuses on the bidirectional negotiation between interlocutors required to achieve successful cross-cultural communication and on the pragmatics of exemplary cross-cultural teaching.

Kathryn L. Kidder was Academic Spoken English coordinator at the University of Florida from 1994 to 2001. She previously taught and administered community college and adult ESL and international language programs.

◈ APPENDIX A: EAP 5836 SEMINAR TOPICS & READINGS

WEEK 1:
Course Introduction
Tips for the first day of class

WEEK 2:
Characteristics of a "Good" Teacher

WEEK 3:
Cross-Cultural Teaching
Interaction 1: Active Listening

WEEK 4:
Interaction 2: Listening and Responding to Questions

WEEK 5:
Interaction 3: Promoting Learning by Asking Questions

WEEK 6:
Prosody as Communication

WEEK 7:
Testing and Grading
Handling Difficult Situations

WEEK 8:
Academic Honesty
One on One With Students

WEEK 9:
Negotiation and Persuasion

WEEK 10:
The Interactive Lecture: Organizing Information and Making Connections

WEEK 11:
Discussion: Leading and Participating

WEEK 12:
Who Are My Students? Pt. 1,
The Undergraduate Student

WEEK 13:
Who Are My Students? Pt. 2,
Diversity, Emergencies

WEEK 14:
Who Are My Students? Pt. 3,
Gender Issues, Course Evaluation

WEEK 15:
U.S. Values
Course Summary and Future Directions

◈ APPENDIX B: EAP 5836 SAMPLE LESSON PLAN
Week 9: NEGOTIATION AND PERSUASION

OBJECTIVES:

- Students will be aware of the interplay of language, culture, and context when dealing with potentially difficult and/or emotional one-on-one situations.

- Students will demonstrate through role-play their ability to deal with such situations.

- Students will improve their English pronunciation with a focus on enunciation.

NEED:

- Role-player(s)
- Video: *Techniques for Teachers* (Wennerstrom, 1991), Office Hrs.
- Videotape and camera set up
- Video: *Crosstalk* (Gumperz, Jupp, & Roberts, 1979), principal scene and notes
- OH: principles for 1-on-1
- Role-play scenarios, include ones provided by Ss

BUSINESS:

- Evaluations of 5836. Thanks. Comments: what can/will/can't change.
- Video analysis form: Continue to use as a guide for microanalysis of tapes. Come to conference prepared to discuss your observations.
- Wordlist: Your choice: 10 words and sentences OR choose another exercise in your book for which you'd like feedback.
- Other concerns?

PRONUNCIATION:

- Pairs practice
- Enunciation: What is it? Do you perceive any cultural barriers in producing this?

NEGOTIATION:

- Use their role-play tapes and/or OH to review principles for office hours/ grading situations + academic honesty.
- *Techniques for Teachers 13D* (Wennerstrom, 1991)
  - — View segment on test failure and test strategies.
  - — Importance of active listening, clarification.

- — What is student asking for? Grade change? Tips to do better? Test taking skills? Math knowledge? Assessment of her abilities/need to drop course? Confidence?
- • View *Crosstalk* principal scene
  - — Remember: goals of each side. Listen! Think of the other's perspective. Use culturally expected modes of disagreement (see notes).
- • View *Techniques for Teachers 13E* (Wennerstrom, 1991)
  - — Saying no: T holds firm in disagreement w/ persistent student who wants to make up work.
  - — *Listen.* Know policy and hold to it where important. Give where you can. Learning is the point.
- • *ITAs Share Scenarios* of situations w/ their students. List on board for role-play.

ROLE-PLAYS:

- • Scenarios students brought and others useful for the particular students.
- • Summarize principles
  - — Dealing with students individually helps them learn the content, understand how experts in the field think, appreciate basis for grading, etc.
  - — It helps you evaluate their background, motivation, abilities, and therefore be a more effective teacher.
  - — Both sides should benefit, feel their goals are met.
  - — That always takes good listening; requires that you have consistent principles and are able to articulate them.
  - — Assume good faith and keep in mind that *learning* is the goal.

ASSIGNMENT:

- • Next we will go back to other classroom teaching techniques, spending 2 weeks on lecture and discussion-leading.
- • Lots of readings re: organizing presentation (see schedule).
- • ** Prepare for miniteach (3–5 min.) = Only Group B
  - — Present a visual you would use in class or to explain your research (OH, board, HO or ?) Follow organizational principles from Comm. 43–44
  - — Teach a process/give instructions interactively: pp. 77–78
- • Wordlist: 10 words/sentences OR choose another exercise in your book for which you'd like feedback.
- • Journal: How's your teaching going at this point?

CHAPTER 3

Situated Support in the First Year of Teaching

Wayne Jacobson, Margy Lawrence, and Karen Freisem

◈ INTRODUCTION

The International Teaching Assistant (ITA) Program at the University of Washington Center for Instructional Development and Research (CIDR) has existed since 1984. Over time, the ITA Program has given us opportunity to reflect on and evaluate the role of instructional support for ITAs and to observe directly how new ITAs negotiate the challenges of their first year of teaching. On the basis of direct observations of ITAs in classes that they teach, data collected from their students, and individual consultations with them during the quarters they are teaching, we have been able to develop and expand our initial ITA preparation and our strategies for ongoing follow-up. Additionally, by working with ITAs when they are already teaching, we are able to situate the instructional support that we provide in ways that research and experience suggest are highly strategic for improving teacher effectiveness.

In the ITA Program's current form, ITAs are required to attend selected workshops during the university's Annual TA Conference on Teaching and Learning at the beginning of the academic year and to participate in ongoing individual consultations with CIDR staff that focus on teaching effectiveness, intercultural communication, and/or language fluency. The focus and frequency of consultations depend on an ITA's prior teaching experience, the nature of his or her teaching assignment, and the instructional support provided by the ITA's department. All ITAs must participate in the ITA Program during their first year of teaching at the University of Washington (UW).

◈ CONTEXT

In the first years of the ITA Program (1984–1988), there were no specific policies regarding language proficiency or instructional preparation for ITAs at UW. During this time, CIDR held a week-long workshop specifically for ITAs at the beginning of the academic year and CIDR staff consulted individually with ITAs to help them improve language proficiency and teaching effectiveness. Although the ITA Program was not required, departments were strongly encouraged to refer ITAs to CIDR.

In 1988 the university instituted an oral language proficiency requirement for ITAs. In 1990 the Graduate School also mandated participation in CIDR's ITA Program for all newly appointed ITAs. As more departments became responsive to the mandate, the number of participants in the ITA Program grew from 25 in 6 departments in 1984 to 160 in 47 departments in 2004.

Until 1998 reporting to departments was limited to providing the names of ITAs who participated. In 1997, in response to requests from the Graduate School and an interdepartmental review, the ITA Program instituted a process for gathering early feedback to help identify and assist ITAs who might be having difficulty communicating effectively with their students. This process was also designed to include departments in planning and implementing appropriate measures to address issues that the process brings to light. A quarterly reporting procedure was also established to document for departments each ITA's work with the ITA Program. Developing these procedures in ways that were responsive to the institution and respectful of the ITAs has posed a major challenge, but as we will show, these procedures have led to a number of unanticipated benefits for ITAs and the ITA Program alike.

In 2003 the ITA Program went through another significant change when CIDR and the Graduate School instituted the Annual TA Conference on Teaching and Learning. As a result, new ITAs now join all other UW teaching assistants at a 3-day conference designed to help them prepare for their teaching assistant responsibilities. After this conference, ITA Program staff continue to follow up individually with new ITAs during their first year of teaching.

These changes, and lessons we have learned because of them, are explained more fully in the following description of the ITA Program, its distinguishing features, and practical ideas for working with ITAs.

◈ DESCRIPTION

The ITA Program is housed in CIDR, a unit of the Graduate School that supports teaching and learning on campus. CIDR provides instructional development for UW faculty and teaching assistants on individual, departmental, and campus-wide levels. ITA Program staff devote part of their time to this work for the UW teaching community, and part to the ITA Program. Three professional staff and up to five graduate student staff members contribute to the ITA Program. The number of staff members varies each year, but the total number of client contact hours devoted to the ITA Program is roughly equivalent to the time of two full-time employees.

During 2004–2005, 160 ITAs representing 47 departments participated in CIDR's ITA Program; 57% of this group came from engineering and natural or physical sciences departments, 23% came from social sciences departments, and 20% came from arts and humanities departments. Approximately one third of the ITAs were new to the United States, one third transferred from other U.S. universities, and one third had already been at UW for at least one year. Approximately one half of the ITAs referred to the ITA Program reported to us that they were new to teaching.

The ITA Program is one component of UW's preparation and support for ITAs. Before they can be appointed as teaching assistants, ITAs must receive a score of 230[1] on the Speaking Proficiency English Assessment Kit (SPEAK) test, administered by

---

[1] The form of the SPEAK test administered by the University of Washington is scored on a 0–300 scale.

the Office of Educational Assessment (OEA) and scored by the ESL Program, or a score of 55 on the internationally administered Test of Spoken English (TSE). ITAs who do not achieve a passing score on the SPEAK test or the TSE are required to take and pass an ESL course designed for ITA preparation. See Appendix A for a list of Internet sites that outline these university requirements for ITA appointments.

ITAs are also asked to meet the same requirements as all other teaching assistants, including participation in the Annual TA Conference on Teaching and Learning and in departmental teaching assistant development and supervision. Because ITA Program clients are involved in these activities at the same time that they are participating in the program itself, CIDR's ITA Program staff coordinate with a wide range of UW offices, programs, and academic departments.

The ITA Program begins with orientation and professional development workshops one week prior to the university's autumn orientation week. In previous years these workshops were provided through the Pre-Autumn Workshop (PAW) for ITAs. PAW lasted 4 days, providing a set of core sessions for all participants as well as concurrent sessions that participants chose according to interests, needs, or teaching assistant roles. For examples of topics typically addressed during PAW, see Table 1.

Starting in 2003, much of the PAW content was integrated into the Annual TA Conference on Teaching and Learning. Departments are now asked to refer newly appointed ITAs to a set of sessions on the first day of the conference that are designed specifically for ITAs. These sessions include an overview of teaching assistant roles in U.S. higher education, a session on teaching undergraduates in the United States, a question-and-answer session with a panel of experienced ITAs, and an overview of the SPEAK test. ITAs then have opportunities during the next 2 days of the conference to attend elective sessions on teaching with other noninternational teaching assistants. These elective sessions address much of the content formerly provided at the PAW, although in sessions designed for all teaching assistants rather than only for ITAs. Table 2 identifies the content of ITA sessions at the Annual TA Conference on Teaching and Learning.

After the teaching assistant conference, ITA Program staff individually follow up with each ITA. They visit classes taught by these ITAs and, in most cases, gather feedback from the students, help them interpret and respond to students' feedback, and consult with them on effective teaching and communication. On average, during each quarter slightly more than half of the ITAs in the ITA Program have classroom teaching assignments, with the remainder assigned to grading and office hours, working as research assistants, and/or preparing to teach during an upcoming quarter.

When data indicates that an ITA may be experiencing difficulty communicating effectively with students (based on language proficiency test results, student feedback, or department feedback), ITA Program staff implement the Early Feedback Process. This process involves the staff observing the ITA in the classroom and collecting written feedback from students early in the quarter. Appendix B provides a sample form for collecting student feedback. If more than one fourth of the students express strong concern about the ITA's ability to communicate, ITA Program staff inform the ITA's department and work with the ITA and the department to develop strategies for communicating more effectively. In the past, these strategies have included increased consultations on both language and instruction with ITA Program staff, assignment of a mentor teaching assistant from the department, and

TABLE 1. SAMPLE PRE-AUTUMN WORKSHOP CONTENT

Day One	Learning Contexts:
	• TA Roles in U.S. Higher Education
	• Who Are Your Students
	Preparing for the First Day of Class
	Assessment of Student Learning
	SPEAK Test Overview
Day Two	SPEAK Test
	Panel of Experienced ITAs
	Teaching Situations (Choose One)
	• Teaching Discussion Sections in Math, Science, and Engineering
	• Teaching Discussion Sections in Social Sciences and Humanities
	• Teaching in Labs
	• Teaching Language Courses
	• Teaching in Study Centers and Office Hours
Day Three	Elective Sessions (Choose Two)
	• Active Learning in Math, Science, and Engineering Courses
	• Avoiding Cultural Misunderstandings in Class
	• Communicating in American English
	• Grading
	• Interactive Problem-Solving
	• Responding to Student Writing
	• Teaching through Discussion
	• Using the Internet in Instruction
Day Four	Challenging Classroom Situations
	Microteaching

closer supervision by the department. In a few cases, ITAs have been reassigned to different teaching assistant responsibilities involving less direct contact with students.

At the end of each quarter, all ITAs referred to the ITA Program receive an End-of-Quarter (EOQ) Teaching Report summarizing their work with CIDR during that quarter. These reports are drafted by ITA Program staff based on data previously discussed with the ITA; ITAs are given the chance to read the report, confirm that it accurately reflects their work with CIDR, and add their own comments. After that, final copies of the reports are made available to each department. Appendix C provides a sample EOQ form.

These early feedback and EOQ documentation procedures were first instituted in 1998, and they emerged in the context of the university's increased emphasis on accountability. At that time, the Graduate School asked CIDR to monitor ITA communication issues in the classroom more closely and to provide supporting documentation. At the same time, an interdepartmental faculty review committee

TABLE 2. ITA PROGRAM SESSIONS AT THE ANNUAL TA CONFERENCE
ON TEACHING AND LEARNING

Day One (am)	ITAs join other UW TAs for an opening plenary and elective sessions on a wide range of topics related to teaching and learning.
Day One (pm)	ITA Program Sessions: • TA Roles in U.S. Higher Education • Who Are Your Students Panel of Experienced International TAs
Day Two Day Three	On the second and third days of the TA Conference, ITAs join other UW TAs for elective sessions on a wide range of topics related to teaching and learning.

recommended that departments receive more information from the ITA Program on each ITA's teaching performance. Responding to these calls for increased monitoring and documentation of ITAs' performance has been one of our greatest challenges as a program (Lawrence & Jacobson, 2003).

These program changes required us to reconcile CIDR's principle of confidentiality for clients and our emphasis on formative feedback with the goals of being collaborative and providing documentation for other program stakeholders. Previously we had kept consultations confidential and focused exclusively on formative feedback, so we were concerned about how the nature and quality of our interactions with ITAs might change if they thought their interactions with ITA Program staff would be reported back to their departments. We also were concerned that gathering feedback early in an ITA's first quarter of teaching might undermine his or her confidence and credibility in the classroom.

In response to these concerns, we piloted a variety of feedback tools for the early feedback process, and we decided to collect feedback using an open-ended form with two questions focusing on what helps students learn and what changes students would recommend, without asking specifically about language. In this way, we hoped to gather the feedback we needed without putting undue negative focus on any ITA. We have also been careful to engage the ITAs collaboratively in every phase of the student feedback process: initial interpretation of the feedback gathered, discussions with the department regarding strategies for addressing issues raised in the feedback, and drafting the EOQ Teaching Report at the end of the quarter. We also defined clearly what was to be reported to departments and what was not; for example, ITA discussion of struggles with teaching or difficulties working with supervising faculty would not be reported, but feedback from students on the ITAs' contributions to their learning would be included in the report.

Responses to these program changes have been generally positive. ITAs report that they appreciate the instructional support they receive from the ITA Program, as evidenced by comments on program evaluation forms and by their apparent attitudes toward their work with us. We have not detected changes in ITAs' willingness to participate in the ITA Program, and many departments have done more to encourage participation in the ITA Program and to make use of the information gathered through observation and feedback processes.

Another indicator of the ITA Program's value has been how ITAs have used program documentation to help demonstrate their teaching effectiveness. For example, each year since we began using our current EOQ system, there have been situations in which an individual student has complained to a department about an ITA and claimed to speak on behalf of all students in the class; in these cases, it has helped the ITAs to have documentation on record indicating that very few or no complaints of this type were raised when student feedback was collected earlier in the quarter. Similarly, departments who make teaching assistant appointment decisions solely on the basis of numerical student evaluations now have additional evidence of teaching effectiveness.

ITAs who have trouble communicating with their students have also benefited from the feedback process. Generally, our experience has been that such an ITA is already extremely conscientious and concerned about students' learning; in these cases the student feedback helps the ITA have a more accurate understanding of students' perceptions and helps document for the department the ITA's efforts to improve. In a few cases, ITAs have wanted to dismiss student dissatisfaction as an indicator of lack of preparation on the students' part. Having a documented record that a significant number of students do not understand them has motivated these ITAs to take more seriously the need to prepare for class and to work on improving communication skills.

The fact that increased communication and collaboration with departments is now built into the structure of the ITA Program has provided additional benefits sas well. We have more opportunities to integrate our own instructional consulting with the content-area expertise and departmental experience of a faculty member or more experienced teaching assistant. Greater departmental collaboration has also raised the ITA Program's profile. We have been called on more often to help departments and individual faculty when they become aware of situations in which ITAs need additional instructional support. This increased departmental awareness has at times brought faculty and non-ITAs to CIDR, as a result of their interactions with the ITA Program, to request the same type of instructional consulting or feedback on their own teaching.

Increased attention to monitoring and documenting ITAs' teaching has also contributed to a greater campus-wide awareness of the fact that all new teaching assistants need feedback and instructional support. Soon after the institution of Graduate School Memorandum No. 15, "Conditions of Appointment for TAs Who Are Not U.S. Citizens," the Graduate School Council passed Graduate School Memorandum No. 14, "Departmental Responsibilities Regarding Instruction by TAs." This policy memorandum established guidelines for teaching assistant preparation and supervision across departments and was motivated at least in part by the recognition that all teaching assistants would benefit from the same type of institutional support that ITAs were receiving.

◈ DISTINGUISHING FEATURES

The consultation-based approach of CIDR's ITA Program allows us to provide support for ITAs at a strategic point in their development as teachers, greatly informs our own practice by bringing us directly into contexts in which ITAs are teaching, and helps us see how the challenges faced by new ITAs compare to challenges faced by other new university instructors.

What New Teachers Need to Learn and How They Learn It

The support that our ITA Program provides is situated in immediate contexts of teaching practice, and places ITA Program staff into situations in which we are able to help ITAs negotiate meaning and action in those contexts. It is not simply a matter of presenting ITAs with general principles of teaching which they will then extend and apply to classroom situations as needed; rather, we are able to help them develop skills and utilize resources to interpret their situations as they experience them, and to test with them the implications of interpretations and instructional choices they make. From this situated perspective, it is not quite right to say that we are helping ITAs learn *from* the experience of teaching, but rather, *in* the experience of teaching (Wilson, 1993, p. 75). There is much in the literature on the nature of learning, teaching, and learning to teach that discusses the importance of understanding teaching as a situated act.

Putnam and Borko (2000) pointed out that it is common to think of knowledge as "something that persons *have* and can take from one setting to another" (p. 12). From this perspective, a person learns general principles at an abstract level and applies them to specific settings; if the person is unable to apply general principles, it is taken as an indicator that he or she has not sufficiently learned the principles. Putnam and Borko argued in contrast that a teacher's knowledge needs to be recognized as contextual; for example, successfully fielding questions in a microteaching session with a small group of fellow novice teachers does not necessarily mean that one will be similarly successful fielding questions with a large group of novice learners. It is not simply a matter of what one knows about teaching, but where one knows it.

Carter (1990) wrote that "teachers' knowledge is not highly abstract or propositional. Nor can it be formalized into a set of specific skills of preset answers to specific problems. Rather, it is experiential, procedural, situational, and particular-istic" (p. 307), suggesting that there are definite limits on what can be learned apart from the experience of teaching. Carter warned, however, that new teachers dropped into "natural settings" (p. 307) of teaching can be easily overwhelmed or distracted by the many things going on; there is no guarantee that a novice teacher will learn what to do in a situation simply because it is authentic. She proposed guided or constructed experiences with a "high degree of situation and task validity" (p. 307).

Participants in our ITA Program, however, are already immersed in natural settings of teaching. Some may have benefited from guided preparation (through an ESL course or departmental preparation), but many have not received formal preparation for their teaching roles outside of ITA Program orientation and professional development sessions. In either case, they face the challenge of taking knowledge gained in one context and putting it to use in another context that is often very different from their own prior learning or experience. To some extent we have responded to this challenge by focusing our ITA Program orientation and professional development on specific issues and contexts that many ITAs are likely to face early in their teaching experience, but our experience also suggests that we can provide the most significant help for new ITAs by consulting with them individually.

In this way we are able to situate instructional support in their first year of teaching, when learning how to teach is necessarily grounded in the immediate experience of teaching.

Grounding Our Own Practice

Through our continuous involvement with ITAs during their first year of teaching, we have also learned lessons about the actual settings in which ITAs teach and the strategies that help them succeed in those settings. This accumulated local knowledge of different departments and their respective teaching situations contributes greatly to our ability to consult with clients in those departments.

Our ITA Program staff represent a variety of professional and academic backgrounds and teaching experience, but the majority of us find our academic homes in languages, linguistics, literature, and education. Yet we find the majority of ITAs referred to our ITA Program are in disciplines that heavily emphasize preparation in mathematics and natural or physical sciences. It has been important for our staff to recognize that different disciplines are taught and learned differently—with distinct ways of organizing and representing knowledge, distinct social and cultural histories, and distinct systems of values and expectations (Donald, 2002; Lee, 1999; Shulman, 1987). Furthermore, undergraduates enter courses in these disciplines at different points in their own academic careers, with distinct learning goals. For example, are students majors, nonmajors, or premajors? Is the course a requirement, an elective, or a prerequisite for later courses in a different major? As a result, we need to be aware that characteristics of effective teaching may differ, in form and substance, from one disciplinary context to another. As instructional consultants working with clients across a wide range of disciplines, our knowledge base needs to extend beyond our teaching experience in our own academic disciplines.

One way of expanding our knowledge base has been to keep informed about different disciplinary conversations on teaching by following publications, Web sites, and discussion lists in the disciplines in which we frequently work. Even more important, however, is our staff's collective history observing the classes taught in these disciplines on our campus. Through the ITA Program we have observed ITAs' classes on a quarterly basis, interviewed students in many of those classes, talked with the ITAs about their perceptions of teaching and learning in their disciplines, and learned from faculty members about their goals and expectations for teaching assistants and students. These interactions have also given us a sense of the challenges presented in particular classes by the balance of majors and nonmajors, for example, or the point in their academic programs at which students take a particular course or sequence. In some departments we have established working relationships with specific faculty members who frequently teach courses to which teaching assistants are typically assigned. This collection of information sources and perspectives has allowed us to develop constellations of local knowledge that helps us ground our instructional consultations in the specific contexts and the immediate challenges faced by teaching assistants in particular teaching situations.

This knowledge gives us a basis from which to present features of good teaching that might apply across multiple contexts, but take specific forms in different disciplines. For example, rather than saying only, "Students need appropriate feedback on performance to benefit from courses" (Chickering & Gamson, 1987, p.

8), we can say, "Students at an introductory level in calculus benefit from feedback of this type, and they tell us they appreciate getting it in this form, at these points in time." This local knowledge also enables us to identify challenges that are characteristic to a given course and to distinguish those from challenges that an individual teaching assistant may face on his or her own due to ineffective teaching strategies.

Our experience has been that this local knowledge base gives us an extra measure of credibility with our clients and their departments. Because we can say, "We've been in a number of discussion sections for this course, and students frequently tell us they have this kind of problem," we are able to demonstrate that our assessment is based not only on opinion or expertise, but also on empirical evidence. Because we are able to say, "Here is a strategy that we've observed other teaching assistants using in this class, and this is how it worked for them," we are able to make a stronger case than if we could appeal only to abstract or generalized principles of good teaching.

In addition to grounding our practice in the context of disciplines and specific departments on our campus, the data we have been able to collect over time and across courses has helped us ground our practice in student perceptions of what helps them learn. Thus as we talk with ITAs about teaching effectively, we can refer to interviews and surveys of students in similar courses during other quarters—both to identify potential learning challenges and to develop teaching and problem-solving strategies. In this way, too, we are able to extend our knowledge base for consulting beyond our own academic disciplines and professional experience as teachers.

In their review of teacher education research, Zeichner and Gore (1990) concluded that new teachers are socialized to the practice of teaching through the classrooms in which they teach, relationships with colleagues, and the cultures of departments and institutions to which they belong. Because we are grounding our work with ITAs in an understanding of the cultures and classrooms within which they function, we are able to help them in this socialization process while they are at a key point in the formation of their teaching beliefs and practices. Furthermore, our instructional support can be in concert with these other critical contextual factors—adding emphasis, reinforcement, and supplemental assistance as needed—rather than being separated from them in time, space, and disciplinary focus.

Gaining Perspective

Finally, because CIDR ITA Program staff are also assigned to consult with noninternational faculty and teaching assistants on instructional issues, we have had the opportunity to observe how issues faced by ITAs compare to the issues faced by their noninternational colleagues. We find, for example, that many instructors (not only new ITAs) find it challenging to express disciplinary expertise in terms that are accessible to novice learners. Consider, for example, these comments by students in an introductory statistics course, taught by a U.S.-born native English speaker:

> He doesn't speak English, he speaks statistics.

> He often speaks in symbols and abbreviations, and not actual words.

> [Students] need more explanation of terms, more "layman explanations."

Our interactions with noninternational instructors suggest that this challenge is not simply a matter of word choice, but frame of reference. One instructor e-mailed this insight after working extensively for two quarters to find better ways of helping his students learn:

> I woke up in the middle of the night recently and had the thought "You're teaching to yourself, not the students." Which is to say, I'm not spending enough time thinking about what the students are going to ask. I prepare by doing a problem myself and breaking it into its elements, but from my point of view. . . . At some level, I have been telling myself that it would make me look dumb to talk about the more trivial (to me) elements of a problem, but that is ridiculous, of course. . . . I kept this idea in mind when I was lecturing Wednesday, and I felt that I went at a slower pace and had more pauses, because I was thinking about times when they surely would be puzzled.

This instructor's observation of his own teaching echoes Brookfield's (1995) observation that the

> best learners . . . often make the worst teachers. They are, in a very real sense, perceptually challenged. They cannot imagine what it must be like to struggle to learn something that comes so naturally to them. Because they have always been so successful in their learning, it's impossible for them to empathize with learners' anxieties and blockages. (p. 62)

These observations are consistent with research findings that a central element of effective teaching from the students' perspective is being able to connect the content of the course to students' prior learning, and to show appreciation of the challenges students face in trying to learn it (Bransford, Brown, & Cocking, 2000; Carson, 1999; UW SOUL, 2001). Instructors who do not make these connections will be viewed as relatively ineffective by their students, whether they are international or noninternational, teaching assistants or faculty.

It is not something to take for granted that noninternational instructors will make these connections any more automatically than international instructors. McBride, Miller, and Nief (n.d.) circulate Beloit College's annual *Mindset List* to remind members of the academic community about the differences between their generation and the generation of incoming freshman, and the American Association for Higher Education has published demographic data to emphasize some of these differences (Hansen, 1998). Others highlight the different life experiences of the increasingly diverse student body compared to the relatively less diverse community of faculty and TAs (University of North Carolina at Chapel Hill, 1997), for example, or the different approaches to learning taken by students who have grown up with relatively easy access to information technology (Brown, 2000). These differences have particular implications for teaching and learning, but all suggest that university instructors can be fairly certain that their students are not like them in life experience or approaches to learning. It is important for all instructors, not only ITAs, to recognize who their students are, what experience and expectations they bring with them to the classroom, and what ways of teaching will be most effective for helping them learn.

Research in higher education indicates that the development of effective teaching practices is best supported by ongoing mentoring and feedback throughout the course of a teaching career (Fox & Hockerman, 2003). Yet we find that many academic departments provide teaching assistants with uneven support in their teaching roles, at best (Austin, 2002; Nyquist et al., 1999). Our work with U.S.-born native English speakers has helped us learn to recognize how challenges faced by ITAs are reflections of the fact that they are new to teaching in their departments and still in the process of being socialized into their academic disciplines (Lewis, 1997; Nyquist & Wulff, 1996). For many ITAs, these challenges may overlap and interact with challenges based on differences in language, culture, or prior experience in different educational systems. But different strategies are required for responding to these various challenges, and viewing ITAs' situations in the context of teaching challenges faced by all graduate students and faculty has helped us develop more strategic approaches to consulting with them on improving their teaching.

⬦ PRACTICAL IDEAS

Based on our experiences in the CIDR ITA Program, we propose the following practical suggestions for others who work with ITAs, whether their main points of contact are before the ITAs start teaching, while they are teaching, or both.

Observe Noninternational TAs and Faculty in the Classroom and Encourage ITAs to Do the Same

Observations of noninternational TAs and faculty in specific disciplines by the ITA program staff as well as the ITA can yield a much greater understanding of disciplinary discourse and practice that can then inform the ITA's subsequent teaching practice. Those working with ITAs can observe clusters of classes in several disciplines and note key discourse patterns, typical instructional practices, and student behavior and interaction with the instructor. Observations by ITAs need to be preceded by a discussion of observation goals and focus. We have found it most helpful for the observer, whether instructor or ITA, to use an open-ended observation approach guided by a few key questions determined in a meeting beforehand (see Classroom Observation, 1998). It is also important to meet afterward and discuss the observation, focusing on what the ITA thinks might work in his or her teaching situation and what he or she might do differently.

Observe ITAs in the Classroom and Gather Student Feedback

Observing and gathering student feedback in the ITA's own classroom forms a basis for discussing effective teaching and communication strategies. The students' perspective can be gained by asking them to write answers to these questions: "What is helping you learn in this class?" and "What is not helping you learn? What suggestions do you have?" Feedback can be collected and typed up in a single report to ensure students' anonymity. In consultation with the ITA afterward, the observer can work to identify themes in the feedback and goals for change. The ITA should leave with a copy of the feedback and a written summary of key points discussed. It is also important to follow up with the ITA by e-mail, another meeting, and/or another observation. This process of observing and gathering feedback not only informs the ITA of how to improve, but also provides the program with information regarding the effectiveness of preservice preparation.

Help ITAs See the Value of Ongoing Reflection and Feedback

Whether a program works with ITAs while they are teaching or prepares them for future teaching assignments, it is advisable to help ITAs develop an appreciation for the situated nature of teaching and the consequent importance of ongoing reflection and self-assessment. Reflective practices and self-assessment can be folded into all aspects of professional development, including workshops and preteaching preparation classes. ITA Program staff can model these practices by being observed and/or implementing classroom assessment techniques (see Classroom Assessment of Teaching and Learning, 1998), whether they work with the ITAs one on one or in a classroom setting, and ITAs themselves can be assigned to practice these approaches throughout their professional development. In addition, ITAs can be encouraged to continue to seek out colleagues who are interested in discussing issues of teaching and learning, to ask colleagues to observe them teach, and to gather midterm feedback from students on their own. They can also be introduced to a variety of other classroom assessment techniques to help them develop a repertoire of strategies for ongoing assessment of student learning and their own teaching effectiveness (see Angelo & Cross, 1993a, for a wide range of classroom assessment techniques, with many discipline-specific examples).

Collaborate with ITAs to Document
Teaching and Learning Experiences

Creating a report that documents work with the ITA program gives the ITA and the consultant an opportunity to summarize and foreground strengths and potential areas for change in the ITA's development; the document can establish a foundation for the ITA's future work on his or her teaching. It can also be a helpful source of information to departments engaged in ongoing work with the ITA. If this documentation is going to be used by departments, our experience tells us that it is important to find out from departments what kinds of information they would find useful, to make the document concise, to include the ITA's voice in the document, and to set clear expectations for the reporting process.

However, even if the only audience for this document is the ITA, producing it still provides an opportunity for the ITA to reflect on and to evaluate teaching experiences in order to learn from and build on those experiences for the future. For the growing number of ITAs whose careers keep them in the United States (Johnson, 1998; Park, 2001), this practice of documenting and reflecting on their efforts to become more effective teachers could become an important contribution to future professional roles in organizing projects, leading teams, and representing their work to scholarly and professional communities.

❖ CONCLUSION

Freeman (1996) noted that "there are people who 'teach' in every society, [but] the term 'teacher' will have different meanings within those societies reflecting tacit, de facto social agreements about the boundaries of the term" (p. 745). We have long understood that many ITAs hold implicit models of good teaching that are based on the different social, cultural, and educational practices they have experienced. It is not always clear, however, how these implicit, prior models affect visible, current teaching practices, or how these models change when a new model is confronted. To some extent we can try to delineate what new ITAs need to learn in order to be effective teachers in U.S. university classrooms, and we can give them some prior notice of important features of teaching that they need to be aware of, but our experience and teacher preparation research both suggest that many important lessons about teaching are best learned in the experience of teaching.

◈ CONTRIBUTORS

Wayne Jacobson is associate director of the Center for Instructional Development Research and coordinator of the ITA Program at the University of Washington.

Margy Lawrence is a senior consultant at the Center for Instructional Development and Research at the University of Washington, where she coordinates services to the social sciences and humanities departments, consults with faculty and teaching assistants in those departments, and consults with ITAs in the ITA Program.

Karen Freisem is a senior consultant at the Center for Instructional Development and Research at the University of Washington, where she coordinates services to the math, science, and engineering departments; consults with faculty and teaching assistants in those departments; and consults with ITAs in the ITA Program.

◈ APPENDIX A: INTERNET SOURCES OF INFORMATION ABOUT THE CIDR ITA PROGRAM

Center for Instructional Development and Research (CIDR)
http://depts.washington.edu/cidrweb/

ITA Program at CIDR
http://depts.washington.edu/cidrweb/ITA.html

ITA Program Workshops at the TA Conference on Teaching and Learning
http://depts.washington.edu/cidrweb/ITAPAW.html

Overview of Prerequisites for ITA Appointments
http://depts.washington.edu/cidrweb/ITAappts.html

> English Language Competence for Admission to the Graduate School
> http://www.grad.washington.edu/Acad/gsmemos/gsmemo08.htm

> Departmental Responsibilities Regarding Instruction by TAs
> http://www.grad.washington.edu/Acad/gsmemos/gsmemo14.htm

> Conditions of Appointment for TAs Who Are Not U.S. Citizens
> http://www.grad.washington.edu/Acad/gsmemos/gsmemo15.htm

> English 102 (English for ITAs)
> http://depts.washington.edu/uwelp/aep/ita.shtml

◈ APPENDIX B: EARLY FEEDBACK PROCESS AND SAMPLE FORM

Selection and procedures for Early Feedback

For international teaching assistants (ITA) who have teaching assignments, and who have received SPEAK scores under 250, TSE scores under 55, or complaints about their communication skills during a previous quarter, a CIDR representative will visit the ITA's classroom and gather feedback from students about their perceptions of the ITA's teaching as soon as possible during the quarter. The CIDR consultant and the ITA will use this feedback to help determine what to address in ongoing instructional consultations that quarter.

In cases in which a significant number of students (greater than 25%) express complaints related to the ITA's communication skills, CIDR and the ITA will also inform the department and collaborate with the department to plan an appropriate response. Ideally, this collaboration will proceed as follows:

The director of CIDR will review the case and contact the appropriate department chair. The chair will be asked to arrange a meeting between selected departmental representatives and representatives of CIDR. Departmental representatives may include the chair, the graduate program coordinator, lead TAs, ITA supervisors, and the ITA. The purpose of this meeting will be to collaboratively design an appropriate response for each specific case. To the extent that funding permits, possible options include

- Increase training, observation, and/or supervision by a faculty member or experienced ITA mentor.

- Refer the ITA to CIDR for instructional consultations.

- Employ a more experienced teacher to team teach with the ITA.

- In exceptional cases where other responses cannot adequately address the issues that have been identified, reassign the ITA to another role. Acquire a more experienced teacher to fill the role from which the ITA was removed, and provide additional training to prepare the ITA for reassignment during subsequent quarters.

CIDR consultants will follow up on the specific plan during individual consultations that quarter, and at the end of the quarter, confirm the extent to which the plan was followed.

STUDENT FEEDBACK FORM

TEACHING ASSISTANT Name: _____

Class: _____ Date: _____

1. What are the teaching assistant's strong points that are helping you learn in this class?

2. Are there any things in this section that are not helping you learn? Please explain.

◈ APPENDIX C: END-OF-QUARTER TEACHING REPORT

Purpose: To document teaching assistants' work with CIDR and to provide departments and the Graduate School with information about the teaching assistant's teaching.

A: Teaching Assistant Information

Name: _____   Quarter / Year: _____

Department: _____   English proficiency shown by: _____

Course Supervisor: _____   CIDR Consultant: _____

Teaching Assistant
Responsibilities:_____   CIDR Services Provided: _____

B: Student Feedback Data

_____ **not collected by a CIDR consultant this quarter**

_____ *collected during week _____ , by _____ class interview / ____ written survey*
For written comments, number of responses:
Number of students' written comments indicating difficulty understanding the TA:

Summary of Student Feedback:

Strengths   *Areas for Change*
•   •
•   •
•   •

C: Observation of Teaching by a CIDR Consultant

_____ **not observed by a CIDR consultant this quarter**

_____ *observed during week ___*

Summary of Observations:

Strengths   *Areas for Change*
•   •
•   •
•   •

D: CIDR Consultant Recommendations

In light of the information gathered this quarter, I recommend that this TA:

_____ continue as assigned

_____ continue with increased supervision and assistance from the department and CIDR

_____ be evaluated by departmental supervisors before being reassigned

_____ not applicable at this time (see comments below)

Additional comments/explanation:

E: TA Comments

(after reviewing the information presented in this report)

CHAPTER 4

Students Teaching Students: Cultural Awareness as a Two-Way Process

Marilyn Miller and Sandy Matsuda

◈ INTRODUCTION

Undergraduates have participated in the International Teaching Assistant (ITA) Program at the University of Missouri–Columbia (MU) since the program's inception in 1986. They have asked questions and rated comprehensibility in language assessments, provided feedback on classroom and cultural skills in the presemester ITA teaching orientation, and provided midsemester teaching feedback to first-semester ITAs. The ITAs have appreciated the opportunity to learn about MU classroom culture, the undergraduates have thrived in their peer-teaching roles, and both groups have enjoyed the opportunity to interact in a positive way. As a result of the benefits for ITAs as well as undergraduates, we sought undergraduate participation when we designed the first ITA course in 1997. In the first few semesters, undergraduates participated in the microteaching portions of the course, just as they had in the presemester orientations. In 2001, the idea of cultural growth through peer-teaching was broadened from the unidirectional concept of undergraduate students teaching ITAs about MU classroom culture, to a bidirectional concept of ITAs and undergraduate students teaching cultural competencies to one another.

To enable undergraduate students and ITAs to appreciate the value of learning cultural information from one another, all of the students needed to be able to see that their cultural development assignments were relevant to the goals of their course. In addition, ITAs and undergraduates needed to see each other as legitimate sources of the needed cultural information. To meet these needs, we linked the undergraduate and ITA courses for an entire semester, developed social ice-breaker activities to introduce the students, and developed peer-teaching activities so that each could be the valued teacher or informant as well as the learner or recipient. In this chapter we discuss the process and evaluation of expanding undergraduate participation to include bidirectional cultural learning through peer-teaching. We describe the university setting, the growth of the cultural peer-teaching program, and the details of linking an undergraduate occupational therapy (OT) course with an intermediate-level ITA course. We also share the action research done to formally evaluate the OT-ITA linking, which shows that not only were ITAs and undergraduate students satisfied with the peer-teaching linking, but also that the cultural competency of both groups increased.

◈ CONTEXT

MU is located in a small city in the central, rural part of the state, halfway between the two major cities of St. Louis and Kansas City. Columbia lacks heavy industry and has a population of approximately 85,000 (Missouri Census Data Center, 2000). Columbia's location creates a decidedly small-town atmosphere, with MU introducing some of the cultural amenities usually found in a larger city.

MU, a land-grant institution and the largest university in the state, is part of a four-campus system that includes Kansas City, St. Louis, and Rolla. Although many MU undergraduates attended high school in large cities, many others come from towns much smaller than the MU campus. Many of the students have neither traveled abroad nor had a friend from another country. Opportunities to interact with students their age from different cultures are limited because of the low number of international undergraduates at MU. In 1987, international students constituted 1.8% of the total undergraduate population. Numbers rose slowly to 3.2% in 1994, but then decreased again to 1.52% by 2004 (UMC Division of Enrollment Management, 2005a, 2005b, 2005c, 2005d). For many MU undergraduates, an ITA may provide their first contact with someone whose language and concepts of teaching and learning are different from their own.

When an undergraduate's first exposure to cultural and linguistic difference is with an international instructor, conflict can occur. In 1986, legislation in Missouri mandated language assessment and cultural orientation for international graduate students who would be teaching. MU responded by creating the Office of Teaching Assistant Training and Development, which provided presemester teaching orientation for all teaching assistants, and, for ITAs, (a) oral language assessment, (b) a 2-week presemester teaching orientation, and (c) midsemester feedback on teaching and language for the first semester of teaching. After 3 years, the teaching assistant office was expanded into the Program for Excellence in Teaching (PET) and began to serve the instructional development needs of faculty as well as teaching assistants. In 2005, the ITA program was moved to the graduate school.

Prospective ITAs whose oral proficiency was insufficient for a teaching assignment and who wanted to develop their proficiency could enroll in the Intensive English Program (IEP) or take a course offered by the English Language Support Program (ELSP), MU's on-campus, self-supported ESL programs. Students who tested out or had completed all available ELSP courses relied on tutors and off-campus classes for further oral language development. For many years, departments tended to have sufficient numbers of U.S. graduate students and ITAs with strong language skills to meet teaching needs, as well as funding for research assistantships and grading assignments for international graduate students with low language skills. Therefore, during the first few years of the ITA program, an ITA course was unnecessary.

However, in the mid-1990s, the undergraduate population began to rise, creating a demand for teaching assistants. At the same time, however, the graduate population was falling (see Figure 1). The increasing demand for teaching assistants, coupled with a decreasing supply, caused departments to rely more heavily on international graduate students. Demand for language assessments rose, as did demand for remedial language courses. To meet the increased need for remedial instruction, ELSP opened additional sections of their courses and IEP created a special summer section for ITAs. When these actions still did not meet the demand, frustrated department chairs turned to the provost for assistance. Because ELSP did not have the resources to offer ITA courses, the provost funded PET to hire a part-time ESL instructor to teach one free, noncredit ITA course called, "Language and Pedagogy for ITAs." After two semesters and increased demand, an advanced level was added and another part-time instructor was hired. Demand continued to rise and, in winter 2001, the ITA courses became three-credit graduate courses in the Department of Educational Leadership and Policy Analysis. In summer 2001, a full-time instructor was hired and taught both levels. Demand for language remediation

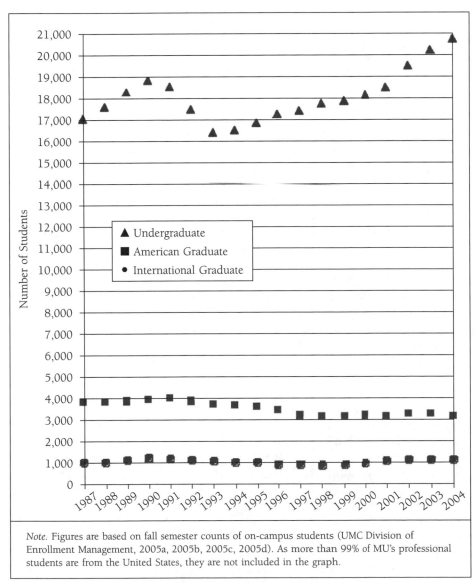

Note. Figures are based on fall semester counts of on-campus students (UMC Division of Enrollment Management, 2005a, 2005b, 2005c, 2005d). As more than 99% of MU's professional students are from the United States, they are not included in the graph.

FIGURE 1. Undergraduate and Graduate Population Changes, 1987–2004

continued to grow and by fall 2002, a second full-time ITA instructor was added. This not only helped meet increasing demand, but also allowed students to take the intermediate and advanced levels from different instructors.

◈ DESCRIPTION

The ITA program at MU consists of a screening component, a presemester orientation for ITAs who pass the screening and receive teaching assignments, a follow-up program in the first semester of teaching, and courses for prospective ITAs who do not pass the screening exam. Undergraduates are involved in all components of the program.

Currently, we use the Speaking Proficiency English Assessment Kit (SPEAK) test as our intake assessment measure and an Oral Presentation Test (OPT) for subsequent assessment. The SPEAK test is administered at the local high school and assessed by two qualified raters. For the OPT, a prospective ITA makes a short presentation on a topic in the ITA's teaching department and answers four–six questions posed by a rating team composed of a faculty member, an ESL instructor, a PET staff member, and two or three undergraduates. The rating team assesses both the language in the prepared presentation and the spontaneous language in the question-answering session. We send a report to the teaching assistant and to the department indicating the teaching assistant's proficiency level and type of teaching permitted (none, office-hour, laboratory teaching, teaching a language course, leading a discussion or review session, or independent teaching).

ITAs who receive an assessment result appropriate for the type of teaching needed in their department must participate in the presemester teaching orientation. We offer a 4-day orientation free of charge the week before the beginning of the fall and spring semesters. The first 3 days are specifically designed for ITAs and include sessions on making presentations, giving explanations and definitions, developing rapport, teaching interactively, asking questions, and handling challenging situations. We also provide the ITAs with two opportunities to give 15-minute lessons and receive feedback on their teaching from a qualified facilitator and two or three undergraduates. On the final day of the presemester teaching orientation, the ITAs join the U.S. teaching assistants for a joint teaching assistant orientation that focuses on some of the same topics, but also includes sessions on issues that are not addressed in the first 3 days, such as grading, technology, and leading discussions.

Those who receive a language assessment level that is too low to teach in their department may take classes from either the campus ESL programs if their language is Level 1 or lower or our ITA classes if their evaluation is a high Level 1 or above. To meet the higher demands for it, each year we offer five sections of our middle-level course, "Communication and Culture for American College Teaching," which focuses on understanding the cultural aspects of the U.S. classroom, developing interactive teaching skills (e.g., organizational, questioning, compensation strategies), and improving fluency at the suprasegmental level. We offer one section per year of our lowest and highest level courses, "Tools for Teaching American Students" and "Instructional and Communication Strategies for Effective College Teaching." The lower-level course focuses on advanced academic listening, discrete pronunciation skills, techniques for laboratory and one-on-one teaching assignments, and an overview of U.S. classroom culture. The higher-level course focuses on more advanced teaching strategies such as presenting with technology, using case studies and problem-based learning, interactive learning, and classroom and course management. The linguistic development is minimal and mainly focuses on reduction, linking, and speech patterns. In all of the courses, ITAs have four microteaching opportunities.

In their first semester of teaching, ITAs must participate in our follow-up program, which is designed to help them make early adjustments to their teaching and thus reduce student complaints and poor end-of-semester evaluations. For the first stage in the follow-up program, gathering midsemester teaching evaluations from the undergraduate students in the class, each ITA may select whether to use the PET Early Feedback form (available in both online and paper formats) or the more process-orientated small-group instructional feedback (SGIF). If the student feedback shows dissatisfaction with overall teaching or language, we ask the ITA to participate in a videotaped teaching observation. After we gather data from the midsemester assessment (and the observation, if needed), we consult with the ITA to discuss what is going well and to give suggestions for teaching improvement.

❖ DISTINGUISHING FEATURES

The distinguishing features of the MU ITA program are the linking of undergraduate courses with the ITA courses and the utilization of reciprocal teaching (J. E. Miller, Groccia, & M. S. Miller, 2001). We now discuss linking the ITA course with two different undergraduate courses: one a topics seminar on becoming a teaching assistant, for seniors wishing to pursue graduate education, and the other an experiential course for juniors in the OT program. In discussing each of these linkings we address the following issues (a) the rationale for linking that particular undergraduate course with the ITA course, (b) the specific procedures and activities of the linking, and (c) the results or effects of the linking. Our discussion of the first linking focuses mainly on the lessons learned and how they influenced the design of the second linking.

Initial ITA-Undergraduate Course Linkings

In the presemester orientation and the ITA courses, ITAs appreciated having undergraduates in their microteaching sessions and highly regarded the undergraduates' advice on improving their teaching. In the presemester orientation we pay undergraduates to participate; however, for the ITA classes, we found that neither pay nor volunteer arrangements have yielded a dependable audience of undergraduates. Because undergraduate input was highly regarded by ITAs and provided cultural development opportunities for undergraduates, we looked for alternate ways of getting undergraduate involvement. In fall 2000, we created the first linking between an undergraduate course and an ITA course when the ITA instructor was also the instructor for a one-hour topics seminar, "EL 360: Preparing to Be a Teaching Assistant," for seniors heading to graduate school. The EL 360 students discussed readings on teaching and learning and observed the teaching of ITAs in microteaching sessions, native-English-speaking (NES) teaching assistants, and ITAs in actual teaching assignments.

Assessment of the EL 360-ITA linking revealed that the ITAs perceived feedback from undergraduates as being valuable. However, only some of the EL 360 students understood how the out-of-class activities benefited their learning, and others viewed the activities involving the ITAs as arbitrary service requirements. This feedback guided the planning of subsequent linking in three ways. First, in planning a linking, we examined the goals of both the undergraduate course and the ITA course to determine which goals could be best met through interaction with students in the other course. We designed peer-teaching activities to meet those goals and reviewed the activities to ensure that they matched course goals. Second, we created ice-breaker activities that would develop the rapport and connection necessary for successful peer teaching to occur. Third, in some cases we sought formal assessment and Institutional Research Board approval to measure change and allow dissemination of results.

Using these guidelines, the linking of courses grew in number and variety and resulted in enhanced learning opportunities for ITAs and undergraduates alike. The number of students participating grew almost tenfold, from 22 students the first year to 201 students 2 years later. In each linking, the goals and objectives of the undergraduate and ITA courses produced unique activities for the ITA and undergraduate peer instructors. In a link between the ITA course and a science methods course, both groups of students learned to use discrepant events and then served as students as well as critics for each other's practice teaching. In a linking with an ESL methods course, the undergraduates designed and led discussion on various cross-cultural language learning issues. These discussions allowed the ITAs to practice their language skills and the undergraduates to gain cross-cultural insights. When an ITA class was linked with an undergraduate textile course, the textile students interviewed ITAs on clothing style and purchasing patterns in their home countries, and the ITAs received feedback on their microteaching lessons.

ITA-Occupational Therapy Linking: An Example

For three fall semesters from 2001 to 2003, the ITA courses were linked with an OT course, "OT 225: Professional Perspectives." In this linking, the goals were to enhance cultural competency for the OT students, to provide the ITAs with authentic teaching experiences, and to develop the communication skills and cross-cultural understanding that ITAs and OT students need to succeed in their respective areas of teaching and health care. This three-semester linking between the OT and ITA courses is used as an example to illustrate the linking concept and the results.

Goals for Linking Occupational Therapy and ITA Classes

Goals for the OT course focused on self-awareness, therapeutic communication, and group process skills. Specific objectives included

- learning to distinguish personal values from client values
- reasoning within a client's value system
- communicating with people from diverse cultures and backgrounds
- conducting interviews that elicited needed information and eased client fears
- developing active listening, group process, and leadership skills

Assignments included interviewing, planning and leading group activities, and role-playing. In preparation for interactions with ITAs, the OT students studied two models of cultural competence (Purnell & Paulanka, 1998; Wells, 1993) and several culturally sensitive assessment tools (MacDonald, 1998).

Goals for the ITA course focused on the pedagogical, linguistic, and cross-cultural skills necessary to teach successfully in a U.S. university. Specific objectives included

- understanding how students learn and the relationship between learning and teaching
- developing familiarity with some of the U.S. teaching behaviors
- improving English language pronunciation and fluency skills
- learning to gather verbal and nonverbal feedback from undergraduates
- broadening awareness of U.S. classroom norms

Assignments included observing good teaching assistants and ITAs in their disciplines, microteaching, role-playing difficult student scenarios, peer review of classmates, and class discussions. ITAs also received individual weekly language tutorials outside of the regular class sessions.

Reciprocal Teaching Activities

We created five reciprocal teaching activities to teach the OT students how to form therapeutic relationships across cultural boundaries, to help the ITAs acquire effective teaching skills, and to develop ITA and OT speaking and listening skills. For reciprocal teaching to be effective, not only did the activities have to be relevant to the course goals of both courses, but also the ITAs and OT students needed to trust one another. To achieve this, two exchanges focused on rapport-building and three focused on content goals of the two courses.

We designed the first exchange, a rapport-building activity, to help ITAs and OT students understand how their cultural beliefs regarding social exchanges differed. Most of the ITAs came from Asian and Eastern European cultures that valued a host-guest relationship in exchanges between strangers, whereas the OT students came from U.S. and Australian cultures that valued independence and perceived equality in exchanges between strangers (M. S. Miller, 1996). To prepare for the first exchange, hosting a breakfast for the ITAs, the OT students reviewed U.S. social hosting behaviors and learned about hospitality expectations in other cultures. They also learned the ITAs' names, majors, and something about their countries of origin; practiced active listening skills; and developed open-ended questions designed to encourage conversation. To prepare for this initial exchange, the ITAs discussed U.S. undergraduate customs and behaviors, met with the OT instructor, and completed a self-assessment of cultural adaptability. The breakfast was held in the Conley House, an 1870s home that is now university property. During the breakfast paired undergraduates and international students conversed for 45 minutes with little intervention from either instructor. OT students practiced hosting, active listening, and asking open-ended questions while international students practiced being guests in a U.S. setting and learned to move out of the guest role by beginning to ask questions of the undergraduates.

In the second exchange, which combined content and rapport-building, OT students were students and consultants for the ITAs' microteaching lessons. ITAs reviewed U.S. college classroom customs for making presentations, giving examples, and building student rapport, and prepared 10-minute field-specific lessons illustrating competence with those behaviors. The OT students participated and asked questions as they would in a regular course. At the end of the lesson, the OT students served as educational consultants by giving cultural and pedagogical feedback, which met the OT course objective of learning to give constructive feedback. They prepared for this exchange by learning to give feedback in an *ego sandwich* (i.e., giving a suggestion for change sandwiched between two statements of strengths). The microteaching lessons were videotaped, which allowed the ITAs to review their verbal and nonverbal communication in light of the input received from the OT students.

The third exchange focused on developing interviewing skills, a content goal for the OT course, and communication skills, a content goal for the ITAs. For this activity, each OT student conducted an out-of-class interview with an ITA to explore the ITA's views on health care in both the home country and the United States. The OT students prepared for the interviews by reviewing cultural assessments, practicing interview skills, writing questions, and then practicing them with an international faculty member who gave them feedback on their skills and questions. The OT students also discussed readings on cross-cultural communication skills (Dyck & Forwell, 1997; Luckmann, 2000) and culturally relevant assessments prior to interviewing (Goode, 2001). The ITAs prepared for the meeting by practicing U.S. norms for asking and responding to questions. After the exchange, the OT students wrote interview reports and the ITAs discussed their experiences.

The fourth exchange took place at an outdoor ropes course and was completed through MU's Experiential Education Program. Prior to the ropes course, OT students learned about group dynamics and the stages of group development, and the ITAs discussed team-building roles appropriate to the activity. The ropes course began with team- and trust-building activities. To prepare for climbing the five-story tower, teams of three students learned to tie secure knots and belay, and then taught these skills to one another. They checked each other's knots and gear for safety and learned a series of verbal commands to use between the ground support team members and the climber. The final step before climbing involved doing a trust fall— where the climber intentionally "fell" and support team members lowered the climber safely to the ground. The team members rotated roles so everyone could climb and learn the importance of the ground support team in helping climbers achieve their goals. At the end of 4 hours, the participants debriefed by generating metaphors, generalizations, and applications of the lessons they had learned at the tower. The OT and ITA course instructors also participated as team members.

The fifth exchange was a second microteaching session in which the ITAs again taught a short lesson, and the OT students participated as students and evaluated the lesson. This was the ITAs' third microteaching lesson (out of four) and for this lesson they used interactive teaching activities and visual aids. The OT students were by now preparing their own group presentations and focusing on similar challenges of being effective teachers to peers, developing awareness of both verbal and nonverbal communication, and using visuals to enhance audience understanding. The results were exchanges between students who were no longer strangers, but true colearners in a process of helping one another learn to use visual aides and to become interactive teachers.

In the second year of the linking, role-playing replaced the second microteaching session and a potluck replaced the ropes course, which had been valuable and enjoyable but too costly. The role-playing activity was reciprocal in that ITAs had to respond to undergraduates pretending to be disruptive students, and OT students had to respond to ITAs acting as international patients who were confused or unhappy with treatment procedures. The room was alive with conversations, occasional laughter, and applause as the students' desire to act overcame their initial reluctance. The success of this exchange depended greatly on the trust relationship built between the students in earlier exchanges. The potluck was the closing exchange of the semester. At this point, the OT students were seasoned in planning group activities and invested in the task of hosting the ITAs. A large map of the world was a centerpiece of conversation and students flagged places they had lived or visited. This final exchange afforded more time for informal conversations and brought closure to the semester's linked activities.

In the third year, the potluck was replaced by conversation hours. These informal gatherings were facilitated by a graduate student and not attended by either instructor. The OT students wrote reflective journals on the experience while the ITAs earned class points for their participation.

ITA-Occupational Therapy Linking: An Evaluation

Assessment from the first ITA-undergraduate linking suggested that the OT-ITA linking would likely have positive results if the peer-teaching activities were carefully designed and rapport-building activities were included. Therefore, we designed an action research project to evaluate the student responses to linking courses and to provide data for sharing those results. We asked both a quantitative research question ("Are there changes in the students' perceived cultural competency?") and a qualitative question ("What was the meaning of the experience for the students?"). We triangulated data collection using pre- and posttests of cultural competency, questionnaires, and student journals. Students were engaged in the evaluating process and we shared the results of the pretest with the OT students, who were able to use the findings to develop communication and cultural competency skills needed to be successful, not just in their courses, but in their future professional work as well.

Participation in the research was voluntary and one ITA declined. There were 86 participants: 39 ITAs and 47 OT students, 3 of whom were international. The ITAs were on average 5 years older than the OT students and more than 80% were male, compared to 3.5% of the OT students.

The first instrument that we used to measure change in perceived cultural competency was the Cross-Cultural Adaptability Inventory (CCAI; Kelley & Meyers, 1992), which measured perceived cultural competency in four areas: personal autonomy, flexibility and openness, perceptual acuity, and emotional resilience. We chose the CCAI for its validity and reliability and because it provided posttest recommendations for developing cultural competency, recommendations that we felt would be beneficial to the students participating in the study.

We administered the CCAI at the beginning and end of the semester and found a positive change in perceived cultural competency overall. The degree of change in total CCAI scores for all students pre- to posttest was significant at the $p < .0002$ level (see Figure 2). Three of the subareas on the CCAI also indicated a significant positive change as well ($p < .05$). The first was in Emotional Resilience, defined as the ability to bounce back, emotional equilibrium, a positive attitude, and a sense of adventure. The second significant change was in Perceptual Acuity, defined as being empathic, attentive to verbal and nonverbal cues, and aware of communication dynamics, all skills that were emphasized in the OT and ITA courses. The third change was in Flexibility and Openness, defined as lacking rigidity, being nonjudgmental, and enjoying diversity. These changes suggest that peer teaching may empower students to develop cultural and professional competencies in ways that build self-confidence and awareness of self and others.

When we separated the U.S. students into two groups based on international travel experience, we discovered some interesting distinctions. The U.S. students with travel experience showed the highest percentage of change, followed by the international students. The U.S. students with no international travel experience changed very little during the semester. This suggested to the OT faculty that incorporating international experience into the curriculum could further enhance cultural competency (see Figure 3).

We used the Self-Assessment Checklist for Communicators (SACC) as our second measure of change in perceived cultural competency in the OT students (Wells, 1993). The SACC measures the level of effort required to communicate in a multicultural setting. We selected the SACC even though it is not standardized

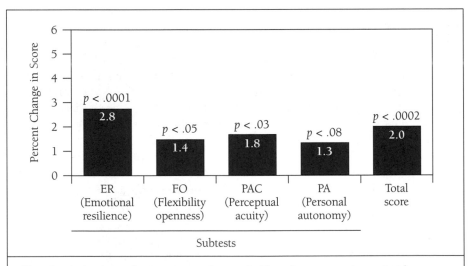

Note. Comparing pre- and posttest scores shows a significant improvement in emotional resilience (ER), flexibility and openness (FO), and perceptual acuity (PAC) subtests and in total scores on the CCAI assessment of cultural competency following five experiential exchanges. Results shown are average values; $N = 86$. Statistical significance was determined by paired student's t test.

FIGURE 2. Percent Change in Cultural Competency Scores of All Students Following Five Experiential Exchange Activities

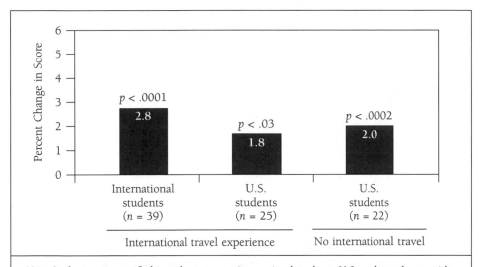

Note. Students were stratified into three groups: international students, U.S. undergraduates with international travel experience, and U.S. undergraduates without international travel experience. Students with international travel experience ($n = 64$) showed significant improvement on the CCAI assessment of cultural competency following five experiential class exchanges. Results shown are average values. Statistical significance was determined by paired student's t test.

FIGURE 3. Percent Change in Cultural Competency Scores of Students With and Without International Travel Experience

because the questions reflect the professional goals important in occupational therapy. On average, the OT scores improved from 55.00 to 59.13, suggesting that after a semester of five exchanges, OT students found communication in multicultural settings easier, but would benefit from further international experiences.

The instructors of the OT and ITA classes developed questionnaires (see Appendix A) and reflective journal questions (see Appendix B) for students to complete at the end of the course. We asked the students to list positive and difficult experiences as well as reasons for their feelings. Using a 1–5 Likert-type scale, the ITAs rated the overall exchange from very positive to very negative, while OT students rated various in- and out-of-class experiences on how each experience contributed to their cultural competency. In their journals, OT students reflected on the experiential exchanges, addressed their emotional reactions (both positive and stressful), and discussed applications to their future as occupational therapists.

Analysis of questionnaires and journals suggested that OT students and ITAs initially had misgivings that lessened with continued contact and additional shared experiences. Although all the ITAs rated the contact with OT students as "mostly positive" to "very positive," some described initial difficulties such as, "When talking with them, it's difficult to express myself precisely. So, sometimes we are unable to get full understanding" and "The most difficult moment is to start [the] relationship." One ITA described the OT students as "friendly, open, even if some of them seems [sic] to be shy, she is willing to help." The OT students had similar initial anxiety. One wrote, "At first I felt this interview was going to be a burden to both the ITA student and myself, but as the interview progressed I found myself seeking more and more information." Another wrote,

> Throughout the experience, my level of comfort greatly increased and I was relaxed and enjoying myself at the end. This was a great experience that opened my eyes to many things, all of which I am trying to incorporate into my everyday life.

Themes in the reflective journals indicated changes in perceptions of cultural competency in the following ways:

- moving from "initial nervousness to being comfortable conversing"
- "learning to trust somebody you don't know"
- "understanding nonverbal communication"
- learning to "listen more" to cope with language barriers

Analysis of the OT questionnaires showed that these students ranked the interviews, followed by the social exchanges and conversation hours, as most helpful in improving their cultural awareness and communication skills. They rated experiences in their OT class higher than experiences with their families and friends or in their workplaces for increasing their cultural awareness. Perhaps most encouraging was the finding that students wanted more rather than fewer interactions with each other. When asked for their recommendations for improving the courses, students suggested that they "be given more opportunity to know each other," "more chance to cooperate, to talk with each other," and "more opportunities for joint work."

The initial research questions were answered. The OT students' perceived cultural competency and the ITAs' language skills improved. The class exchanges were meaningful for the ITAs and the OT students, and the experience of linking and evaluating the classes enlightened the instructors as well.

◈ PRACTICAL IDEAS

We offer five practical suggestions for those thinking of linking an undergraduate course with an ITA course or program.

Focus on Student Learning Goals

Focus on student learning goals throughout the planning, implementing, and evaluating stages. In finding a course and an instructor with which to link, list the goals for the ITA course and think about how undergraduates could provide authentic instruction in meeting those goals. Consider the knowledge and skills of the ITAs that would make them good teachers for U.S. students. When designing activities, attend to all three domains of learning: attitudes, skills, and knowledge. Increase student investment by designing activity guidelines that require student input in the final design and execution of an activity. Review each activity in light of whether it will help students achieve the course goals. If it seems that the results of an activity do not match the course goals, set the activity aside or redesign it. Do not include an activity just because it seems enjoyable or you hate to waste it. State the relevance and importance of each activity in your syllabus and your course orientation. Give students shared responsibility for planning, implementing, and evaluating exchanges. Evaluate whether or not the goals have been met by soliciting feedback throughout the course, and take student assessments and recommendations seriously.

Be Flexible

Be flexible while planning ahead and trying to anticipate student challenges or resistance. In-process change is necessary in most teaching experiences, especially when you are designing something new. In-process changes can help build rapport, lower resistance, and even augment learning. For example, one semester the ITA class met at 7:30 am, but the OT class started at 10:00 am. To participate in the microteaching sessions, the OT students had to come to campus much earlier than usual. Coffee and donuts were introduced as incentives. These helped dissipate some of the resistance, kept the students awake, and even provided a cultural learning experience for the ITAs, most of whom came from cultures where eating and drinking in class would be considered rude.

Increase Risk Gradually

Increase risk gradually to help develop students' confidence and competency. Rather than expecting students to leap across chasms, ask them to step just beyond their comfort zone, become comfortable with the new state, and then take another step. For example, before interviewing the ITAs, the OT students tested their interview questions on a friendly foreigner and received feedback on their questions and interviewing technique. Likewise, the ITAs practiced pieces of a lesson before creating and performing a 10-minute lesson in front of U.S. undergraduates. Another sound strategy for building confidence is to order experiential activities from the least threatening (informal, one-on-one conversations, in our case) to the more threatening (performing trust climbs and doing and critiquing microteaching lessons).

Seek Support

Seek campus support and connections for practical suggestions, resources, and even financial support for facilitating course linking. In addition to utilizing the traditional academic resources, seek out allies and resources in student services (e.g., international student centers, experiential education programs) and administrative services (e.g., instructional and faculty development offices, general education programs, service-learning programs, honors programs). When looking for an undergraduate course with which to link, talk to faculty members who teach skills or concepts that fit with the ITA course goals. For example, faculty who value internationalization, international language, cross-cultural competence, college learning and teaching issues, or communication skills might be interested in linking their courses with the ITA course.

Approach the Project as Research

Approach incorporation of linking as you would any educational innovation, by treating it as educational research. Including a research approach in your plans will allow you to share your innovation with others, provide you with evaluative data to assist in dissemination of the results, and hopefully provide evidence to ask for further funding if you want to continue the project. Approaching your project as research entails some additional work, mainly getting institutional approval for your project and adding a measurement component to the plan. Before approaching another instructor to create a linking, become familiar with the regulations of the campus Institutional Research Board (IRB). Discuss with an IRB officer the types of activities you envision including in the linking, the types of assessment tools you might use to measure change, and the means of dissemination (e.g., print, Web site, photos, video) you hope to use, as well as your plans for protecting student anonymity and guaranteeing informed, voluntary consent. To determine which measurement tools to use or make, consider the changes that you hope will occur and the tools that will help you triangulate the research.

◈ CONCLUSION

Linking courses and designing reciprocal teaching activities require extra thought, time, and energy; however, the benefits definitely outweigh the costs as we saw from our project. First, there was the bonus for instructors that this was a powerful learning experience in many ways, including a renewed respect for the power of students teaching one another, the joy of learning from one's students, and the satisfaction in seeing students gain respect for those who are different. Also, because several of the instructors were new to the campus, this experience accelerated their own learning about the campus resources and culture.

Second, students in both courses benefited. Their awareness and acceptance of cross-cultural difference increased and they became more capable of seeing issues from the perspective of the other. This experience moved them closer to the OT goal of being able to reason within the value system of a client and the ITA goal of creating a learning environment in which students sense enough cultural familiarity to learn effectively.

Third, students teaching one another not only increased student interest and involvement, but also created a more authentic and rich learning environment.

Finally, it was just plain fun. Students enjoyed the activities and asked for more. It is well known that if an activity stimulates interest and engages students, they become more involved and motivated and therefore learn more.

Encouraging students to teach one another is a humane, student-centered way to provide an individualized teaching and learning situation. Structuring environments and activities for reciprocal teaching-learning is limited only by our imagination and energy. In a world threatened by deeply rooted cultural misunderstandings, developing ways to enhance cross-cultural communication skills and sensitivity is essential. Teaching one another and intercultural development can be woven into the fabric of all learning experiences. In addition, further experimentation and research in these areas can help improve student learning, faculty collaboration across disciplines, and the recognition that designing and sharing classroom action research is not only possible, but also highly valuable to students and instructors.

❖ ACKNOWLEDGMENTS

We would like to acknowledge and appreciate the support of all the instructors who linked their courses with the ITA courses: Chris Fox and Pamela Pollock, ITA instructors; Amy Wheeler, Karen Hebert, Melissa Wagoner, and Angela Heckman, undergraduate research assistants; as well as the International Center, the Program for Excellence in Teaching, and the Department of Occupational Therapy at the University of Missouri–Columbia.

❖ CONTRIBUTORS

At the time of the research, Marilyn Miller was interim director of the Program for Excellence in Teaching, coordinator of the New Faculty Teaching Scholars Program, adjunct professor in the Department of Educational Leadership and Policy Analysis at the University of Missouri–Columbia, and was chair of the TESOL ITA Interest Section in 2001–2002. She is currently an educational consultant in the Washington, D.C., area. Her instructional interests include enhancing communication across linguistic and cultural differences, internationalizing U.S. universities, and promoting interactive teaching and learning in higher education, and she has presented nationally and locally on these topics. She is coeditor with James Groccia and Judith Miller of *Student Assisted Teaching: A Guide to Faculty-Student Teamwork* (Anker, 2001) and coeditor with James Groccia of *Building Your Academic Portfolio* (Stylus, 2006).

Sandy Matsuda is assistant professor in the Department of Occupational Therapy at the University of Missouri–Columbia. Her research and instructional interests include developing cultural competencies in occupational therapy students, incorporating the use of complementary therapies from other cultures in occupational therapy treatment, and furthering the use of problem-based learning and peer teaching in the teaching of health-related professions. She participated in the Global Scholars Program, served as a member of the advisory board for the Program for Excellence in Teaching, and participated in the University of Missouri New Faculty Teaching Scholars Program.

❖ APPENDIX A: INSTRUCTOR-CREATED QUESTIONNAIRES

Questionnaire for ITA Students

These answers are for research purposes only and will not be used to identify you.

A. CODE name _____

B. Gender (Please circle)   Male   Female

C. Age: _____

D. How long have you lived in the United States? _____

E. Have you ever lived in a country other than the United States?
    For how long? _____

F. Was your contact with undergraduate students mostly positive or negative for you?

1	2	3	4	5
very positive	mostly positive	neither positive nor negative	mostly negative	very negative

G. What were the most positive parts of the exchange?

H. What were the most difficult moments for you?

I. What activities in this class corresponded to what you will be doing as a teaching assistant?

J. What changes would you recommend for future classes?

Thank you for participating in this study of cultural adaptation!

Questionnaire for OT Students

Your answers are for research purposes only and will not be used to identify you.

A. CODE name _____

B. Gender (Please circle)   Male   Female

C. Age: _____

D. List any international languages that you currently speak.

E. Have you ever lived in another country? For how long? Where?

1. What personal experiences have you had that helped you learn about, or from, people of other cultures or subgroups?

2. What has *most* influenced your beliefs about people from different cultures or subgroups?

3. Do you have one or more friend(s) outside of classmates from a different race or culture?   Yes _____ No _____

4. How would you rate the depth of your learning about diversity in the following situations? (Circle your response)

	Not at all	Intro- ductory	Moderate	In-depth
Experiences in my family	0	1	2	3
Experiences with my friends	0	1	2	3
Experiences in this class	0	1	2	3
Experiences in other college classes	0	1	2	3
Experiences in my workplace	0	1	2	3
Other: (please specify) _____	0	1	2	3

(e.g., travel, languages learned, social groups)

6. Which experiences listed below helped improve your cultural awareness and/or ability to communicate with cultural sensitivity this semester? (Circle your response)

	Not helpful	A little helpful	Moderately helpful	Helpful	Very helpful
Readings on "Communicating with Cultural Sensitivity"	0	1	2	3	4
Presentation on South Africa culture	0	1	2	3	4
Breakfast conversations with ITAs	0	1	2	3	4
Participating in ITA microteaching	0	1	2	3	4
Interview with Dr. Hdeib	0	1	2	3	4
Interview with ITA partners	0	1	2	3	4
Presence of international students in OT classes	0	1	2	3	4
Alpine Tower experience	0	1	2	3	4
Group presentations on cultural sensitivity	0	1	2	3	4

7. If you were planning a professional development seminar on multicultural issues in health care for your profession, what would you do? What questions do you have that you would like answered?

Questions adapted from Cockrell, K. S., Placier, P. L., Cockrell, D. H., & Middleton, J. N. (1999). Coming to terms with "diversity" and "multiculturalism" in teacher education: Learning about our students, changing our practice. *Teaching and Teacher Education, 15,* 351–356.

◈ APPENDIX B: JOURNAL REFLECTIONS

Do not put your name on this paper. Your handwritten responses will be typed by a research assistant. The following questions relate to your Alpine Tower experience or other experiential exchanges we have completed in this class. You may elect for your responses not to be used in any summary for presentation or publication by checking the blank below and turning this page in with your answers.

___ I do not wish for my comments on the following questions (please circle) to be included in any summary for presentation or publication outside this class.

1. 2. 3. 4. 5. 6. 7. 8. 9. 10. 11. 12. 13. 14.

I. Self-awareness
  1. How did any of the experiential exchanges increase your self-awareness?

II. Values
  2. Was this experience mostly positive or negative for you? What made it so?
  3. How were values evident in your climbing team?

III. Communication

4. What did others on your team or facilitators do to attend to your personal needs before, during, and after an experience?

5. (Nonverbal) What mannerisms or behaviors did the facilitators, your teammates, or teaching assistant partners use which added to or detracted from gaining your confidence?

6. (Verbal) What did the facilitators or your teammates do that helped increase your motivation? Describe the effectiveness of their strategy.

IV. General questions

7. (for OT students) What activities corresponded to what you will be doing in classroom, lab, and clinic settings in Occupational Therapy?

8. (for international students) What activities in this class corresponded to what you will be doing as a teaching assistant?

9. What helped you adjust to the learning required in this class?

10. What can you do in a new setting to assume responsibility for your own learning?

11. What were the best moments for you in this semester's experiential exchanges?

12. What were the most difficult moments for you?

13. In what ways were you a "helper" and in what ways were you "helped"?

14. What changes would you recommend for future classes?

CHAPTER 5

Classic Challenges in International Teaching Assistant Assessment

Greta J. Gorsuch

◈ INTRODUCTION

At U.S. universities, efforts to provide instruction and assessment for international teaching assistants (ITAs) have been on the scene for two decades (e.g., Hinofotis, Bailey, & Stern, 1981; Shaw & Garate, 1984). The ITA Development Program at Texas Tech University can be counted among the earliest of these. The initial component was the ITA Summer Workshop, which has been held since 1980. The workshop was founded "in response to the need of academic departments to assess and improve the skills of their international teaching assistants" (ITA Training Program, 1998, p. 1). Twenty-four years and three directors later, the primary purpose of the workshop remains "to help provide excellent instruction to all Texas Tech students" (p. 2) by supporting the ITAs at the outset of their teaching careers. For many years, the ITA program was centered around the summer and the fall semester: There was the summer workshop and a follow-up course (LING 7000) in the fall for ITAs who had not been recommended to teach. However, starting in 2001, an additional LING 7000 course was offered in the spring. At that time, the ITA program became a year-round venture.

The Texas Tech ITA program, like many others, has developed in four main areas: "a testing component along with instructional components in spoken language, intercultural communication, and teaching skills" (Smith, 1994, p. 53). These are classic areas of focus in that issues related to them are never wholly put to rest; interest in ITA assessment is never far away. ITA educators want to know what assessment procedures and instruments are workable and which ones will tell them what they need to know about ITAs' communicative abilities. This chapter describes the Texas Tech ITA program, with a special focus on ongoing revision of an ITA performance assessment and the theoretical, practical, and ethical bases for the rating criteria used.

◈ CONTEXT

Texas Tech enrolls 23,000 undergraduate and 4,300 graduate students per year in 191 undergraduate and graduate degree programs (Texas Tech Department of Institutional Research, 2004). Each year, approximately 300 new international students arrive. Of these, 240 were employed as ITAs in 2002 (Texas Tech

Department of Institutional Research, 2003). The ITA program provides instruction and assessment services to the entire university and is funded by the provost. All departments are required to comply with *Operating Procedure 32.19* (Texas Tech University, 2005), which was formulated in response to state legislation. All nonnative-English-speaking (NNES) teaching assistants are required to have their language ability assessed. The director raises awareness of the program through mailing campaigns, annual phone calls to departments, and maintaining a Web site. Approximately 120 ITAs are assessed and instructed per year.

The Department of Classical and Modern Languages and Literatures provides classrooms, a level four language learning lab, and the program director. See Table 1 for program components matched with personnel and their roles.

TABLE 1. TEXAS TECH ITA PROGRAM COMPONENTS

Component	Personnel	Role
Fall and spring academic-year courses (LING 7000; 14 weeks)	Director	Course instructor, SPEAK test administrator, videotaped teaching demonstration rater
	Graduate advisors	Videotaped teaching demonstration observers and questioners; comment on ITAs' performances; respond to questionnaire on authenticity, appropriateness of teaching demonstration (see Appendix A)
	Department chairs	Report on successes and failures of ITAs using telephone interviews
Summer workshop (3 weeks)	Director	Hires four ESL instructors, administers program and all assessments
	Lead instructor	Offer leadership, develop curriculum and materials
	Instructors	Teach workshop classes; rate SPEAK tests, curriculum, and ITA assessment input
	High school seniors/ University freshmen	Observe ITAs' teaching demonstrations, comment on form, help with student/ teacher role-plays
	Experienced ITAs	Participate in panel discussion
	Graduate advisors	Videotaped teaching demonstration observers and questioners; comment on ITAs' performances; respond to questionnaire on authenticity, appropriateness of teaching demonstration
	Department chairs	Report on successes and failures of ITAs via telephone interviews

The ITAs vary in number, nationality, and discipline. Attendance at the summer workshop fluctuates between 40 and 70 participants, with approximately 30 students per year attending the academic-year courses. In addition, 30–40 more ITAs are assessed without being required to attend further courses. ITAs come from over 30 countries including China, India, and Mexico. ITAs are offered teaching assistantships in over 25 departments including biology, chemistry, and music. The ITAs' ages range from 24 to 40. In 2004, 51% of ITAs had previously taught in their home countries, and 49% had not. ITAs' English communication abilities vary widely; Speaking Proficiency English Assessment Kit (SPEAK) test scores range from 20 to 60.

ITA performance assessment is a process fraught with practical, ethical, and theoretical issues. Because assessments must be continually validated, ITA educators have to keep abreast of discussions on performance assessment. These discussions are a necessary part of the context in which ITA educators operate. One significant thread of these discussions—performance assessment criteria—is the focus of this chapter. Hiiemae, Lambert, and Hayes (1991) stressed the importance of "serious consideration of language competency before an international student is given a teaching assistant appointment" (p. 127). Which instruments and procedures should be used for ITA screening is an issue of debate. Scholars discuss using multiple-choice English proficiency tests, such as the Test of English as a Foreign Language (TOEFL; Dunn & Constantinides, 1991), and general-purpose performance assessments, such as the old version of the SPEAK test or the Test of Spoken English (TSE; Gallego, Goodwin, & Turner, 1991). However, there is a general consensus that teaching simulations are appropriate for capturing ITAs' abilities to use English to teach U.S. undergraduates (Carrell, Sarwick, & Plakans, 1987; Ford, Gappa, Wendorff, & Wright, 1991; Gallego et al., 1991; Smith, 1994). Common sense suggests, therefore, that "prospective [ITAs] . . . need to be observed in language use situations similar to those they meet in their roles as TAs" (Briggs, 1994, p. 63).

Many performance assessments call upon ITAs to teach a prepared lesson to simulate future situations in which they will use English. The ITAs' performances of such is rated using specific criteria (see Appendix A for the ITA Presentation Evaluation form used at Texas Tech). Hinofotis et al. (1981) developed an early set of criteria that was adapted from an ESL oral presentation checklist (p. 107) and further developed through a validation procedure. The criteria pertained to ITAs' "language proficiency," "delivery," and "communication of information" (p. 123). "Communication of information" included traits that are associated with good teaching (e.g., Hahn & Hall, 1991), such as development of explanation, use of supporting evidence, and ability to relate to student. Smith (1994) stated that "typical" ITA performance assessments include criteria on "teaching skills," including "organization," "clarity," and "sufficient level of redundancy" (p. 53). An instrument in a well-known ITA development textbook (Smith, Myers, & Burkhalter, 1992) has a "teaching skills" category that includes specific criteria: "organization of presentation," "use of blackboard and visuals," "teacher presence," and "audience awareness" (pp. 174–177).

Arguably, these criteria go beyond assessment of ITAs' English communication abilities. Many state and university policies stipulate only that ITAs' ability to communicate in English be assessed. So is it fair to use additional teaching skills criteria to assess ITAs if they can be granted or denied employment on the basis of that assessment? In the following sections, arguments for and against including teaching skills criteria in ITA performance assessments are discussed underscoring the practical, ethical, and theoretical issues involved.

Arguments for Including Teaching Skills Criteria

Using teaching skills criteria in ITA assessments certainly has practical value. From an English for specific purposes (ESP) viewpoint, ITA assessments should mirror a program curriculum based on empirical descriptions of ITAs' needs (Shaw & Garate, 1984). These needs include "the language, culture, and pedagogy of the U.S. university classroom" (Smith, 1994, pp. 55–56). In an ESP framework, a program of "pedagogic activities and materials" (Shaw & Garate, 1984, pp. 29–30) would be developed and assessed, which conflates ITA program assessment with ITA candidate assessment. Assessments comment on the success of the program by examining the achievement of ITAs. And why not help ITAs improve their teaching skills? Hinofotis et al. (1981) suggested that teaching skills figure in U.S. undergraduates' evaluations of ITAs. Further, Bauer (1991) found that ITAs themselves were concerned about classroom management issues, in addition to language problems. From an institutional viewpoint, it makes sense to encourage good teaching among teaching assistants, regardless of their nationality. Interest in good teaching at the university level has grown (e.g., Dinerman, Feldman, & Ello, 1999), and good teaching skills may help worthy ITAs compensate for poor language skills (Smith, 1994).

From a theoretical viewpoint, including teaching skills criteria in assessment may be necessary to fully explore ITAs' communicative competence. Adopting the communicative competence model of Bachman and Palmer (1996), one can argue that knowledge of rhetorical organization and cohesion intersects with some of the teaching skills criteria listed earlier in this chapter (development of an explanation, use of supporting evidence, organization of presentation). Strategic competence also comes into play as ITAs use compensatory linguistic and nonlinguistic strategies to communicate with U.S. undergraduates (e.g., use of blackboard and visuals), and ITAs must tap into their sociolinguistic competence in order to use and comprehend idioms and cultural references (e.g., audience awareness). If these aspects of communicative competence are not taken into account when judging ITAs' performance, it may not be possible to adequately predict how ITAs will do in future teaching situations.

Arguments Against Including Teaching Skills Criteria

From an ethical viewpoint, ITA educators must consider the fact that not all ITAs have teaching experience. It may not be fair to assess neophyte teachers on teaching skills they cannot possibly possess. ITAs are graduate students and apprentices in their fields, and they require learning over time and contact with fellow teaching assistants and faculty mentors to learn to effectively communicate with undergraduates (Sheridan, 1991). If ITAs are awarded or denied employment partially on the basis of their teaching skills, and native-English-speaking (NES) teaching assistants are not, this may constitute discrimination (e.g., McNamara, 1996, p. 40). NES teaching assistants are likely hired with the assumption that they are neophyte teachers. Why should ITAs, who are also neophyte teachers, be forced to demonstrate teaching skills that they have had no chance to develop before being hired? Thomas and Monoson (1991) argued that "legislation should ensure that all instructors be provided with ways to develop their pedagogical skills; oral, written language abilities" (p. 391).

The majority of ITAs are apprentices in their disciplines and have yet to develop pedagogical content knowledge, "the capacity of a teacher to transform the content knowledge he or she possesses into forms that are pedagogically powerful" (Shulman, 1987, p. 15). Limited pedagogical content knowledge may explain Zukowski-Faust's (1984) description of chemistry ITAs' inability to explain chemical theories. Most likely, teaching skills criteria on ITA performance assessments (development of an explanation, use of supporting evidence, audience awareness) tap into pedagogical content knowledge. This may point to a source of bias in ITA performance assessments that include teaching skills criteria. ITAs who have teaching experience may do better because they score higher on the teaching skills criteria, whereas ITAs who do not have teaching experience may score lower.

Finally, from a practical viewpoint, it may not be appropriate for ESL specialists to assess ITAs on teaching skills that are not necessarily relevant to the teaching done in specific departments. Some departments have elected to conduct teaching assistant professional development within their departments (e.g., Ambrose, 1991). As Wulff et al. (1991) argued, "the ways academics stimulate inquiry, generate knowledge, and present understandings is specific to particular disciplines" (p. 115). Further, departments "know firsthand the nature of the content and the setting in which instruction will occur" (Weimer, Svinicki, & Bauer, 1989, p. 58). Because the ITA program at Texas Tech traditionally included teaching skills criteria in ITA performance assessments, whether or not to include these criteria has been a continuing challenge.

◈ DESCRIPTION

As stated earlier, the ITA Development Program at Texas Tech University has two instructional components: a three-credit course (LING 7000) and the summer workshop. Twice a week, in 90-minute classes, pronunciation instruction is provided using computer programs; pronunciation textbooks with video- and audiotapes; and in-class practice using pair, group, and community language learning techniques (Stevick, 1976). LING 7000 also focuses on the communicative functions of answering student questions, using examples and visuals, and making transitions. The current textbooks are Smith, Meyers, and Burkhalter's (1992) *Communicate: Strategies for International Teaching Assistants* and Wennerstrom's (1989) *Techniques for Teachers*. Individualized, longitudinal feedback is a cornerstone of LING 7000. ITAs complete a mini class assignment every third or fourth class meeting. For these assignments, ITAs prepare and teach a 4- to 5-minute lesson, defining a term, giving examples, and completing other tasks as they put into practice the elements of communicative functions covered in a given unit. Mini class assignments are videotaped and ITAs are encouraged to view the video in the privacy of the instructor's office. Each student keeps his or her own copy of the ITA Presentation Evaluation form (see Appendix A). When an ITA does a mini class assignment, he or she hands the form to the instructor, who dates it and makes notes and ratings about which criteria seem applicable to the performance. For example, for the unit on making transitions, the ITA Presentation Evaluation form includes criteria for discourse competence. Each ITA's form becomes a longitudinal record of improvement on specific criteria. ITAs in LING 7000 are also required to spend one hour per week on independent study in the language learning lab.

The ITA Summer Workshop is free of charge to ITAs, and room and board are provided for newly arrived ITAs. The workshop meets 8 hours per day, 5 days per week. Mornings are devoted to English communication skills for teachers (e.g., describing visuals, responding to questions), talks on university practices and policies (e.g., academic integrity, teacher and student conflict), and other activities such as role-plays with university undergraduates. Afternoons are devoted to language skills development (see Gorsuch, Stevens, & Brouillette, 2003).

ITAs can receive one of three recommendations after taking LING 7000 and the summer workshop: first, teach with routine supervision; second, teach with close supervision; and third, no teaching and a recommendation to take further LING 7000 or summer workshop course work. Recommendations are based on four assessments: two 15-minute videotaped teaching demonstrations using the ITA Presentation Evaluation form, the SPEAK test, and instructors' assessments of ITAs' performance in LING 7000 and workshop classes. The target score for a teaching recommendation for the SPEAK test is 50 at Texas Tech, and students must earn consistent ratings of 4 or above on all criteria on the ITA Presentation Evaluation form.

◈ DISTINGUISHING FEATURES

Development of the ITA Presentation Evaluation form has been one of the distinguishing features in the evolution of the program. Formal videotaped presentations last 15 minutes, including time for audience questions. The ITAs define a term or explain a process, and the audience consists of instructors, other ITAs, graduate advisors, and, in the summer workshop, university undergraduates. Next, the ITAs watch their own videotaped performance and attend an individual feedback session with one or more instructors. Although the assessment procedure has not changed greatly during the past 5 years, the ITA Presentation Evaluation form has undergone several revisions (the sixth version appears in Appendix A). The precursor to the ITA Presentation Evaluation form included many of the criteria used in Smith et al. (1992, p. 173), such as pronunciation, grammar, fluency, manner of speaking, teacher presence, and method of handling questions. Unlike the 7-point ascending scale in Smith et al., on the Texas Tech form the rater had to fill out in longhand descriptive information for each criterion. This instrument had a number of other problems, including rater fatigue and excessive subjectivity. It was also impossible to subject the data to conventional reliability and validity analyses. Subsequently, Version 1 of the ITA Presentation Evaluation form was developed. Table 2 describes the revisions that have been made to this form and the rationales for them. Version 3 included criteria on rater familiarity and complexity of topics. At that time, the fact that ITA candidates chose topics of varying difficulty was an issue of concern. Raters and graduate advisors felt that ITAs who chose harder topics did not perform as well. As a result, graduate advisors provided a list of topics that freshmen students were likely to cover in courses that ITAs would teach. ITAs now choose a topic from that

TABLE 2. REVISIONS MADE IN THE ITA PRESENTATION EVALUATION FORM, 1999–2003

Revision	Rationale
Version 1. Added a 5-point rating scale for each criteria	To address the issue of unclear criteria and criteria subjectivity by allowing for quantitative analyses for interrater reliability and construct validity (intercorrelations)
Version 2. Added prose descriptions of behavior under each point on the 5-point scale	To clarify the constructs and improve rater training
Version 3. Some criteria culled (e.g., teacher presence); remaining criteria organized under Language Skills, Teaching Skills, Interaction, and Overall; two new criteria on (a) rater familiarity with the presentation topic, and (b) raters' estimate of topic difficulty	Some criteria (e.g., teacher presence) has very low interrater reliability (suggesting little construct validity) and low correlations with ITAs' Overall scores; reorganization helps conceptualize the criteria; raters and graduate advisor feedback suggests inclusion of topic specific criteria
Version 4. Criteria for "pronunciation and use of field specific vocabulary" added	Rater feedback
Version 5. Open-ended questions on "points that helped" and "points that hindered" where raters can comment on issues of concern; rater familiarity and difficulty criteria dropped	Rater feedback; multiple regression analysis suggests some variance in Overall score unaccounted for. Perhaps persistence of specific kinds of comments made by raters in the open-ended items will suggest additional criteria.
Version 6. General Teaching Skills category abolished. New criteria written to reflect aspects of communicative competence related to language use in classrooms. Criteria reorganized under Linguistic Skills, Classroom Communication Skills, and Overall. Prose descriptions of scores of 1, 2, 3, and 5 are removed, and prose descriptions of 4, the target score, are moved to free up space for criteria-specific rater comments. An asterisk is placed under 4 on all criteria scales to indicate the target score.	Consideration of arguments for and against the use of teaching skills criteria, refocusing of program on developing ITAs' language skills; rater feedback

list for their videotaped teaching presentations. Henceforth, the rater familiarity/difficulty criteria were removed.

Version 6 includes criteria that reflect aspects of communicative competence as they relate to communication in classrooms to underscore the importance of language skills for classroom use. The focus of the program is on the language skills ITAs need to communicate in classrooms rather than on teaching skills, and the program provides ample opportunities to practice use of that language. Use of the blackboard, for example, is demonstrated as a means to reinforce verbal messages, rather than as a teaching skill in and of itself. Test designers have many different perspectives that can influence how the competencies are described and assessed (Bachman & Palmer, 1996; Brindley, 1995, p. 150), and this process also occurred in the ITA program at Texas Tech.

The Texas Tech ITA program has several additional distinguishing features that center on the following areas: (a) increasing instructor involvement in curriculum revision (Gorsuch et al., 2003), (b) using background analyses of cultural and teacher development issues to develop a more refined vision of ITAs' needs and the educational cultures in which they operate (Gorsuch, 2003), and (c) continuing validation and revision of an ITA performance assessment instrument based on quantitative and qualitative information. The current ITA Presentation Evaluation form is by no means final. Future revisions will be based on both quantitative and qualitative analyses as illustrated in Table 3. The telephone interviews have been added to compensate for de-emphasizing ITAs' teaching skills in the ITA Presentation Evaluation form and to more fully explore the communicative competence of ITAs in specific language use situations.

◈ PRACTICAL IDEAS

Gather Information From Many Sources

To keep fresh and relevant ideas flowing, information should be continually gathered, both formally and informally. Information can be collected formally through questionnaires or interviews answered by ITAs, ITA program staff, departmental representatives, or U.S. undergraduates. Items can address specific concerns such as whether graduate advisors feel teaching simulation procedures are authentic, whether ITAs feel their ratings are accurate and informative, and whether raters feel the meanings of specific criteria are clear. Information can also be gathered informally through unplanned contacts, conversations, or experiences.

Use Personal Research Interests to Guide the Program

Personal research interests should be used to guide the long-term growth and vitality of the program and to promote diversity in the ITA education field. For instance, research in teacher development and performance assessment has contributed to the development of assessment instruments used in the Texas Tech program. Research in other areas, such as communicative task design or diverse styles of feedback to errors, will also serve the interests of ITA education.

Discern and Look Beyond Tradition

As discussed earlier, ITA education has developed various traditions, one of which is to adopt an ESP approach for curriculum generation and for ITA program and candidate assessment. This approach has aided in the development of many excellent ITA education curricula and assessments (e.g., Shaw, 1994; Shaw & Garate, 1984; Smith, 1994), but it is important to look critically at its widely held assumptions that ITAs require preparation in pedagogy and that they should be screened partially on the basis of pedagogical skills. The latter assumption should not be accepted without question; rather, it requires further, sustained consideration. It is important, as a

TABLE 3. QUANTITATIVE AND QUALITATIVE ANALYSES

Quantitative Analyses	Rationale
Interrater reliability correlations between raters on all criteria and on Overall criteria	To estimate reliability between raters
Correlations between criteria	To determine whether some criteria are redundant (very high correlations suggest two criteria are measuring the same thing); to determine whether criteria under Linguistic Skills correlate with each other and not with criteria under Classroom Communication Skills
Correlations between criteria and Overall	To determine which criteria are positively or negatively correlated with ITA candidates' overall communicative success (Brindley, 1995, p. 151); criteria with nonsignificant relationships with ITAs' Overall scores might be dropped
Compare group means on each criteria divided by differing levels of teaching experience	To explore whether ITAs without teaching experience are biased against, and on which criteria
Rasch analysis on raters and each criteria	To explore rater bias and to determine whether some criteria are more difficult than others (i.e., should a target score of 4 be expected on all criteria?; S. Ross, personal communication, March 18, 2003)

Qualitative Analyses	Rationale
Group interviews with raters	To gather feedback on clarity of criteria, rater fatigue, and ease of instrument use
Telephone interviews with department chairs and graduate advisors	To estimate the extent to which ITAs' scores on the Overall criteria predict ITAs' success in actual teaching.

practical idea, to discern curriculum or assessment traditions that are currently in place in national and local ITA educational contexts and to understand their theoretical and pragmatic origins. ITA development staff or program directors may wish to build on these traditions or look beyond them for the answers they seek.

◈ CONCLUSION

This case study described the ITA Development Program at Texas Tech University and reported on one area of challenge and change specific to the program—the development of assessment instruments and the criteria for the ITA Presentation Evaluation form. More ongoing analysis is needed, both quantitative and qualitative. Further research will offer significant opportunities for healthy debate and discussion, which will continue to enrich this program.

◈ CONTRIBUTOR

Greta J. Gorsuch is associate professor of applied linguistics and former director of the ITA Development Program at Texas Tech University. Her interests focus on socialization and language learning, fluency development, teacher learning through curriculum design, and language testing practices. She lived in Japan for many years, earning an EdD from Temple University, Tokyo campus.

◈ APPENDIX A: ITA PRESENTATION EVALUATION V. 6

ITA Name: _____ Date: _____

Rater: _____ Time: _____ Room #: _____

Linguistic Skills

1. Word stress (*expectation, similar*)

Target: 4 ITA makes a few errors, but comprehension is not impeded.

  1   2   3   4   5   Problematic field specific terms or expressions:
Low   * High

2. Vowel clarity (a, e, i, o, u, diphthongs)

Target: 4 ITA makes a few errors, but comprehension is not impeded.

  1   2   3   4   5   Problematic field specific terms or expressions:
Low   * High

3. Consonant clarity (t, s, z, b, v, sh, th, zh, etc.)

Target: 4 ITA makes a few errors, but comprehension is not impeded.

  1   2   3   4   5   Problematic field specific terms or expressions:
Low   * High

4. Spoken grammar and usage

Target: 4 ITA makes a few errors, but comprehension is not impeded.

  1   2   3   4   5   Problematic sentences, expressions, phrases:
Low   * High

5. Speech flow

Target: 4 ITA seems to speak fairly easily. There are a few unnatural thought groupings and pauses, a few incomplete sentences/phrases, a few false starts, but comprehension is not impeded.

  1   2   3   4   5   Specific problems:
Low   * High

6. Discourse competence (classroom specific language used in explanations, announcements, etc. that express transition, sequence, etc. *first, second, then, I have an announcement, an important concept is, to review, on a different topic, now I want to move on to,* etc.)

Target: 4 ITA uses basic discourse markers most of the time. Listeners are generally able to follow the ITA's line of thinking.

1   2   3   4   5   Specific problems:
Low   * High

7. Handling of questions (use of language to negotiate questions and answers, and clarify question meaning)

Target: 4 ITA is generally able to respond to questions by acknowledging the question, confirming understanding by repeating or paraphrasing the question, asking for clarification where necessary, and confirming listener comprehension of the ITA's answer.

1   2   3   4   5   Specific problems:
Low   * High

8. Examples (use of language to create effective examples to explain field specific concepts)

Target: 4 ITA makes adequate attempts to make content relevant to students by using examples, analogies, or stories that are relevant to students' experiences.

1   2   3   4   5   Specific problems:
Low   * High

9. Detection and repair of communication breakdowns (use of language to detect listener noncomprehension, and use of clarification sequences to repair breakdowns in communication)

Target: 4 ITA demonstrates general awareness of listener comprehension using comprehension checks with adequate wait time, and other verbal strategies such as *You look like you have a question*, etc. ITA demonstrates, where appropriate, the basic ability to use clarification requests to repair communication breakdowns.

1   2   3   4   5   Specific problems:
Low   * High

Classroom Communication Skills

10. Compensation (use of strategies to underscore and supplement ITA's intended message; e.g., use of visual cues, blackboard, and OHP; verbal repetition and recycling of key words, phrases, and sentences)

Target: 4 ITA uses basic compensation skills which generally enhance listener comprehension. ITA uses the blackboard, OHP, etc., when appropriate to use or introduce a term, and/or repeats and recycles verbal cues adequately.

1   2   3   4   5   Specific problems:
Low   * High

11. Eye contact (ITA maintains eye contact with a variety of listeners, faces listeners while explaining items written on the blackboard)

Target: 4 ITA maintains adequate eye contact, looking at a variety of listeners, in such a manner as to express openness and awareness of listeners. ITA faces listeners while explaining terms, illustrations, etc. on the blackboard.

  1   2   3   4   5   Specific problems:
Low   * High

Overall

12. Overall, how comprehensible is the ITA? Would you want this candidate as a teacher?

Target: 4 ITA is generally comprehensible. ITA shows a general ability to communicate in the English language in classroom situations.

  1   2   3   4   5   Specific problems:
Low   * High

Additional Items

What helped or hindered your comprehension of the ITA's presentation? (i.e., use of humor, rate of speech too slow or too fast, voice volume, speech mannerisms, etc.)

    Points that Helped   *Points that Hindered*

PART 2

Beginnings, Challenges, and Growth

CHAPTER 6

The Evolution of an International Teaching Assistant Program

Carol Piñeiro

❖ INTRODUCTION

Boston University is currently recognized as an important research institution. The university has an endowment of almost $700 million with additional grants and contracts of more than $250 million. The fourth largest independent university in the United States, it has more than 30,000 students from 50 states and 135 countries. The largest entity at Boston University is the College of Arts and Sciences (CAS), with 23 departments and about 10,000 undergraduates enrolled each year. The graduate school of CAS has 20 departments and almost 2,000 students studying for advanced degrees; about half of these students are from other countries. During the past 30 years, the chemistry and physics departments, housed in the same building, have developed into a major research center, attracting more than $40 million in external grants and contracts.

Because the number of U.S. students studying for graduate degrees in the sciences was on the decline, these departments began to accept more international students and to include a teaching assistantship in their scholarship package (National Science Foundation, 2000). Although the Test of English as a Foreign Language (TOEFL) scores seemed to indicate a high level of proficiency, the directors of graduate studies found that it was otherwise and recognized the need for remedial English language development. They approached the Center for English Language and Orientation Programs (CELOP) and asked if the instructors there could give the international teaching assistants (ITAs) special classes. About a dozen students, primarily from China, were offered weekly tutorials focusing on pronunciation and presentation techniques. These classes, which began 20 years ago, were the beginnings of the ITA program.

❖ CONTEXT

Although the majority of ITAs needing English instruction were in the chemistry and physics departments, others in anthropology, biology, computer science, economics, geography, international relations, mathematics, modern foreign languages and literature, and sociology were also required to take the classes. (Other schools and colleges, like engineering, also have a number of ITAs, but they do not take part in the program because they are not connected to CAS. Rather, they sponsor proprietary sessions led by faculty members or graduate student mentors to help orient and assist the ITAs.) As mentioned before, the majority of the ITAs in the sciences are from China, but others also come from Latin America, Europe, Russia, the former Soviet bloc countries, North Africa, South Asia, and East Asia.

Continuing the trend of the 1980s, the number of ITAs steadily increased throughout the 1990s, with more and more applicants from China being accepted to the university. About two thirds of the incoming graduate students in the chemistry department were Chinese, which prompted the chair to begin funding summer orientations ranging in length from 1 to 3 weeks in the 1990s. For several hours a day, CELOP instructors led groups of 20–30 ITAs in activities that involved pronunciation, listening comprehension, U.S. culture, academic discourse, spontaneous speeches, error correction, teaching techniques, and videotaped presentations. At the end of these orientations, the instructors provided written evaluations of the participants' skills, and most of them were advised to continue language development in tutorials at the language center during the academic year.

As the number of ITAs increased, so did complaints from undergraduates about instructors with poor communications skills. These complaints took the form of letters to the editor in the campus newspaper, *The Daily Free Press*, or comments on surveys by the CAS Student Forum about the quality of academic life at the university. In extreme cases, parents called the president's office to say that because of an ITA's lack of proficiency in English, their son or daughter was failing a course. In response to these complaints, the dean of the CAS graduate school requested funding from the provost and instituted a mandatory ITA orientation program for all departments in 1998. The program included 30 hours of instruction as well as on-campus housing at a cost of approximately $1,000 per student.

At the same time, similar complaints about the detrimental effect of ITAs on the quality of education at U.S. universities echoed at universities around the country and surfaced in the local press (Abel, 2002; Clayton, 2000; Dorsey, 2000). Furthermore, a study by an economics professor at Harvard showed that undergraduate economics students taught by ITAs received 0.2 grade points less on their final course grades than students taught by native-English-speaking (NES) teaching assistants (Borjas, 2000). The investigator concluded that the ITAs' poor communication skills were, for the most part, responsible for this discrepancy. Such information served to strengthen the commitment of the provost and the deans of CAS to continue funding the preparation of ITAs in order to maintain the quality of undergraduate education at Boston University.

◈ DESCRIPTION

This section describes the orientation program and its components as well as the academic-year program.

Orientation

The 10-day orientation program begins the latter half of August and includes orientation to the city, the university, and the departments, which takes about 50 hours. Thirty of these hours are classes taught by CELOP faculty, and the remaining 20 include presentations by the International Students and Scholars Office, the Off-Campus Housing Office, computer lab coordinators, and graduate students' advisors. The ITAs are housed in a dormitory on campus and are given meals in the cafeteria. The 30 hours of instruction are divided into 3-hour blocks in the morning or afternoon over the 10-day period (see Table 1). Depending on the number of students, they are placed into diverse groups by mixing genders, nationalities, and majors, with 15–18 students per group and 3–4 ESL instructors.

TABLE 1. ORIENTATION SCHEDULE: INTERNATIONAL TEACHING FELLOWS ORIENTATION, BOSTON UNIVERSITY

3-Hour Sessions	First Part	Second Part
Session 1	Introduction to ITA program Overview of syllabus Characteristics of good teacher: reflection and discussion	Videos of U.S. classrooms with note-taking and small-group discussion
Session 2	Rotation of 3 groups: — SPEAK test in language lab — Video: *Role of the Graduate TA* (1995) — Spontaneous speeches	Continue rotation
Session 3	Pronunciation: word stress Review of classroom expressions and terms Explaining a visual from field on OHP (in pairs)	Video: *Cold Water* (Ogami, 1987) Viewing and questions for discussion
Session 4	Pronunciation: sentence stress Article: *Foreign TAs' First Test: The Accent* (Clayton, 2000) Reading and discussion	Video: *College Freshman Survival Guide* (1992) Review of idioms; listening comprehension and summary
Session 5	Pronunciation: final consonants Begin BARNGA simulation (Thiagarajan & Steinwachs, 1990)	Continue BARNGA simulation Debriefing
Session 6	Videotaped presentations: Teaching a concept from field (individual)	Evaluation by peers and instructors (Playback and self-evaluation at later time in language lab)
Session 7	Classroom vocabulary and idioms Practical situations: idiomatic usage	University culture: stereotypes in small, self-defined groups Flip chart presentation
Session 8	Pronunciation: sentence structure, linking, blending Defining terms	Interactive teaching: presenting a process (in pairs)
Session 9	Pronunciation wrap-up Problem solving strategies Program evaluation	Proper dress and good grooming Panel by second-year ITAs
Session 10	Department information surveys Hints for success: effective classroom communication	Video: *What Students Want* (1993) reflection and discussion

In addition to language classes and department orientations, the orientation offers social activities, such as an outdoor barbecue with NES teaching assistants, a Red Sox baseball game, and a final reception at the conclusion of the orientation. Students also explore Boston, look for apartments, and shop for furniture as they become acclimatized to a new environment and bond with their future colleagues.

The associate dean of the graduate school of the CAS oversees the entire orientation, posting an announcement on the CAS Web site, keeping track of attendees, arranging for housing and meals, and taking care of other such details. In addition to administrative staff, second-year ITAs serve as volunteer guides around campus and as speakers on a final panel addressing the concerns of the first-year ITAs.

Instructors

The associate director for academic programs at CELOP hires instructors, who are senior lecturers in ESL and hold master's degrees or doctorates in TESOL or related fields. Together, they formulate the curriculum for the orientation program, modifying what was taught in previous years and refining the content. One of the instructors serves as the coordinator, determining class lists and schedules and acting as liaison among the different entities involved in the orientation.

ITAs

Whereas up to 100 new ITAs enter the CAS during the academic year, only about 60–70 participate in the orientation. Native English speakers from Australia, South Africa, or the United Kingdom are excused. Nonnative English speakers who have received undergraduate or master's degrees in the United States are normally excused from the program. Students from South Asia are invited to attend, even though their schooling has been in English, because they often need to modify or reduce their accents.

Assessment

The Speaking Proficiency English Assessment Kit (SPEAK) test is administered on the first day of the orientation in the main language laboratory on campus. Afterward, each tape is duplicated and scored by two qualified raters from CELOP (their compensation is $20 per tape). Unlike the state universities, where according to mandate ITAs must receive a score of 50 in order to teach, there is no cutoff score at Boston University. Due to funding limitations, ITAs must teach during their first year in order to receive support—unless a department has enough second-year ITAs to fill all the teaching slots. In this case, the less proficient first-year ITAs are assigned the responsibility of grading.

The SPEAK test is used mainly to determine whether an ITA needs further language instruction during the academic year. However, professors tend to choose those with scores of 50 or more to lead discussion sections, although even those with 45 are sometimes assigned such classes. In departments such as chemistry or physics, which offer dozens of introductory undergraduate courses each semester, ITAs with 30s and 40s are assigned to supervise labs, and it is this practice that generates complaints. (Recently, however, an ITA from the Modern Foreign Language and Literature Department received a 20, the lowest score, and was still allowed to teach because Spanish was the medium of instruction. Although he was effective during class, when students spoke in English after class, he had a difficult time.)

Microteaching is also an important part of the assessment process. About halfway through the orientation, the ITAs must give a prepared presentation in which they teach a concept from their field. The videotaped presentation lasts 5–10 minutes and is given in a small-group setting. It is evaluated by an instructor, two peers, and later through video playback by the ITA.

Content

Because two thirds of the students in the orientation program are from China, much time is spent on improving oral skills through activities that involve practicing of pronunciation, classroom expressions, idioms, and vocabulary. Time is also dedicated to presentation techniques, peer teaching, university culture, and short readings. Half of the 30 hours is spent in small groups, and the other half is spent in one large group, viewing and discussing videos or taking part in simulations (see Table 1).

- **Readings:** Readings have included "Conversational Ballgames" (Sakamoto & Naotsuka, 1982), "Ways of Reasoning" (Althen, 1988), "Stereotypes" (Adler, 2002), and *American Cultural Patterns* (Stewart & Bennett, 1991). The reading assignments are usually given for homework and discussed the next day in class. Occasionally, role-plays or skits are used to illustrate the points made in the articles.

- **Videos:** Some of the videos shown are *Cold Water* (Ogami, 1987), *College Freshman Survival Guide* (1992), *Role of the Graduate Teaching Assistant* (1985), and *What Students Want* (1993). After students view certain scenes, the instructor gives them time to answer questions or discuss relevant topics in small groups.

- **Pronunciation:** Instructors use exercises from the two books used during the academic year, *Communicate: Strategies for International Teaching Assistants* (Smith, Meyers, & Burkhalter, 1992), and *Speechcraft: Workbook for International TA Discourse* (Hahn & Dickerson, 1999b). Students usually practice pronunciation in pairs for short periods every day.

- **Vocabulary:** Terminology from each subject area is chosen from the two textbooks and practiced in small groups of ITAs in the same field. Instructors teach stress and intonation patterns and reinforce them daily with short practice sessions.

- **Presentation Techniques:** Instructors introduce effective techniques from *Communicate* (Smith et al., 1992) to the students and provide plenty of practice through assignments like using the board to teach a process, using the overhead projector to explain a visual, and teaching a concept from one's field in the videotaped microteaching assignment.

- **Simulations:** Another activity that encourages communication is *Barnga: A Simulation Game on Cultural Clashes* (Thiagarajan & Steinwachs, 1990). After taking part in the simulation, the ITAs participate in a debriefing, during which they talk about the feelings they experienced and the strategies they used to cope with unexpected situations. Instructors try to make connections between the card games and future cross-cultural encounters, helping ITAs become more aware of the power of the beliefs, assumptions, and expectations of their culture. Despite the ITAs' familiarity with the superficial aspects of the United States, *Barnga* helps them realize that it might be more difficult to become acclimated than they had at first expected.

- **Evaluations:** At the end of the orientation, the participants fill out an evaluation of the program, and the instructors fill out an evaluation for each student, rating communication and presentation skills and recording his or her SPEAK score and band descriptor. Copies of the evaluations are sent to the department chairs and used by the coordinator to place students in tutorials and seminars during the academic year.

Academic-Year Program

The components of the ITA program during the fall and spring semesters include tutorials, seminars, observations, and evaluations. This section explains each element in detail.

Tutorials

A few weeks after the academic year has begun, the coordinator places the ITAs who scored below 50 on the SPEAK test in tutorials, small one-hour classes of 2–4 students that focus on improving pronunciation and fluency. Those who scored below 40 on the SPEAK test are given two tutorials per week, and those who scored above 40 are given one tutorial per week. Each student is given the text and audiotapes of *Well Said* (Grant, 2001) so they can practice at home or in the language lab. *Speechcraft: Workbook for International TA Discourse* (Hahn & Dickerson, 1999b) is used for second-year ITAs who requested—or were required by their departments—to take tutorials again. Newspaper and magazine articles relevant to the students' majors are also read and discussed.

Seminars

Communication seminars, 90 minutes in length, are larger classes of 8–14 students focusing on teaching techniques, U.S. culture, classroom vocabulary, and idioms. Units from *Communicate* (Smith et al., 1992) that were not done in the orientation are covered in the seminars. Instructors also videotape microteaching sessions and give feedback, show professional development videos and discuss techniques, and show segments of television programs or films to explore linguistic or cultural content.

Observations

The instructors observe labs and discussion sections once a semester and fill out an observation form. Afterward, the instructor discusses the form with each ITA and gives constructive feedback and suggestions for improvement.

Evaluations

Instructors write personalized evaluation forms for each ITA, with a general rating of communication and presentation skills and a description of strengths and weaknesses. The instructors give each student a copy of his or her form at the end of the semester; the forms are also sent to department chairs and kept on file by the coordinator. ITAs who wish to transfer to another university often ask their ESL instructors for letters of recommendation; these evaluation and observation forms provide the basis for such recommendations.

◈ DISTINGUISHING FEATURES

Teaching Requirement for First-Year ITAs

Although a handful of international graduate students receive scholarships and simply take courses during their first year, the majority receive teaching assistant-ships and are required to teach, regardless of their SPEAK scores, as mentioned before. This has been problematic when an ITA's proficiency has interfered with quality of instruction in science labs or has impeded communication during discussion sections. Despite the fact that most graduate students admitted to the CAS have scores of 600 in the paper-based TOEFL and 250 in the computer-based TOEFL, the fluency and comprehensibility of some students, particularly those from China, do not always reflect such proficiency, as evidenced by the generally low ratings some ITAs receive on undergraduate students' evaluations.

Some departments used to arrange telephone interviews with Chinese appli-cants to determine their listening and speaking skills. However, these were found to be generally ineffective because students either recited a prepared speech or got so nervous they were not able to formulate coherent answers. This method of interviewing students was therefore abandoned after a few years, and another form of screening was sought to bring in graduate students with better English skills.

Virtual Interviews

Possible Site on Campus

In the fall of 2001, the directors of graduate studies in the chemistry department asked the ITA coordinator to investigate the feasibility of videoconference interviews. The coordinator found several sites on campus, such as the corporate facility in the manufacturing engineering department, which housed large-screen televisions that used Internet Protocol (IP) or Integrated Services Digital Network (ISDN) lines. The cost, however, was prohibitive at $50 per hour for an IP connection and $200 per hour for an ISDN connection, plus a bridging service charge to connect to a corporate site in China where the interviews could be held. The resulting cost would have been greater than a trip to China.

Actual Site on Campus

A better site for videoconference interviews was the Access Grid (AG) facility in the computer science department, which housed a network of audio, video, and computer equipment that enabled two-way communication over IP lines in a conference room setting. The AG network, funded by the U.S. Department of Energy and operated by the Argonne National Laboratory at the University of Chicago, comprises nodes at universities, government laboratories, and research firms (http://www.accessgrid.org). They are used for computational science and engineering, scientific visualization, computer graphics, and other high-performance require-ments. It turned out that Boston University departments could use the facility free of charge, and the AG Web site revealed that a few universities in China also had nodes:

Beijing University of Aeronautics and Astronautics, Chinese Academy of Science, and Tsinghua University, all in Beijing. The stage was set for videoconference interviews that would hopefully solve the problem of accepting applicants who were scientifically savvy but linguistically lacking.

Pilot Project

The ITA coordinator contacted Tsinghua University in late January 2002, and the administrators of the node were enthusiastic about hosting the interviews in February. Due to the Chinese New Year and the ensuing winter vacation, however, it was not possible. Beijing University of Aeronautics and Astronautics though, eagerly agreed to set up a test date to check the connection between Boston and Beijing. The systems were found to be compatible, and an easy, effective form of screening ITAs was about to become a reality.

Because of the time difference, the session began at 7:00 am in Boston and 8:00 pm in Beijing. Despite the fact that only a few applicants responded to the e-mailed invitation, the interview was a resounding success. Sitting together at a long table, the Chinese students could see and hear the interviewers and vice versa. Each side asked questions and responded with answers. Thoroughly pleased, both sides agreed to make arrangements for the interviews earlier the next year so they would proceed more smoothly.

Second Year

In 2003, the videoconference interviews were scheduled in both Beijing and Shanghai, recently connected to the Chinese Educational Resource Network. They started in late January and resumed after winter vacation in late February and ran through early March. The chemistry and physics departments of the CAS and the College of Engineering participated, and almost 100 applicants were interviewed by admissions teams. The ITA coordinator devised an evaluation form to rate the oral proficiency, listening comprehension, and general communicative competence of the applicants and to predict if they would perform well as teaching assistants (see Table 2).

The departments were very pleased with the process, commenting that virtual screening was the wave of the future because it took the guesswork out of the admission of international students (Fitzgerald, 2003). In 2004, the interviews were again held in Beijing and Shanghai, and another site, the University of Science and Technology of China in Hefei, was added with great success.

Independence of the ITA Program

ITA programs can be housed in many places at a university: a center for teaching and learning or teaching excellence, a dean's or provost's office, or a language center. Boston University's ITA program is housed in the Center for English Language, which gives it more autonomy than if it were housed in one of the other two areas. Any full-time ESL instructor is eligible to teach in the program, and the coordinator and instructors are free to modify the curriculum and arrange their own schedules. Although part of the perceived problem with ITAs at Boston University is that there are no objective standards that must be attained (e.g., a certain SPEAK score) before they start teaching, that is also part of the solution. With the first-year teaching

TABLE 2. INTERVIEW EVALUATION FORM

Name _____ M / F   Date _____

University _____ Dept. _____

1 = Poor   2 = Fair   3 = Average   4 = Good   5 = Very Good

Skills		Rating				Comments
Enthusiasm/comfort	1	2	3	4	5	_____
Fluency	1	2	3	4	5	_____
Grammar	1	2	3	4	5	_____
Pronunciation	1	2	3	4	5	_____
Vocabulary	1	2	3	4	5	_____
Listening comprehension	1	2	3	4	5	_____
Ability to answer questions	1	2	3	4	5	_____
General communicative competence	1	2	3	4	5	_____

Strong points:

Weak points:

Based on the interview, this applicant's communication skills appear to be

__ inadequate / __ barely adequate / __ adequate / __ quite adequate / __ strong enough

for TEACHING ASSISTANT duties

requisite, the ITAs must sink or swim. Many admit that, although it was difficult at the beginning, they learned more English from their students in labs than from English instructors in seminars. This exposure to the language and culture of the undergraduates, coupled with tutorials and seminars, has been crucial to making great strides in a short period of time.

◈ PRACTICAL IDEAS

Three suggestions to strengthen ITA programs are forming regional networks, promoting awareness on campus, and making use of undergraduates' talents. Regional networks allow directors, coordinators, and instructors to come together to discuss issues and solve problems. Promoting ITA programs on campus can enlighten administrators, faculty, and students to the efforts made to improve the cultural and linguistic comfort levels of ITAs and to the contributions that the university community needs to make. Making use of the time and talent of undergraduates will add a new dimension to the experience of ITAs as well as their students.

Form Regional Networks

When the New England International Teaching Assistants Network (NEITAN) started in the late 1990s, the former coordinator of the ITA program at Boston University came back to campus brimming with ideas. She wrote a proposal suggesting that our program emulate others in the area that required ITAs to achieve a mandatory score on the SPEAK test and a good evaluation in microteaching before being allowed to teach. She lobbied for change, but not much happened. The departments said that it would be too costly to support the ITAs for an entire year without requiring that they lead labs or discussion sections. One of the few outcomes of her campaign to raise standards was the formalization of the August orientation program, which was surely a step in the right direction. Although she was unable to put into practice all the ideas presented at NEITAN meetings, the group remains an important means of sharing ideas and lending support.

Promote Awareness on Campus

Make the ITA program more visible to the departments by attending faculty meetings and getting to know the directors of graduate studies. When there seems to be a problem with a particular ITA or class, alert the department to the situation so they can respond before the campus newspaper publicizes it.

Participate in campus events. For example, during the annual Technology Showcase, where professors demonstrate how they use technology to facilitate student learning or course administration, the current coordinator publicized the virtual interviews in China. Several professors expressed interest in the process for screening ITAs the following year. Because the program is housed in the Center for English Language, departments unfamiliar with the work of the instructors needed to become more aware of them and the services they offered.

Involve Undergraduates in the ITA Program

When a letter to the editor appeared in the campus newspaper, *The Daily Free Press*, the coordinator issued an open invitation to undergraduates to attend the seminar classes. Only two students responded to the invitation, and she asked them to prepare suggestions to give to the ITAs. Before the students spoke, however, she asked the ITAs to talk about their schooling and their English language education. Most of them were from China, but a few were from Latin America, Southern Europe, North Africa, Turkey, Greece, and Israel. The ITAs gave short presentations about their countries and spoke about having little contact with native English speakers until they started attending the university in a large city. They also spoke of memorizing grammar and vocabulary to get a high score on the TOEFL, but not being able to actually communicate in English. After the ITAs had finished discussing their backgrounds, the undergraduates appeared to have a different attitude toward the ITAs—one of newfound respect and understanding. As the undergraduates gave advice, it was more like a dialogue than a monologue, and they left the seminar with a broader understanding of the ITA experience and its inherent challenges.

◈ CONCLUSION

The enrollment of international graduate students has been rising steadily for the past 20 years, and there seems to be little indication—despite the current political climate—that the trend will change. Talented students from other regions of the world who are offered the opportunity to study at some of the finest institutions in the United States, without the burden of tuition, will continue to come. There seems to be a slight improvement in the oral and aural proficiency of applicants to graduate schools in the past several years. Greater emphasis is being placed on acquiring communicative competence through the establishment of standards and the monitoring of teacher education programs (Liao, 2001; McClosky, 2003)—although passing standardized tests like the TOEFL and Graduate Record Examination (GRE) is still vital to gaining entrance to U.S. universities. In China, TESL summer camps in the provinces are springing up for middle-school children; native English speakers with university degrees, regardless of major, are invited to teach there, perhaps in preparation for the 2008 Olympic Games. These are all signs that future ITAs from China will come with increased language proficiency.

Demographic trends show that an increasing number of U.S. students are expected to enter graduate degree programs in the sciences (Mangan, 2002). It is also expected that students from other countries will possess improved language skills and greater ability to present information in a cogent and appealing fashion to U.S. undergraduates. ITA programs should prepare for such changes. Nevertheless, until that day comes, coordinators must continue to design programs that are more effective and to prepare ITAs to be more comfortable in academia and more proficient and knowledgeable about their roles as classroom instructors.

◈ CONTRIBUTOR

Carol Piñeiro was coordinator of the ITA program at Boston University from 1999 to 2003. She has a doctorate in educational media and technology from Boston University and is currently teaching both the online and on-site versions of "English for Medical and Health Professionals." She is the author of *Grammar Form and Function Teachers' Manuals* (McGraw-Hill) and *English for New Americans* video series (Living Language/Random House), and a contributing author to *Mega English CD-ROMs* (Macmillan), *Market Leader Online* (Longman), and *Communicator I and II* (Prentice Hall/Regents).

CHAPTER 7

From Complaints to Communication: The Development of an International Teaching Assistant Program

Catherine Ross

❧ INTRODUCTION

Administration

In January 1998 the International Teaching Assistant (ITA) Program at the University of Connecticut, a Research I, flagship institution, changed from a program run by a half-time graduate student to a program with a full-time director. This change occurred at a critical time in the history of the university. A new office for Undergraduate Education and Instruction (UE&I) had been created, with an agenda to promote change in the way undergraduate education was viewed on the campus. One of the priority initiatives for the new UE&I vice provost was to deal with the complaints about ITAs by requiring departments to adhere to a policy of language proficiency testing for ITA appointees. The administration hoped that a change in policy would lead to a change in the departmental hiring practices, which would, in turn, lead to a change in the undergraduates' perception of the quality of undergraduate instruction at the university.

Because the ITA program is housed in the Institute for Teaching and Learning, which has no power of enforcement over departments, we had to find a way both to implement and to enforce the English proficiency policy to fulfill the vice provost's agenda. Three factors aided in this transition: (a) the ITA program had an advisory board consisting of various department heads and deans and they had drafted the policy and set the required minimum Speaking Proficiency English Assessment Kit (SPEAK) test score at 50, (b) the graduate school's representative to the advisory board had agreed that the graduate school should be the enforcement agency because they process all teaching assistants' appointments as they are sent by the departments, and (c) the ITA program had a full-time assistant who was skilled in database management. Departments were informed that by the following fall 1998 semester, all ITAs had to have their oral English proficiency tested in order for the graduate school to process their payroll authorization, and the graduate school would check the ITA program's database for compliance.

◈ CONTEXT

Departments

Due to a general departmental skepticism about the validity of the SPEAK test as a measure of spoken proficiency, a microteaching test was added to enhance the credibility of the testing process. The microteaching provided an alternative way to certify those students who fell into the borderline area. Not only did this test have higher face validity for the ITAs and their departments, but it also allowed for the participation of departments and undergraduates in the assessment process, thus putting the opposed stakeholders in the same room to reach agreement on the comprehensibility of an ITA's English. Department heads could hear directly from the undergraduates that they could not understand an ITA's English and could no longer point to the director of the ITA program as the problem. Although only about one third of the borderline group of ITAs was certified using the microteaching test, departments were satisfied that their concerns had been addressed. The ITA program had demonstrated its flexibility regarding the assessment process and its readiness to work with the departments in a positive way.

The ITAs

The next issue of concern was the perceived quality of the ITA courses. The ITAs, according to various department heads and advisors, reported that the classes were "a waste of time" and "did not help their English." This was due in part to the class size, 15 students per section, and the ITAs' disinclination toward pair work or any activity involving their peers as language partners. The classes were completely revamped; the ITA program capped enrollment at 12, chose new textbooks, hired undergraduates to assist the ESL instructors in providing more talk time per ITA, and added two videotaped presentations and playbacks per semester for each student. The reaction was immediate: There were far fewer problems with absenteeism in the courses and far more students wanting to enroll in them.

The Undergraduates

At this point the ITA program now had the components in place to function effectively for three of its four constituents: the ITAs, the departments, and the administration. However, the ultimate goal of changing the undergraduates' perception of the quality of instruction remained elusive. There was a pervasive belief on campus that part of the "UConn experience" was having a class "taught by a teaching assistant who spoke broken English" (Cardillo, 2002, p. 4). Clearly this attitudinal change would be a long-term project.

◈ DESCRIPTION

Previously housed in the Institute for Teaching and Learning, in January 2001 the ITA program became part of a larger entity, the Teaching Assistant Programs, which offers professional development and orientations for all teaching assistants on topics such as effective teaching, running a discussion section, diversity, and academic dishonesty. The director of the Teaching Assistant Programs reports directly to the associate vice provost for undergraduate education, who is also the director of the

Institute for Teaching and Learning, and to the ITA program advisory board, which meets twice a year.

The University of Connecticut has approximately 1,500 teaching assistants teaching in any given semester, and about one third of them are ITAs. The ITA program serves about 150 new ITAs every year with orientations, classes, testing, and teaching consultations. The majority of the ITAs are from China, followed in number by students from India, and then a mix from other countries: Turkey, Russia, Ukraine, Spain, Brazil, Italy, Korea, the Philippines, Nigeria, Kenya, France, Columbia, Egypt, Iran, and Pakistan to name just a few. In terms of disciplines, most are from the School of Engineering (civil, mechanical, electrical, chemical, and environmental), followed by mathematics, computer science, statistics, economics, the natural sciences, and business. There are also a few every year from linguistics, history, communication sciences, sociology and anthropology, and modern and classical languages.

The ITA program has one full-time director and one full-time assistant to the director. The director oversees the orientations, the scoring and administration of all tests, the hiring of the adjunct faculty who teach for the program, and the hiring of the undergraduates who assist with the classes. Other duties include consultations for video playbacks, class observations initiated either by the teaching assistant or by an undergraduate complaint, interventions in classes where a problem has developed, prescreening to assess potential ITA candidates for departmental admissions committees, offering workshops for teaching assistants, writing a teaching assistant handbook, and attendance at various conferences. The assistant to the director manages the office; helps with the Spoken English Test-10 Minute Version (SET-10) test administration; and maintains both the Microsoft Access database used by the graduate school and the program's Web site (www.tap.uconn.edu), which includes registration capability for all orientations, tests, and classes.

The ITA program offers three semester-long, noncredit classes every semester with multiple sections as needed: the "ITA Course" for those who score 55 or higher on the SET-10, the "Oral Communication Course" course for those who score between 45 and 54, and the "Accent Modification Course" for those who score 55 or higher on the SET-10 and have a recommendation from the director. The courses are taught by adjunct ESL instructors who are hired each semester according to enrollment needs. These instructors have master's degrees in ESL and usually work part-time for other programs, such as the University of Connecticut American English Language Institute. In addition to employing the ESL instructors, the ITA program hires undergraduates from all majors as in-class partners for the practice exercises.

The ITA program offers a one-week orientation for new ITAs before each semester, in August and January. In addition to the oral English assessment, the ITAs receive both pedagogical and cultural preparation. The workshops consist of the following:

- a panel discussion with experienced ITAs
- the video *Teaching in America: A Guide for International Faculty* (1993) and discussion
- information on cross-cultural communication problems in the classroom

- a tour of a local high school and a meeting with the assistant principals to go over the high school curriculum

- a discussion of the chapter "Help! My Professor (or Doctor or Boss) Doesn't Talk English" (Martin, Nakayama, & Flores, 1998)

- the video *Respect on the Line* (Ahluwalia, Barker, & Ross, 2001) and discussion

- first-day-of-class practice

- microteaching practice

- informational sessions on the English policy and testing requirements

After the orientation, the three classes previously mentioned are offered every semester. The classes start one week after the university classes begin and because the ITAs have been screened during the presemester orientation, they know what, if any, classes they need to take. Because all of the courses offered by the ITA program are noncredit, ITAs do not receive a grade for completing a course. Teachers fill out final evaluations with recommendations for each ITA in the class, but ultimately the ITA must pass the SET-10 and/or microteaching tests. Students do not pass or fail the classes; they only pass or fail the proficiency tests. This decision was made to avoid confusion over students passing the course but not passing the proficiency tests.

The SET-10 and microteaching tests are offered throughout the year, with the largest number occurring in August during our orientation. In addition to the August test dates, microteaching tests are offered in early December, mid-January, and early May so that students can be certified for the following semester. This schedule brings the total number of proficiency tests for the year to about 250 and the total number of microteaching tests to about 130.

Three courses are offered as part of the program. The lower-level course, the "Oral Communication Course," is intended for students with lower proficiency levels. The class meets three times a week, 2 hours each session, with Fridays being the lab component. Many of these students have difficulty with all aspects of oral English: pronunciation (at phonemic, word, and sentence levels), vocabulary, syntax, and grammar. The textbooks currently in use are *Communicating on Campus* (Hemmert & O'Connell, 1998) and *Well Said* (Grant, 2001). They are augmented by some small-group open conversation on topics in the University of Connecticut's *Daily Campus* newspaper with the undergraduates in small groups and various other group tasks such as debates.

The "ITA Course," for students who will likely need only one semester of English support, meets on Tuesdays and Thursdays for 3 hours a week. Currently the textbooks are *Speechcraft: Workbook for International TA Discourse* (Hahn & Dickerson, 1999b), and *Presenting in English* (Powell, 1996). The students prepare several presentations in this course, and they are videotaped at the beginning, middle, and end of the semester. The end-of-semester microteaching can count toward certification to teach, assuming the student receives a minimum score of 55 on the SET-10.

The "Accent Modification Course" is offered through the Speech and Hearing Clinic in the Department of Communication Sciences and is taught by a graduate student in the final year of master's degree work in speech pathology. It is funded by the ITA program budget and 16 students can enroll in this course each semester. The course focuses primarily on phonemic-level problems, although students also work on speech rate, intonation, and voice modulation. The ITAs undergo an initial screening for hearing problems and a diagnostic interview. They are reassessed at midterm and at the end of the course.

◈ DISTINGUISHING FEATURES

Handling Student Complaints

In the fall of 2000, a contentious editorial in the *Daily Campus* student newspaper added to the pressure to find a way to reach the undergraduates (Goodwin, 2000, p. 4). This editorial targeted an ITA inappropriately and the negative tone was compounded by the message that nothing could be done about a problem with an ITA except to live with it as a fact of college life.

What follows is an illustration of how the ITA program director proceeded in this and similar cases. The director met with the students in the ITAs' classes to discover the reasons for dissatisfaction. In order to ascertain this, Small-Group Instructional Diagnostics (SGID) were carried out. When the students were dissatisfied with the course, the actual cause often turned out not to be language, as indicated in the editorial, but pedagogical issues. Students were upset, for example, when ITAs read Microsoft PowerPoint slides in class. They wanted more spontaneous interaction with the material, examples from real-world situations, and a chance to ask questions and have them answered. Sometimes, an ITA was so soft spoken in class that students could not hear what he or she said. All the comments were respectful and the suggestions legitimate. It soon became clear that undergraduates attributed the problems to language proficiency rather than to teaching style and classroom communication patterns that were at odds with their expectations. The ITAs read the students' comments and met with the director of the ITA program to discuss the outcome of the SGID in order to make adjustments in their teaching style.

Based on the outcome of such interventions, the director asked the advisory board to allow her access to the classes in which undergraduates had reported problems. The purpose was twofold: to find out how reliable the undergraduate complaints about language were, and to provide the chance to interact with undergraduates. This access could be gained by allowing students to complain directly to the ITA program, something not previously formalized. With skeptical approval from the advisory board, the director published a letter to the editor in the *Daily Campus*, informing students that complaints about ITA issues could be made directly to the ITA program by e-mail, by phone, or on the Web site. The response, coming on the heels of the widely publicized and highly emotional debate in the *Daily Campus*, was immediate. In a week there were 14 complaints on the director's desk: 7 from mathematics courses, 2 from statistics, 1 from economics, and 4 from linguistics.

The information obtained in the observations that followed led to several insights that had an effect on the preparation the ITAs receive and on approaching undergraduates about this topic. One insight was that a common theme was discovered in the complaints from the mathematics department. The students were frustrated with the curriculum set by the department and by their perception that their ITAs were unwilling to help them because they would not slow down the presentation of the material. This pattern was observed in the initial seven complaints and reaffirmed in subsequent semesters. Because most of the students in these lower-level math classes are freshmen, they do not always understand the difference between a faculty member and a teaching assistant. They do not realize that ITAs do not have the power to change the curriculum or the test dates, which are set by the department to be the same across all sections. Compounding the problem of ignorance, the ITAs were not explicitly addressing their role at the university in the classroom so that the students would know the limits of their ability to help them. The situation was remedied by having the ITAs complete an adaptation of a "minute paper" assessment (Angelo & Cross, 1993b, pp. 370–377). They asked their students to take one minute at the end of a class and write an anonymous answer to the question: "What could we do to improve your learning in this class?" The ITA read and summarized the responses and in the next class was prepared to discuss the students' requests and comments, with the goal of stating which suggestions would be implemented and which were beyond the power of a teaching assistant. For ITAs, the use of the minute paper was an empowering experience, allowing them to take control of their classes and at the same time establish communication with their students on the previously hidden assumptions and agendas that caused so much frustration for both parties. The undergraduates were likewise empowered and given an opportunity to express their feelings about the class and give input directly to the ITAs in a nonthreatening way.

In a concurrent development in the spring of 2001, the issue of ITAs was introduced into the curriculum for the First Year Experience (FYE) courses that the majority (80%) of freshman take in their first or second semester. These courses are one-credit courses taught by faculty, staff, and administrators. Students deal with academic and university-life issues related to the process of transitioning from high school to college. The Institute for Teaching and Learning did a workshop for the FYE instructors on the issues surrounding ITAs and introduced the video *Respect on the Line* (Ahluwalia, Barker, & Ross, 2001) as a tool for promoting discussions of civility in the classroom. Using the Classroom Disruption scenario, the facilitators promote a discussion of classroom behavior and civility, give tips on how to communicate in a positive way with an ITA, and discuss the role of teaching assistants in general in the university structure. Students are also advised that complaints may be directed to the ITA program if they feel unable to resolve the problem themselves.

If undergraduates want to make a complaint they can send it in an e-mail, anonymously if they choose, or they can simply call and request that the director of the ITA program observe their lab or class. The complaint is then investigated without further involvement from the student. Once a complaint is received, the director notifies the department, verifies the time and location of the class, and e-mails the ITA to arrange a date for the visit. After the observation, the director meets with the ITA for an individual consultation.

The response to this outreach effort has been tremendous, and the number of complaints from freshmen dropped from 12 in the fall of 2001 to 2 in the fall of 2002. Finally, almost 4 years after the reshaping of the ITA program had begun, the fourth constituency, undergraduates, was being reached in a way that promoted greater understanding of the problems with and the solutions to working with ITAs. The perception of the quality of the ITAs' instruction has finally started to shift, as evidenced in a recent editorial in the *Daily Campus* (Shores, 2003), in which the author argues that "a little patience" and coming to class "actually having read the readings" will "guarantee you will magically understand the majority of what is being spoken" (p. 4).

Teaching assistants and ITAs can likewise submit requests for help or ask for advice by going to the Web site. The ITAs have used this option to ask for help interpreting student evaluations, to ask for observations, and to ask for advice on how to handle certain situations.

Troubleshooting Observations

During the observation the director always sits in the back of the room to be as inconspicuous as possible and to hear student comments about the ITAs. The director's goal during an observation is to record what happens in all aspects of classroom interaction. To this end, initial notes are made on the appearance and location of the room and any physical factors such as ambient noise or excessive heat. The number of students is also noted as well as how many arrive late. The notes on the ITAs' behaviors have included, for example, the presence or absence of behaviors such as greetings at the beginning of class, the use of transitions in moving from one activity to another, and the use of nonverbal behaviors such as eye contact and smiling. No attempt is made to categorize behaviors; the goal is a detailed description of all that happens. Student behaviors are also noted, for example, who asks questions; who talks during the explanations; and how they respond to the ITA's questions, to the material, and to the ITA.

Shortly after the observation, the notes are typed into a report that is given to the ITA in a meeting. The report consists of three parts: a descriptive summary, comments, and recommendations for the teaching assistant. The descriptive summary of the class includes what was covered, said, asked, or done. The comments section provides an opportunity to point out problems and/or praise various aspects of what happened in the class; it is the evaluative portion of the report. The recommendations section contains suggestions and goals for improvement. The director decides whether there will be a subsequent observation. This decision is based on the severity of the problems and the students' reactions to the ITA, as well as the ITA's receptiveness to the suggestions and the plan for improvement.

First Year Experience Links

As stated earlier, the issue of ITAs became part of the curriculum for the FYE classes that freshmen take, in either their first or second semester at the university. Using the video *Respect on the Line* (Ahluwalia, Barker, & Ross, 2001), the FYE instructors promote discussions on civility and how to manage classroom communications with an ITA. To provide the students with a chance to reflect on how their behavior can contribute to communication breakdowns, FYE instructors also assign a chapter titled "Help! My Professor (or Doctor or Boss) Doesn't Talk English" from the textbook *Readings in Cultural Contexts* (Martin, Nakayama, & Flores, 1998). Students respond to the reading in an online chat (all FYE courses are Web-based). The responses are remarkable in demonstrating how much of the undergraduate response to ITAs is seemingly subconscious, yet still appears to be open to self-examination. Most of the students admit that they are uncomfortable with taking classes from ITAs, but they go to great lengths to defend their beliefs in equality and to make the case that this kind of diversity is a good thing for the university. Many students admit that they have not been patient enough with their ITAs and that, in fact, they were able to acclimatize to their ITAs' accents after a few classes. Some students actually pointed out that their peers use the ITAs as scapegoats for their own laziness and lack of preparation in the class. But even these students felt it necessary to say that it is often a struggle to understand the ITAs' English, and that given a choice, they would not choose to have an ITA again, especially for the classes they find difficult (chemistry, math, and statistics were often mentioned). Even though some students remain unconvinced that they should accept any responsibility for their communication challenges with the ITAs, this exercise is beneficial in that it helps them to better articulate their problems and to see that many of their peers have successfully found ways to negotiate this classroom terrain. There is also additional benefit in giving the undergraduates a safe space in which to vent their frustrations and to hear and learn from their peers.

Another unanticipated bonus of these FYE class discussions is that complaints about ITAs are now forwarded by the FYE instructors in cases where the student is hesitant to bring the matter to the attention of the department or the ITA program director. Further, since FYE instructors meet regularly, they are able to compare notes and alert the director in cases where there may be multiple complaints about either a faculty member or an ITA. Many of the FYE instructors are able to help the students identify the underlying cause of their problems by asking them about their study habits and whether or not the students have tried meeting with the ITA during his or her office hours. By talking with the students about their complaints, the FYE instructors effectively weed out frivolous complaints and, even better, they are able to give the students advice on coping strategies. As a result, the ITA program director receives much more specific information as to the nature of the complaint and this allows the option of having the departments handle the situations that are related to curricular or departmental decisions as opposed to situations when the student is not able to understand an ITA's English. Clearly the benefits of talking with the undergraduates about the ITAs in their FYE classes has brought about a new level of discourse on campus.

◈ PRACTICAL IDEAS

Prepare ITAs to Be Explicit About Their Role

All teaching assistants need to be made aware of the potential for misunderstanding due to cross-cultural miscommunication and the undergraduates' misperceptions about the decision-making authority that ITAs have over the curriculum, pacing, and assessment in the courses they teach. It is critical for ITAs to make explicit what they can and cannot change in a course. This discussion needs to occur on the first day of class and can be introduced in two ways: through the clear delineation of ground rules in the course syllabus and through the use of a teaching assistant information sheet (see the Appendix).

The syllabus is an underutilized tool; departments or supervising professors often prepare a generic syllabus for their teaching assistants, and the teaching assistants do not know what additional information their students might need or that it is critical to put into writing information that is often only stated verbally. In the ITA professional development that is conducted by the Institute for Teaching and Learning, new teaching assistants are taught to think of the syllabus as a classroom management tool. This means that in addition to giving students their name, e-mail, and office hours on the syllabus, ITAs also provide them with a clear statement of the learning objectives for the course, a detailed and explicit assessment and grading rubric, and a statement of the ground rules for the class. The ground rules necessarily reflect the specific context of each course. Although no instructor wants to appear too heavy handed on the first day, presenting this information on the syllabus actually reassures the undergraduates about the quality of the class and their role as participants in the learning process, which in turn enhances the credibility of the instructor.

Another aspect of the teaching assistant experience that needs to be made explicit is the definition of a teaching assistant and the implications for classroom decisions. This discussion can be short and based on a handout like the one from the chemistry department (see the Appendix). It should not only delineate the teaching assistants' duties from a departmental perspective, but also give contact information for the person(s) responsible for issues that the teaching assistants cannot handle, such as the department head or supervising professor. It should include information about the certification process for ITAs so that students realize there is a university standard for English proficiency. This sheet should be provided on the first day of class along with the syllabus, but should be discussed separately.

Prepare ITAs to Use Formative Assessment

In addition to using the syllabus and a teaching assistant information sheet, all new teaching assistants, especially ITAs, should be prepared to do a formative assessment like the minute paper in the third or fourth week of class. The minute paper and a slightly longer, four-minute paper (McKeachie, 2002) are a means of opening the lines of communication with students in the second or third week of classes.

This simple technique allows teaching assistants to learn the undergraduates' perspectives on how the class is going while fostering an opportunity for further discussion of the topics covered on the first day of class. It is particularly useful for giving ITAs a way to talk to their students and to build rapport with them by discussing the ideas and requests submitted. This assessment also allows a quick release of the tension and involves both sides in discussion and finding solutions. In most cases teaching assistants are able to carry out this assessment and the ensuing discussion without any additional help. The ITA program introduces the use of formative assessments in the ITA orientation as a cross-cultural communication tool and in the orientation for new teaching assistants as a classroom management tool.

Reach Out to Undergraduates

Preparing the ITAs for their role requires dispelling prior beliefs and misperceptions and raising awareness among undergraduate students about the role of ITAs in research universities. An increasing number of colleges and universities offer classes similar to the FYE classes, and these types of courses typically offer the best access to the largest numbers of freshmen, with the added advantage that freshmen students are very likely to have ITAs as instructors. Working with freshmen is the most efficient way to ensure a sea change in attitudes because they will carry these ideas with them throughout their 4 or 5 years at the institution. The instructors of these first-year courses welcome the information and assistance provided by the ITA program because they are the ones who hear the complaints about ITAs and want to know how to advise their students. They look for ways to help their students become independent learners and see the value in giving these undergraduates problem-solving tools such as those listed at the end of Martin, Nakayama, and Flores (1998):

- It's okay to talk about language and cultural differences.

- Respond emphatically.

- Focus on what you can understand rather than on what you miss.

- Listen actively.

- Take a stand against prejudice.

- Don't panic. Be patient. (pp. 157–158)

Bringing the undergraduates into the educational loop is the real key to making the classroom communication problems disappear.

◈ CONCLUSION

Despite the initial fears, establishing a complaint system for undergraduates has had a positive effect on both the undergraduate view of the university and its concern for their classroom experience. More unexpectedly, many of the ITAs themselves have come to consider the ITA program director as an advocate who has enabled them to gain their footing in the U.S. classroom. The use of formative evaluation early in the semester has proven to be a powerful tool for ITAs to establish good relations with their students and to hone their teaching methods.

Although the ITA program has not completely eradicated the myth of the ITA who can't speak English, the University of Connecticut now has a more productive dialogue occurring than at any time in the past. By giving the undergraduates an outlet for venting their frustrations, and the ITAs a tool to create a dialogue about those frustrations, both groups have been empowered to resolve problems in a productive and civil way.

◈ CONTRIBUTOR

Catherine Ross is currently the associate director of the Institute for Teaching and Learning at the University of Connecticut. She has worked in ESL for 20 years, has a master's degree in both ESL and Russian, and received her doctorate in Russian from the University of Texas at Austin in 1998. Her research interests are adult second language acquisition and how language, pedagogy, and culture interact in university classrooms.

◈ APPENDIX: CHEMISTRY TEACHING ASSISTANTS

The instructors for the lab and discussion sections of this course are called teaching assistants (TAs). All of the TAs in the chemistry department are graduate students with either a bachelor's or master's degree in chemistry or chemical engineering.

They are all in the doctoral program and have been admitted after a rigorous screening process. (Chemistry admits only 10% of its applicants for graduate school.)

Some of your TAs are international students. Many of them have taught in universities and colleges in their home countries. They have all passed English proficiency exams (written and oral) and have been cleared to teach by the university's Institute for Teaching and Learning.

The four instructors in Chem 127/128 are committed to giving as fair and as even a course as possible. We do not want your grade to depend on who your lecturer or TA is. As a result, the course is rigidly structured and the TAs are allowed very little flexibility or creativity. They do not decide the format of the discussion section or the grading scheme for your unknowns. All the quizzes that are given are checked over by one of the instructors, and only one TA (not necessarily your own) makes the quiz for a particular time period. So, if you have a question, a complaint or a problem with the format for labs and/or the discussion sections, see your instructor. Your TA has little or no input in the process.

At the end of the semester, your TA hands to your instructor a record of your work. This includes all the points that you have accumulated for all the tasks that you have completed in lab and discussion. He/she also gives the instructor a descriptive summary of your performance. This summary is very important to your instructors. It is used to decide borderline cases, and is often quoted when you ask us to write a letter of recommendation for you. Since your lecture section has at least 175 students, your instructor does not really know you as well as your TA does. Your TA however, does NOT decide your grade for the course. Your instructor does that.

Your TA also has strict guidelines to follow for make-up labs and quizzes. The information sheet that you have been given (also posted on WebCT) explains those guidelines. Only your instructor can decide make-ups for hour exams.

We hope that you can see that even if Chem 127/128 is taken by a large number of people, it is personalized by your small sections of 16 with a TA. Your TA can be an enormous source of help to you. They are all successful students of chemistry. Take advantage of their youth, enthusiasm, and expertise. Be aware, however, that major responsibility for the structure and mechanics of the course is not theirs.

Note. This document created by the Chemistry Department at the University of Connecticut.

CHAPTER 8

The International Teaching Assistant Program at the University of Utah

Diane Cotsonas

◈ INTRODUCTION

The involvement of undergraduates in the professional preparation of international teaching assistants (ITAs) greatly benefits both groups and enhances learning and instruction in ITA classes. At the University of Utah, the ITA preparation program has included undergraduates since 1996. Undergraduate student involvement has contributed to raising awareness of the importance of intercultural communication, enhancing communication among undergraduate students and ITAs, and improving ITAs' listening and speaking skills. In 1998, approximately one fifth of the teaching assistants were international students. Needless to say, their effect on the university and the undergraduate student population has been significant. The involvement of undergraduates has brought an experiential component to ITA preparation that would be impossible through instruction alone. The participation of undergraduates in sessions on intercultural differences and as volunteer students in microteaching practice sessions has provided ITAs with experiential input on what they can expect to encounter when they take on, for the first time, their instructional roles as lab assistants and as instructors in undergraduate classrooms in the United States. Undergraduate students are the primary stakeholders in successful ITA professional development efforts. They benefit from having better instruction and from their communication and encounters with ITAs both within and outside the classroom.

Involving undergraduates in ITA preparation has not occurred without challenges, especially in the area of undergraduate recruitment and facilitation of experiential interaction between undergraduates and ITAs. This chapter describes some of the efforts made at the University of Utah to deal with the challenges we have encountered and explains how these have helped shape the present-day program.

◈ CONTEXT

The University of Utah's ITA program was recently moved to the graduate school. Previously housed in the university's instructional development unit, the ITA program was the only program in that unit for which participation was required, which created problems with issues of enforcement. It is anticipated that administration by the graduate school will provide the credibility and authority necessary to accomplish the program's objectives. The ITA program coordinator, a three-quarter-time academic staff appointment, is the only year-round position solely dedicated to ITA preparation. During workshops, instructors are hired from other campus units, mainly from the English Language Institute. Plans are underway to add personnel and to make the coordinator a full-time position.

The majority of the ITA candidates come from China and India, but more than a dozen nationalities are regularly represented. The College of Science and the College of Engineering register the most students, but students from 18 or more different academic units are represented. Table 1 presents demographic information of the graduate student participants in the Pre-Fall ITA Workshops from 2002 to 2004.

Undergraduate students serve as cultural consultants. They come from different departments on campus as a result of hearing about the program from different sources. The ITA program has made recent efforts to expand the pool of volunteers to include a wider variety of majors. See Table 2 for an example of the demographics of undergraduate participants at a recent workshop.

◈ DESCRIPTION

From the first mandatory ITA workshop in the fall of 1992 to the fall 1995 workshop, ITA preparation at the University of Utah consisted of a 2-week, presemester workshop conducted by the English Language Institute, the University's intensive English program. Some undergraduate students and high school seniors were involved, but for the most part this was an ITA-centered workshop.

In the spring of 1995, the Alumni Association commissioned an Institutional Perception Study to learn more about what current and college-bound students thought about the university. One of the recommendations was to expand ITA professional preparation because the focus groups all listed the comprehensibility of ITAs as an area of concern. In the interest of expanding the support and preparation of ITAs into the academic year, the dean of the graduate school asked the linguistics program to take over the ITA workshop so it would take place in an academic unit and provide ongoing support during the semester. That same year, the university hired 35 new teaching assistants called university teaching assistants (UTAs). Those assigned to the linguistics program observed and evaluated ITAs campus-wide during the 1995–1996 academic year and worked with two linguistics professors to create a new workshop format. In the fall of 1996 an additional UTA was added to linguistics, and the team of five conducted the first 2-week workshop following the new format. The workshop was called "Teaching and Learning Across Cultures." It continued to provide instruction to ITAs in teaching strategies and language

TABLE 1. DEMOGRAPHICS OF INTERNATIONAL GRADUATE STUDENTS 2002–2004 PRE-FALL WORKSHOPS

Year	No. of Countries	No. of Departments	Gender of ITAs
2002	20	16	F: 30 M: 62
2003	14	20	F: 20 M: 75
2004	19	24	F: 14 M: 47

TABLE 2. DEMOGRAPHICS OF UNDERGRADUATE CULTURAL CONSULTANTS

Gender	Major	Class	Heard About Through:
M	Biology	Senior	Student club
F	Undecided	Freshman	Unknown
M	Mechanical Engineering	Freshman	LEAP (accelerated freshman-year program)
M	English/Classics/Asian Studies	Junior	International Center
M	Political Science	Junior	Transfer orientation

development, but it took the professional preparation to the next level, combining the ITA cohort with an undergraduate liberal education class that satisfied the university's diversity graduation requirement. The idea behind this new workshop format was to break down the barriers that prevent people from understanding and appreciating those who are different from them and, in so doing, increase both their willingness and their ability to communicate with one another. Because the workshop involved ITAs and undergraduate students, it effectively transformed what might have been considered the so-called ITA problem into an opportunity for developing cross-cultural communication skills for all participants.

For the first hour of the day, the professors taught the two groups separately. One met with the ITAs while the other met with undergraduates enrolled in his 2-week diversity class. After this first hour, the two groups came together to share a meal, to participate in activities addressing linguistic and cultural diversity, and to prepare microteaching sessions. During the semester, the two UTAs conducted one-on-one tutorials, held monthly seminars, and coordinated outings with the 30 international graduate students who participated.

During the summer of 1997, ITA preparation was moved into the university's instructional development unit, the Center for Teaching and Learning Excellence.

In August of 1997, a new pair of UTAs coordinated the workshop in much the same way as before, collaborating with the same two professors and providing ongoing support during the academic year. Relying on two new UTAs each year to get the workshop up and running proved difficult, and the need for continuity in the form of a year-round position became increasingly clear. In 1998, the position of ITA program coordinator was created, and one of the UTAs from the 1997–1998 year was hired for the position. She organized the 2-week workshop, collaborated with the linguistics professor on workshop content and materials, and conducted the ITA sessions. During the semester, observations, consultations, and tutorials continued. Rescreenings of ITAs who were conditionally cleared or not cleared were added to the programming.

Every year, the number of ITAs in each workshop continued to increase, but the number of undergraduate students declined in recent years. It was very difficult to recruit students for an intensive class that was held during the 2 weeks before the regular academic term commenced. Table 3 gives an overview of how many ITA candidates and undergraduate students were involved from 1996 to 2004. Nevertheless, the workshop was extremely effective and it continued to bring together ITA

TABLE 3. PARTICIPANT NUMBERS 1996–2004

Academic Year	International Graduate Students (Approximate)	Undergraduate Students Involved (Approximate)
1996–1997	30	35 (class)
1997–1998	32	40 (class)
1998–1999	41	8 (class)
1999–2000	50	45 (class)
2000–2001	90	35 (class)
2001–2002	130	50 (class)
2002–2003	128 (including new Pre-Spring Workshop 2003)	20 (cultural consultants)
2003–2004	119	15 (cultural consultants)
2004	Pre-Fall Workshop 2004: 103 prescreened; 66 admitted	8 (cultural consultants)

candidates and undergraduates in a similar format from 1996 to 2001. A number of changes were made. Some were temporary, such as a condensed one-week workshop brought on by the university's conversion from a quarter system to a semester system, and some more permanent, such as an elimination of the postmicroteaching consultations that was necessitated by a quadrupling of the number of candidates.

In 2002, the professor who had been directing the program discontinued teaching the undergraduate class concurrently with the ITA workshop. Instead, the class was held as a regular semester-length class. Undergraduates in the class continued to engage with prospective ITAs during the semester, but the resource of undergraduates from the class during the presemester workshop was no longer an option. Because the undergraduates played such a key role in the presemester workshop, a new component was created: the Cultural Consultant Program. Undergraduate volunteers took the place of the undergraduates from the diversity class. As a result, the level of participation and intensity dropped substantially, but scheduling became much more manageable.

The Spoken English Test (SET), an automated test administered over the telephone, is required to determine who is admitted into an ITA workshop. Students with less than adequate scores are advised on the resources available to improve their oral English proficiency and given a chance to retest later for admittance into the next workshop. From 2002 to 2005, the workshop format has continued to evolve. The level of undergraduate involvement is quite low at present, but the commitment to increase undergraduate participation remains. Plans to involve service-learning students will likely increase undergraduate involvement as cultural consultants. ITA preparation has continually changed over the years, mostly due to increased numbers, but also because of the advent of prescreening that has allowed for a more homogenous group in terms of language skills. A prespring workshop, observations, and midsemester student evaluations have been added, and one-on-one consultations have been more readily available to ITAs than ever before.

Two presemester ITA workshops are held each year. The Pre-Fall ITA Workshop is held in August during the 2 weeks prior to the first day of fall semester classes (see Appendix A for a sample schedule), and the Pre-Spring ITA Workshop is held in January, the week before the first day of spring semester classes (see Appendix B for a sample schedule). The majority of candidates arrive in time for the August event. The January workshop was started in 2003 to accommodate those who were not admitted into the August workshop, those who missed the August event due to visa problems, and students admitted for the spring semester and whose departments needed their instructional services during the spring semester.

Collaboration with the International Center has resulted in a comprehensive new student orientation to lead off the Pre-Fall ITA Workshop. This orientation provides students with information about culture shock, university policies, services and resources both on campus and around Salt Lake City, and keeping in compliance with visa regulations. After the orientation, SET results are distributed and the group disbands for a break. After the break, the two groups (admitted and not admitted) return to separate sessions. Those who have been admitted to the workshop receive their materials and an overview of the upcoming workshop. Those who have not been admitted attend presentations and receive information about the resources available to help them improve before retesting for the next workshop.

◈ DISTINGUISHING FEATURES

Undergraduate Students as Cultural Consultants

In 1996, the approach of the university's ITA program broke new ground when it involved undergraduate students as a way to mentor ITAs and to enrich the undergraduates' own cross-cultural understanding. This was an innovative approach to ITA professional growth and has distinguished the program ever since. The 1996–2001 presemester workshops involved undergraduates at an unprecedented level, and although they were challenging to carry out, the level of intensity that characterized those 5 years was rewarding and effective. Undergraduates have been invaluable as cultural informants, giving ITAs a safe and objective party to answer their questions and give them impartial feedback.

Undergraduate participation is currently accomplished through the Cultural Consultant Program. We strive to increase undergraduate participation from the departments that send the majority of ITA candidates. Undergraduates who have complaints about their teaching assistants are frequently uncomfortable voicing their concerns to the teaching assistants during the semester. However, during the workshop, because the cultural consultants are not the ITAs' real students, they give ITAs critical feedback about their teaching skills and English proficiency. Cultural consultants who participate in the workshop come away with a better understanding of the challenges all teaching assistants encounter and the additional challenges that ITAs face. When undergraduates share this understanding with their classmates, it becomes a powerful way to promote cross-cultural understanding on campus.

Prescreening Techniques

The use of the SET as a phone-based prescreening for workshop admission is another distinguishing feature. Administration of the Speaking Proficiency English

Assessment Kit (SPEAK) test worked when there were 20–30 students registered for the workshop, but as the numbers climbed it became increasingly difficult and eventually impossible to use the SPEAK test because the human resources for scoring simply were not available. It became imperative to find a test that provided results more quickly. Even in 1998, when there were 40 students in the workshop, it was difficult to get SPEAK tests scored in time to use for workshop admittance or clearance purposes, and the reality was that all candidates, despite low levels of proficiency, went through the workshop. The SET has made it possible to prescreen large numbers of students in a short amount of time—a necessity in a program with limited resources and staff. In 2006, when Educational Testing Service begins to administer the new Test of English as a Foreign Language (TOEFL), which includes a speaking component, we expect that the need for the SET will diminish and it will eventually be replaced because the TOEFL is already required for university admission. University administrators are also considering accepting scores from the International English Language Testing System, which includes a speaking component.

Microteaching Sessions

An additional distinguishing feature of the program is the videotaped microteaching practice and testing. Practice microteaching sessions are videotaped and ITAs receive oral feedback after the session. Written feedback is provided by the instructor, peers, and undergraduates. Candidates view the videotape with an instructor and on their own and post a self-reflection to the program Web site. Exit testing is accomplished using the teaching test, a final microteaching that is also videotaped.

Interactive teaching and active learning is new to many ITAs. We have found that microteaching reduces the discomfort considerably, so new ITAs enter both their teaching assignments and their roles as students better prepared. On workshop evaluations, microteaching is by far the workshop component that ITAs most often cite as being the most useful. Microteaching is used primarily as a chance for ITAs to develop an awareness of what they are doing well and what they need to improve upon. All microteaching sessions are videotaped and used in ongoing professional development. Rather than use a single microteaching session as a high-stakes exit test, we use it as a teaching tool first and as a screening tool second. Practice microteaching gives ITAs an opportunity to receive feedback, to view their videotapes, and to make changes, thus giving a final microteaching that better reflects their abilities. As a result, they are much more relaxed when they take their microteaching test.

The undergraduate cultural consultants also learn from the microteaching experience. They learn strategies for listening to different world Englishes and they learn that it is not only acceptable to ask for clarification when they have difficulty understanding, it is highly desirable. The only complaint our ITAs have had about the presence of undergraduates during microteaching is that they are too nice. Many of the undergraduates are afraid they will insult the ITA if they say they do not understand or ask them to repeat or rephrase. The undergraduates are given tips and a chance to practice strategies that allow them to raise their questions and concerns in a way that is sensitive to cultural and personal differences and constructive in nature. They learn to give feedback with a focus on how to make changes, not to simply say that the changes are desired.

Web-Based Technology

The ITA program Web site (*ITA Program at the University of Utah*, 2005), created in 1998, and the use of Web-based technology are further distinguishing features. Initially set up as a central location for prospective ITAs to access information before their arrival, it expanded to include information that ITAs and undergraduates need before, during, and after the workshop. The Web site also serves as a place where staff and faculty can find information about requirements, dates, and registration information. Use of Web-based technology to enhance communication and encourage self-directed learning has greatly enhanced the program. As the number of new ITA candidates in the program grew, workshop organizers looked for ways to expand the opportunities for discussion and reflection on the topics and issues addressed during workshop sessions. Over the years, the ITA program has used WebCT (http://www.webct.com/) and Nicenet (http://nicenet.org/) for a variety of purposes, including to increase opportunities to discuss cross-cultural issues and to give more detailed microteaching feedback. We found that many students who were characteristically quiet when in a large group found it easier to express their opinions and concerns when they had the option of posting on the Web site.

WebCT tools help us make the most of the limited time we have for workshop sessions by continuing the dialogue after hours. The Web site is accessible only to the cohort of ITAs, their cultural consultants, and the workshop staff and organizers. WebCT technology is used to facilitate continued interaction among undergraduates and ITAs and has provided a key tool allowing the ITAs to post self-reflections about their teaching. This, along with follow-up assignments and resources, makes WebCT tools remain useful long after the workshop ends by providing self-directed learning opportunities.

◈ PRACTICAL IDEAS

Recruit Undergraduates as Cultural Consultants

Recruiting undergraduate cultural consultants is a challenge, particularly at a commuter campus like the University of Utah; however, we have developed several successful approaches. These include asking the academic counseling unit to send e-mail flyers to the undergraduate advisor in each department and posting flyers in buildings all over campus, particularly in the departments from which we are interested in recruiting more students. Future plans include collaborating with professors of designated service-learning courses, linguistics courses, and courses taken by international studies majors. Additional areas that may provide successful partnerships include student clubs, the alumni association, and entities that seek to further internationalize the campus.

Create Sites and Resources for ITAs' Oral English Improvement

In addition to traditional ESL classes offered on our campus, we also have a club that provides conversation classes and social and cultural activities. The International Student Council offers many activities, and because the activities involve students with many different first languages, English is spoken as the common language. Furthermore, the International Center has started a language exchange where students studying various foreign languages trade tutoring with native speakers of the language they are studying.

Include Videotaped Microteaching

Practice microteaching is time intensive but infinitely useful for ITAs at all levels of English proficiency. Require ITA candidates to attend their peers' microteaching sessions and stress that they can learn as much by observing others' teaching as they can by watching their own sessions. Provide preparation for your audience on how to give feedback. Even a 15-minute session on the rationale and goals of microteaching makes the sessions much more effective.

Create Web-Based Course Tools

Make your Web interface easy to navigate so energy is expended on the assignment, not on finding the proper place to post. Use the student areas of the Web interface; it gives students ownership of the site and allows an outlet for creativity. Post photos of participants, instructors, and support staff so students can connect names with faces early on. If your institution does not host WebCT or a similar system for your use, consider using the free systems available on the Internet. Use only the features you need; do not try to use all of them—it is better to use one or two well than to use six or seven poorly. Post assignments as well as readings or links to sites that supplement topics raised during your sessions. Allow time for your instructors to respond to each self-reflection. Students especially appreciate written feedback from the instructors, and it is easier to make detailed suggestions in writing when there is more time. Acknowledge the positive aspects of the presentation first, and frame the negative aspects as items that can be improved upon.

Collaborate With Other Units on Campus

Communicate with other campus entities that provide services or have requirements your students need or must fulfill. In the past, our workshop schedule prohibited ITAs from attending other important orientations and activities, but our partnership with the International Center has been instrumental in allowing ITAs to focus on our program, now that their anxiety about other important aspects of their lives has been addressed and significantly reduced during the orientation. If your program is presemester and campus-wide, communicate and collaborate with departments that have preparation programs for teaching assistants and try to synchronize the timing of orientations and workshops.

Student government, alumni associations, and others should know about the screening and preparation programs for ITAs so they can disseminate this information to the student body or to individuals who lodge complaints through their offices. If you have a community service unit, encourage ITAs to volunteer because it is a wonderful way for them to learn about your off-campus communities. Other departments and units that can offer collegiality and human resources include the languages department, the linguistics department, the school of education, the intensive English program, and the instructional development center.

◈ CONCLUSION

In recent years, there has been much discussion both nationwide and at the University of Utah about diversity, intercultural communication, and the internationalization of campuses. International graduate students are a rich resource not only as research assistants and teaching assistants, but also as contributors to the diversity and internationalization of our campus. ITA preparation at the University of Utah has evolved and greatly changed over the years. In the exciting process of shaping the program, we have relied on the strong traditions of pioneers in the field, incorporated the innovative ideas of visionary professors, and addressed the necessity to be practical during times of staffing cuts and budget constraints. In the decade since ITA professional preparation was first offered on our campus, the program has striven to offer all of its graduate students the information and strategies they need to break down linguistic and cultural barriers. They are therefore better able to share and maximize their strengths, thus assuring their success as teachers and learners on our campus. The use of technology, the involvement of undergraduates in ITA preparation, and the collaboration with other units on campus have all served our goal of furthering teaching and learning across cultures at the University of Utah.

◈ ACKNOWLEDGMENTS

I would like to thank my colleagues who have shared their insights into ITA work with me over the years, especially those I have met through TESOI's ITA Interest Section. In addition, I want to express my gratitude to David Chapman, dean of the Graduate School, for his invaluable support and guidance, and to his predecessor, Ann Hart, for having the foresight to begin ITA training on our campus.

◈ CONTRIBUTOR

Diane Cotsonas is the ITA program coordinator at the University of Utah. She was also a teaching assistant when she began working with ITAs.

◈ APPENDIX A: SAMPLE UNIVERSITY OF UTAH PRE-FALL ITA WORKSHOP SCHEDULE

WEEK ONE

MONDAY: International Center New Grad Student Orientation

1:00–1:20 pm	Registration
1:20–1:30 pm	Welcome by International Center
1:30–2:00 pm	Ice Breaker/Greetings
2:00–2:45 pm	Immigration Regulations
2:45–3:00 pm	Break with Light Refreshments
3:00–3:20 pm	Student Health and Insurance
3:20–3:30 pm	Q&A, Break
3:30–5:00 pm	Spoken English Test (SET) Overview and Test (ITA program)

TUESDAY: International Center New Grad Student Orientation

1:00–1:20 pm	Video: *Coming & Going—Intercultural Transitions for College Students* (2003)
1:20–1:40 pm	Culture Shock & Quiz
1:40–2:00 pm	Campus Safety and Security (Campus Police)
2:00–3:00 pm	International Block Party at the Union
3:00–3:30 pm	Q&A, Closing, Evaluations, Attendance stamps
3:30–4:00 pm	Break
4:00–6:00 pm	Meet for Transportation Activity & Dinner (light rail to downtown SLC)

WEDNESDAY: Beginning of ITA Workshop

1:00–1:30 pm	Check-in & Introductions; Welcome from University Administrators
1:30–2:30 pm	Video & Discussion (Undergraduate students): *Teaching in America* (1993)
2:30–2:40 pm	Break
2:40–3:30 pm	Teaching as Communication/How Students Learn
3:30–3:40 pm	Break
3:40–4:30 pm	Functional English for the Classroom
4:30–5:00 pm	Microteaching Overview, Debriefing & Assignments

THURSDAY

1:00–1:45 pm	Video & Discussion (Classroom Management): *Respect on the Line* (2001)
1:45–2:00 pm	Break
2:00–2:45 pm	Interactive Teaching/Active Learning/Teaching & Learning Styles
2:45–3:00 pm	Break
3:00–4:30 pm	Microteaching Practice: Group 1
4:30–4:40 pm	Break
4:40–5:00 pm	Debriefing & Assignments

FRIDAY

1:00–4:30 pm	Teaching Tests: Group 1 Candidates Teach; All Candidates Must Attend
4:30–5:00 pm	Workshop Evaluation, Receipt of Clearance Results: Group 1

WEEK TWO

MONDAY & WEDNESDAY

1:00–2:00 pm	Instructional Session: Focus on Spoken English Skills
2:00–5:00 pm	Practice Microteaching: Group 2 Monday, Group 3 Wednesday

TUESDAY & THURSDAY

1:00–4:00 pm	Teaching Tests
4:00–5:00 pm	Workshop Evaluation, Receipt of Clearance Results: Group 2 Tuesday, Group 3 Thursday

◈ APPENDIX B: SAMPLE UNIVERSITY OF UTAH PRE-SPRING ITA WORKSHOP SCHEDULE

MONDAY

Time	Session Title
12:00–12:45 pm	Check-In/Icebreaker
	Welcome and Overview
12:45–1:45 pm	TA Roles, Education in the United States
	Teaching as Communication
1:45–2:00 pm	Break
2:00–3:30 pm	Giving Presentations
	Language & Communication Skills for the Classroom
3:30–3:45 pm	Break
3:45–4:15 pm	Wrap-Up

TUESDAY

12:00–12:50 pm	Slang, Idioms, and Dialects in North American English
12:50–1:00 pm	Break
1:00–1:50 pm	Crash Course in North American English Pronunciation: Speaking "American"
1:50–2:00 pm	Break
2:00–3:00 pm	Discourse Organization
3:00–3:15 pm	Break
3:15–4:15 pm	Listening Skills: Common Student Questions
4:15–4:30 pm	Break
4:30–5:00 pm	Wrap-Up

WEDNESDAY

12:00–12:50 pm	Video & Discussion: *Teaching in America* (1993)
12:50–1:00 pm	Break
1:00–2:00 pm	Video & Discussion: *Respect on the Line* (2001)
2:00–2:15 pm	Break
2:15–3:15 pm	Microteaching
3:15–3:30 pm	Break
3:30–4:30 pm	Microteaching
4:30–4:45 pm	Wrap-Up

THURSDAY

1:00–1:30 pm	Review of Teaching Test Process
1:30–1:45 pm	Break
1:45–4:30 pm	Teaching Tests
4:30–4:45 pm	Wrap-Up

FRIDAY

12:00–12:30 pm	Workshop Evaluation, Clearance Letters
12:30–1:00 pm	Review of Spring Semester Follow-up
1:00–1:30 pm	Wrap-Up

CHAPTER 9

An Intensive Workshop for International Teaching Assistant Preparation

Thomas J. Schroeder and Dennis M. Kohler

INTRODUCTION

In 1984 the School of Graduate Studies at Utah State University (USU) extended an invitation to the faculty in the Department of Languages and Philosophy to develop a program of instruction for "foreign graduate students" to prepare them to be teaching assistants in their departments. At that time, the international graduate student population at USU was approximately 22%. The international students were rarely given instructional assignments and the graduate school recognized the potential of this intellectual resource, especially given the rapid increases in undergraduate enrollments.

In its 20 years of subsequent operation, the program has graduated a total of 411 participants into classrooms and laboratories across the campus. The majority of international teaching assistants (ITAs) who graduated from the program have been successful in their instructional assignments. They have received satisfactory evaluations from their students and have completed their departmental responsibilities as teaching assistants.

Several graduates from the program have earned recognition as college-level teaching assistants of the year, and one ITA was the recipient of the Robins Award, the university-wide graduate teaching assistant of the year award. On the other hand, the issue of comprehensibility of ITAs has periodically been a topic in the student newspaper and has become a campus-wide issue.

Figure 1 shows the distribution, by geographical area, of all the participants in the USU ITA program between 1985 and 2004. Although 512 students participated in the program, only 411 were certified to become ITAs.

CONTEXT

A team of faculty members accepted the invitation to develop an ITA professional development program for the graduate school. The team consisted of a linguist with a background in English for specific purposes and four faculty members from the Intensive English Language Institute (IELI) at USU, then a part of the Department of Languages and Philosophy. The team proposed to develop a 2-week presession program for prospective teaching assistants, followed by a weekly seminar during the session for those participants who were subsequently awarded teaching assistantships by their departments (Cole, Rawley, & Carkin, 1985; Lackstrom, 2002).

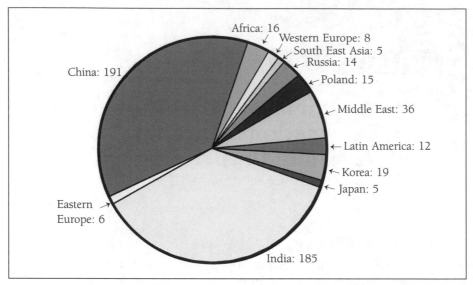

Africa: 16
Western Europe: 8
South East Asia: 5
Russia: 14
Poland: 15
Middle East: 36
Latin America: 12
Korea: 19
Japan: 5
China: 191
Eastern Europe: 6
India: 185

FIGURE 1. Distribution of ITA Program Participants by Geographical Area, 1985–2004

The pilot program was carried out September 16–27, 1985. Funding for the follow-up seminar was not available and that part of the proposal was not implemented. In subsequent years, workshops were funded on an annual basis by the graduate school, where the funding continued to reside. The workshops were conducted under the leadership of a director and carried out by teaching faculty, all of whom were members of IELI or the Department of Languages and Philosophy. These assignments were undertaken on a voluntary, extracontractual basis.

The need to prepare additional graduate students to begin their teaching assignments later in the academic year led to the expansion of the program in the 1991–1992 academic year. The workshop evolved from a single session offered prior to the start of the academic year to two sessions. The second workshop session was offered in seminar format two nights a week during the winter quarter. Again the staffing of the workshops was on an extracontractual basis.

The program was institutionalized in the 1993–1994 academic year. After 8 successful years of the program, it was recognized that no one had a contractual responsibility for the continuation of the program. The IELI faculty members who had been loyal to the program needed to lessen their loads, and staffing the workshop was getting increasingly difficult. The university transferred the funds that had been used to run the program to the IELI budget. IELI had become an independent unit within the college in 1985. The IELI director assumed the directorship of the ITA program. The majority of the funds added to the IELI budget were dedicated to creating a half-time coordinator position responsible for carrying out two workshops annually. The program has continued in this form to the present.

The most recent enhancement to the program was made in the 1996–1997 academic year. Since the inception of the program, we recognized that the preparation given to ITAs in the workshop was only the beginning and that each ITA deserved to be supported during his or her first experience in the classroom or lab.

The graduate school accepted a proposal for a follow-up program to be held during the first semester of an ITA's teaching career. This follow-up program involved a previsit meeting, an observational visit of the ITA in the classroom, and a postvisit debriefing. The pilot program also brought the group of ITAs together for a weekly seminar. This follow-up support has continued to be funded by the graduate school.

Currently, USU advertises its emphasis on excellence in undergraduate education. The university demonstrated this excellence with statistics showing that only 8% of classes are taught by graduate students and only 1% by nonnative English speakers. The graduate school established a university-wide mandate that all international students must certify through the ITA workshop before being permitted to work with students in any instructional role. This mandate provides a centralized control over departments that historically operated with a great deal of autonomy. The graduate school sponsors the workshop and is responsible for monitoring the departments for compliance. The budget for the program primarily supports personnel wages with some supplies and equipment for an enrollment of 25–30 students in the presession workshop and 12–18 during the semester.

In preparation for the initial workshop in 1985, an observational study was proposed and undertaken. Ten classroom videotapes of a group of selected international and native-English-speaking (NES) teaching assistants were taken during the winter and summer quarters. The teaching assistants were from the biology, chemistry, economics, mathematics, and physics departments and consisted of four U.S. students and six students from China, India, and Japan. Transcripts of the taped lessons were made and then analyzed for features that constituted effective teaching. These transcripts and tapes became the central instructional materials in the program; the emphasis on clearly identified features of classroom discourse and behavior, as observed in authentic classroom environments, has characterized the program from its inception to the present day (Cole, Rawley, & Carkin, 1985; Lackstrom, 2002).

All international graduate students are informed of the ITA workshop when they receive acceptance materials from the university. The workshop administers an in-house Speaking Proficiency English Assessment Kit (SPEAK) test to prospective participants. The graduate school requires a SPEAK score of 45 for admission into the workshop. Another criterion for participation in the workshop is a departmental commitment of a teaching assistantship for the fall semester. If the workshop does not reach the maximum enrollment, students with other departmental assistance, such as research, may be admitted.

In recent years, the instructional faculty has included two IELI faculty members in addition to the coordinator. All faculty members have a master's degree in TESOL and they teach in the intensive English program. Their areas of specialization within TESOL include cross-cultural communication, spoken discourse, and instructional technology. In addition to the workshop coordinator, five faculty members within IELI have had experience with the workshop. One of the workshop's strengths is that, in addition to teaching instructional modules, all faculty members work as critiquers in the practicum sessions. Each faculty member works with small groups that vary daily. Therefore, the variety of expertise of the faculty as a group is available to participants for the duration of the workshop. Each practicum group also has the assistance of a hired American classroom assistant (ACA), whose responsibilities include operating video equipment in practicum and final presentations, giving feedback and facilitating peer critique of taped lessons, and providing authentic undergraduate input on cultural issues and classroom behaviors.

An important component in the organization of the ITA program is the advisory committee that was established by the graduate school to provide the ITA workshop with formative feedback. Committee members include the dean of the graduate school, the IELI director, the ITA workshop coordinator, representatives from departments that regularly employ ITAs, currently teaching ITAs, and a group of undergraduate student body officers. The committee meets once a year in the spring. This group is given the final report of the workshop that includes evaluation results, comments from the current year's two workshops, and recommendations. The advisory committee recommends initiatives for the following year.

◈ DESCRIPTION

The ITA workshop is a pass/fail, doctoral-level (IELI 7920: College Teaching Seminar), credit-bearing workshop conducted twice yearly: once prior to the commencement of the fall semester, and again during the fall semester. The prefall workshop meets for 7 instructional days followed by a day of final presentations. The fall semester workshop meets twice weekly for 8 weeks. Each meeting day (or week, in the case of the in-semester workshop) consists of morning and afternoon sessions of instructional modules, followed by an afternoon session of the practicum module.

Throughout the course of the workshop specific characteristics of effective ITAs are presented and reinforced in the instructional modules and the practicum module (see Table 1).

The workshop is divided into two types of modules. Classroom instructional modules are characterized by faculty-fronted lessons, group discussions, and guest presentations. The practicum module is characterized by ITA presentations of undergraduate-level lessons and group critiques. Table 2 provides a sample workshop schedule.

TABLE 1. CHARACTERISTICS OF EFFECTIVE ITAs EMPHASIZED IN THE WORKSHOP

competence		understanding		questioning	
	organization		lecture sequences		reviews
friendliness		interaction		summaries	
	presenting terms		presenting concepts		
topic announcements		conclusions		comprehension checks	
	telling "why"		enumeration		
wait time		real-world examples		giving hints	
	topic restatements		framing the lesson		
preview-present-recap		self-disclosure		markers	
	movement		greetings		
definitions		problems		solidarity	

TABLE 2. SAMPLE WORKSHOP SCHEDULE

	Morning	Afternoon
Day 1	• Introduction (History and Rationale, Goals and Objectives) • Cross-Cultural Perspective of a U.S. Classroom	• Teaching Environments and Practices • Practicum
Day 2	• Classroom Management • Attending Training • Cross-Cultural Perspective of a U.S. Classroom	• Teaching Environments and Practices • Practicum
Day 3	• Classroom Management • Student Voices • Learning Styles/Myers-Briggs Type Indicator (Myers, 1977)	• Teaching Environments and Practices • Practicum
Day 4	• Office of Affirmative Action/Equal Opportunity • Classroom Management • Cross-Cultural Perspective of a U.S. Classroom	• Teaching Environments and Practices • Practicum
Day 5	• Learning Styles/Myers-Briggs Type Indicator (Myers, 1977) • Classroom Management	• Teaching Environments and Practices • Practicum
Day 6	• Classroom Management • Student Voices • Open Forum/Discussion with Experienced ITAs	• Teaching Environments and Practices • Practicum
Day 7	• Americans with Disabilities Act Presentation • Cross-Cultural Perspective of a U.S. Classroom	• Teaching Environments and Practices • Practicum Rehearsal of Final Presentation
Day 8	Final Presentation Taping	
Day 9	Awarding of Certificates and Closing of Workshop	

Each classroom instructional module provides between 1 and 7 hours of instruction. The instructional topics of each module are shown in Table 3.

The practicum module is designed to give the participants practice in implementing a *tool bag* approach to accomplish the classroom fundamentals. The tool bag approach is the self-selection and implementation of a number of techniques and methods from a larger set of possible techniques available to the participant. The fundamentals, as goals of the practicum session, are sequenced in the order of student-centered instruction, interaction, organization, and directed teaching, with

TABLE 3. INSTRUCTIONAL MODULES, HOURS, AND GOALS

Instructional Module Name	Hours	Topics
Introduction and Rationale	2	• History and rationale of the ITA Workshop • Outline of the goals and objectives of the workshop
Cross-Cultural Perspective of a U.S. Classroom	5	• How cultural values influence attitudes and practices in the classroom • Participant attitudes toward education as shaped by cultural influences • Why ITAs should study culture • Participant perspectives of the United States • Cultural expectations of teachers and students • Values discussions (doing, measurable achievement, pragmatism, individualism, equality, effort optimism, and competition)
Teaching Environments and Practices	7	• Proven teaching practices • Video reinforcement of teaching methods
Classroom Management	5	• Strategies and tools for management of the classroom environment in a manner acceptable to the U.S. student • Management tools, the syllabus, office hours, operating procedures, atmosphere, room arrangement, record keeping, the nature of the U.S./USU undergraduate student, student's preparation, student behavior and motivation, testing and grading, identifying and developing strategies for dealing with conflict, prejudice, idiomatic differences, and teacher evaluations
Classroom Language	2	• How language is used in the U.S. classroom • Coding of classroom discourse (Sinclair & Coulthard, 1975) • Language use to create a feeling of solidarity, bonding moves, having the student's perspective • Language use for instructional organization, wait time, restatement, topic announcement, markers, checks, risks and goals, intention of student questions, comprehension checks • Types of questions, where questions fit in the lesson, questions to develop meaning
Attending Training	1	• Provide training in making the speaker the focus of attention. • Listening attentively, showing communicative interest, nonverbal following (eye contact, head nodding, mirroring), and verbal following (questioning, topic repair, paraphrase and summarizing, identification)

Continued on p. 125

TABLE 3 (CONTINUED). INSTRUCTIONAL MODULES, HOURS, AND GOALS

Instructional Module Name	Hours	Topics
Learning Styles and Myers-Briggs Assessment (Myers, 1977)	3	• Differences in learning styles, instructional preferences, social interaction preferences, information processing preferences, and personality • Implications for the classroom are presented including the potential for assuming a classroom role different from one's dominant personality.
Office of Affirmative Action/ Equal Opportunity	1	• Legally defined discrimination and the procedure for filing complaints • Training in recognizing and avoiding issues of sexual harassment
Americans with Disabilities Act	1	• Legal protections and accommodations given to special needs students as identified by legal description

each fundamental a prerequisite to the next. Each practicum session begins with a brief description of the assignment for the following day. The assigned lessons consist of personal introduction, presentation of syllabus, presentation of terms or concepts, and presentation of problems or procedures.

Daily practicum presentations take place in small groups that meet in separate classrooms. Each group consists of 5–7 workshop participants, an ACA, and a faculty member. Each workshop participant presents a 10-minute teaching lesson to the group, which is videotaped. The participants and workshop staff engage in a critique after each participant has completed his or her lesson. The purpose of this critiquing segment is to give each participant feedback on the effectiveness of his or her classroom skills in a simulated teaching environment. The workshop goals and instructional concepts are emphasized in the daily critique. The practicum evaluators focus on the participants' ability to perform the specific, sequenced tasks as mentioned earlier.

◈ DISTINGUISHING FEATURES

The ITA program at USU is distinguished in its intensive workshop format and the modules that have been designed for ITA professional development. This section describes samples from the practicum module and an algorithmic approach to conflict management taken from the classroom management instructional module. It also describes the use of *authentic voice* and a personality measure, the Myers-Briggs Type Indicator (Myers, 1977), which is used as an introduction to learning styles.

Samples From the Practicum Module

The teaching practicum is the formative core of this ITA program. The foundation of the specific instructional template given to the students for the practicum module sessions is the analysis of the classroom discourse of effective teaching assistants. The participants in the workshop consistently rate this as the most valuable and essential feature of the workshop. In keeping with the authentic voice component of the workshop, participants select sample lessons from textbooks used in the courses they will teach.

The daily practicum is divided into three major sections: instruction, teaching presentation, and video review or critique. The day before each practicum session, participants receive instructions for preparing the following day's practicum. These instructions include a description of the required content, a review of important instructional elements discussed up to this point in the workshop, and advice for success. Figure 2 shows the assignment given for the fifth session of the practicum.

Application and subsequent evaluation of the use of specific techniques and methods introduced in the tool bag approach, as seen in Appendix A, give way to the more holistic instructional goals for the preparation of the final teaching presentation. This is evaluated for suitability to teach and for comprehensibility in a teaching role. Appendix B shows the assignment given for the last day of the practicum module.

Each participant prepares a 10-minute teaching lesson for each day of the practicum. Participants are divided into groups of 5–7 ITAs, one faculty member, and one ACA. Each participant's teaching is videotaped. During the course of the lesson other members of the participant's group serve as learners for the presenter. Participants are encouraged to be interested students, to show attending signals to the presenter, to interact with the presenter when offered, and to answer questions appropriately when asked.

Once each participant has finished, the videotapes are viewed and critiqued by the faculty member. Participants are encouraged to ask questions, to engage in dialogue with other members of the group, and to give and receive input on each day's presentation. Each group member, ACA, and faculty member acts as a reviewer.

Appendix C shows a sample of the peer evaluation questions used for the third practicum session. The peer evaluation questions change daily and follow the sequence of the instruction.

The greatest challenge of the practicum module lies in the fact that the teaching simulations can only approximate an authentic classroom environment and the kind of classroom reality within which the ITAs will find themselves. Classrooms of typical undergraduate students would clearly be preferred.

Algorithmic Approach to Conflict Management

This material is presented as 2 hours of the classroom management section of the instructional modules. This segment of the ITA workshop draws its teaching methodology from the algo-heurestic theory of learning (Landa, 1976, 1993; see also Kearsley, 2001; Meuller, 1997; Zhou, 2001). The content comes from two sources: Rivers (2002) and Internet student profiles of three area high schools as reported by USU.

The components of this course section are divided into background knowledge, instruction of the algorithm, and practice. Because this material comes relatively late in the workshop, it can build on the participants' knowledge of the material contained in the other instructional modules previously discussed.

First, the ITAs begin a discussion with the instructional goal of discussing and deciding on possible solutions to a problem. The examples for problems are drawn from real classroom scenarios that commonly present challenges for ITAs in the U.S.

classroom. These include, for example, students talking in class, students handing in homework late, miscommunication among students and instructors, or students failing to respond to a disorganized structure in the classroom.

The participants are asked to build a set of solutions to each problem. The interaction between the participants and the instructor opens a discourse whereby an explicit description of the algorithm is achieved. Next, the following distillation of "Five Steps to Conflict Management" are introduced (Rivers, 2002). Each step is defined and discussed, and examples are given:

> Step 1. Listen first and acknowledge what you hear, even if you don't agree with it, before expressing your experience or point of view (attending).

> Step 2. Slow down and give your listeners more information about what you are experiencing by using a wide range of "I-statements" such as "When I saw . . ." or "I felt . . ."

> Step 3. Translate your (and other people's) complaints and criticisms into specific requests, and explain your requests.

> Step 4. Ask more open-ended questions.

> Step 5. If you need to have a long, complex, important, or emotion-laden conversation with someone, briefly explain your conversational intention first and invite the consent of your intended conversation partner. (pp. 4–7)

Next, the following is an example of an explicit algorithm that was constructed in previous ITA workshop sessions:

> If a student comes to me with the problem, I must first attempt to understand the problem by listening. If the problem is something I have the authority to fix, I must ask consent to help. I must then give the student my point of view with "I-statements." If I cannot help, I must find help for the student elsewhere. If I can help the student I must give specific requests to the student and explain why I am asking the student to follow the requests. I must remind myself throughout to ask questions to promote discussion.

The following mnemonic device, which was derived through past workshop interaction, can help participants remember the algorithm, LACY HaRE:

> **L**isten (What is the problem?)

> **A**uthority (Do I have the power to help?)

> **C**onsent (Ask permission to help.)

> **Y**our Opinion (I-statements)

> **H**elp (Where can I go if I don't have the answers?)

> **R**equests (Tell the student what I want them to do.)

> **E**xplain (Justify why I think this will help.)

The practice component is twofold. The first component is video observation. The workshop participants view a videotape containing several sample role-playing scenes. Each scene features a participant from previous workshops engaged in a role-playing scenario with previous ACAs. The participants are asked to evaluate the performance of the ITA on the videotape using the tables shown in Appendix D.

The second component of practice is role-playing. The participants receive situation descriptions and then role-play either a student or an ITA. Appendix E shows examples of role-playing scenarios. After each role-play, the class as a whole discusses the action the ITA took, offering suggestions and commentary.

At the completion of the second practice session, the students gain a heightened awareness of possible conflicts as well as a method for resolving those conflicts in their role as teaching assistants.

Authentic Voice

The use of authentic voice is another distinguishing characteristic of the program that is present in most of the instructional materials. The presence of ACAs in the practicum sessions gives an authentic voice to workshop participants as they develop their style in the simulated classroom. The authentic voice is also heard in a panel presentation from former graduates of the workshop who have been working as teaching assistants for at least a year. This panel, included as an instructional module, gives the participants an opportunity to hear about the actual experiences of their senior colleagues and peers.

Further, the instructional modules of the workshop are designed to impart specific information to the participants following the goals of good classroom instruction. These instructional hours provide a model or template of the essential teaching style that the workshop promotes. This style is student centered and interactive, and it uses organizational frames with learning as the goal.

An Introduction to Learning Styles

Administering the Myers-Briggs Type Indicator (Myers, 1977) to all the participants in the workshop, and the personal knowledge gained from this assessment, has also proven to be another distinguishing and unifying part of the workshop. All workshop staff members are encouraged to participate. As an introduction to learning style differences, participants learn about the variations among members of a group and gain insight into each other's personality characteristics. This activity also enhances the individualized and differentiated instruction in the practicum sessions.

❖ PRACTICAL IDEAS

Consider Institutional Challenges When Developing the Program

The comprehensibility of ITAs is a politically volatile issue. There is a constant tension between two needs: departments want ITAs to teach classes because of the intellectual resource that they bring, and undergraduates want NES teaching assistants. The international graduate students recruited by the departments have excellent intellectual qualifications and highly developed research skills. The composition of the undergraduate student body at USU is more homogeneous than at many other Research I institutions around the country and, as a result, students often lack cross-cultural understanding and awareness. In this context, both constituencies exert pressure on the workshop.

Consider Organizational Structure Within the University

At USU, the workshop is housed in the IELI, which is situated in the College of Humanities, Art, and Social Sciences. However, the School of Graduate Studies is the workshop's main client. Therefore the existing administrative structure creates an environment where neither of these organizations feels a proprietary interest in the program's development. Seeking additional funding from either of these most obvious sources is seen by both as a request from outside. Furthermore, the departments that most extensively use the workshop are housed in other colleges. The optimum organizational structure for the program within the university has not yet been identified.

Gather Input for Decision Making

Curricular decisions within the program have been made based on input gathered from four sources. First, each workshop is evaluated by all the participants, by both qualitative and quantitative measures. Second, departments are periodically surveyed to determine their current uses of ITAs and their preparation needs. Third, the graduate school's advisory committee gives university-wide input to the program. Finally, the collective knowledge of the participating faculty members contributes to curricular decisions by means of regular debriefings following the workshops and the input of a focus group. Given ITAs' high visibility in the educational process, it is important to get regular feedback from the people the workshop serves: the departments, the graduate school, and the undergraduate student population. Keeping all constituencies satisfied is a balancing act.

Match Instruction to Participant Population

The most significant change in the participants' backgrounds throughout the history of the workshop has been in the area of teaching experience. The workshop was originally designed to meet the needs of international students who come to the United States with teaching experience and who require a sociocultural adaptation to the distinctive environment of U.S. classrooms. Issues of student-centered education and interactive environments were key instructional goals. Recent participants in the workshop, however, are recruited immediately from undergraduate school and have no teaching experience. This change has necessitated more emphasis on the fundamentals of instruction, such as organization of content and classroom management.

Provide Follow-Up Support

Preparing international graduate students to be effective teachers in U.S. undergraduate classrooms is a long-term process. The workshop provides ITAs with only rudimentary preparation. It is in their first classroom teaching assignments that the lessons of the workshop become meaningful. Once the semester begins and the pressures of a teaching assistant's position are added to the pressures of full-time graduate school, ITAs feel severe time pressures. Follow-up support from the workshop and reinforcement of reflective teaching practices during this first semester is essential, but it must be sensitive to the ITAs' time constraints and academic pressure.

◈ CONCLUSION

USU has demonstrated a commitment to the excellence of its undergraduate education and views this as a key point in recruitment and the image it markets. It has also demonstrated a belief in the value of international education and the presence of international students on the campus. During the past 20 years, the preparation program for ITAs has been a part of both of these goals. International graduate students have been recruited by departments and have been promised departmental support in the form of teaching assistantship. These ITAs have had an effect on undergraduate education across the campus. In fact, a former president of the university was quoted as saying, "In order to be prepared for the globalized future, having an ITA should be a part of every student's undergraduate education." The overall goal of the ITA professional development program at USU is to make that experience with an ITA a most positive one for the undergraduates at the university.

◈ CONTRIBUTORS

Thomas J. Schroeder is an associate professor at Utah State University. He is the coordinator of teacher training for ITAs and has been on staff since the workshop's inception in 1985. His interests include culture and its influence on behavior, cross-cultural education and communication, personality psychology and the education process, and reflective teaching.

Dennis M. Kohler was an adjunct faculty member at Utah State University. He was on the staff of the ITA workshop from 1989 to 2003. He has worked as a professor of English at universities in Korea and Kuwait. His interests include the application of technology to second language teaching and learning, and teaching methods.

APPENDIX A. SAMPLE PRACTICUM MODULE ASSIGNMENT

At this point in the practicum you should have some well established techniques for maintaining solidarity with the class. An interactive presentation style should also be developing. Problem solving presentations lend themselves well to an interactive format. Problem solving also requires careful attention to organizational preparation, particularly to "one-step-at-a-time" development.

OBJECTIVE

Present a Procedure and/or Solve a Problem from your field. Show the students **how to do** something. The three most common methods for doing this are:

1. Present the procedure in general form. Work through an example.

2. Present one step of the general form and work that step of an example and continue for each step.

3. Present and solve an example problem. Using the solution, present each step of the general form.

The 10-minute lesson should be addressed to an undergraduate audience.

POINTS OF EMPHASIS

In your lesson remember the following:

Opening Part of Lesson

1. Greeting for solidarity and interaction

2. Review the previous content

3. Frame the lesson's content

Middle of the Lesson

4. Tell students how to succeed—what they should remember (will be on the test)

5. Use questioning and elicits to involve the students

6. Explain why this material is important to the subject

7. Use Examples

8. Use "one-step-at-a-time" organization

9. Use topic announcements and restatement

10. Use questioning to develop the lesson

End of the Lesson

11. Tell the student what they should have learned today

Throughout the Lesson

12. Use wait time and markers

13. Be student centered

14. Attend to the audience

15. Handle student questions well

16. Recognize—Repeat—Answer—Confirm—Move On

17. Use good board technique

18. Use the board in an organized manner

19. Teach, have clear, nontrivial, instructional goals

◈ APPENDIX B. FINAL PRACTICUM MODULE ASSIGNMENT

Objective

Rehearse the presentation you will give as your final presentation for evaluation. This presentation may be one that you have given previously. It may be either a term/concept or a problem/procedure. As you prepare this presentation do not be concerned with covering a certain amount of material. The final tape is a sample of a lesson (a representative piece of a whole). It will not be evaluated with a checklist identifying all the elements we have discussed in the workshop. It will be evaluated on the basis of how well the following workshop goals are demonstrated in the 10-minute segment.

Points of Evaluation

In your lesson today be certain to accomplish the following:

- ▶ **Be Comprehensible**
  - Slow down
  - Talk out
  - Announce
  - Restate
  - Wait

- ▶ **Teach, Don't Lecture**
  - Have the students' learning as the perspective

- ▶ **Be Interactive**
  - Check comprehension
  - Involve the students in the lesson

- ▶ **Use Directed Teaching Behaviors**
  - Organization
  - Clarity
  - One-step-at-a-time in correct sequence
  - Good board use

Be your own person. Be comfortable and confident. You can do it! Have Fun!

◈ APPENDIX C. SAMPLE PEER EVALUATION FORM

In order to help your classmate know where he or she needs to improve, please give the best feedback you can.

(1) Could you understand the presenter?

100%————————75%————————50%————————25%————————0%

Loud enough? _____ Clear enough? _____

(2) Pace of delivery

5————4————3————2————1

   too fast   just right   too slow

(3) Who was the presenter talking to?

The camera?   One person?   Everyone?   The wall?

(4) How confident was the person?

5————4————3————2————1

calm, in control   scared, nervous

(5) Was the person's pronunciation understandable?

100%————————75%————————50%————————25%————————0%

(6) Did you notice a specific problem?

(7) Did the presenter use questions to check your understanding?

5————4————3————2————1

Well designed   Not Consistent   No questions

(8) How did the presenter show that he/she was attending to you as the student?

(9) How interesting was the presenter?

5————4————3————2————1

enthusiastic   stayed awake   low energy

(10) How did the presenter establish solidarity with you, the student?

APPENDIX D. SAMPLE TABLES FOR STUDENT EVALUATION OF VIDEO SCENES

Rate the ITA's performance in the following categories (1 lowest, 5 highest):

	1	2	3	4	5
Identification of the problem					
Restatement of the problem to show understanding					
Explanation of ITA perspective (needs)					
Controlling without offending					
Maintains acceptable authority					

Check the box if each of the following steps was accomplished.

	Step 1. Listen
	Step 2. I-statements
	Step 3. Specific requests explained
	Step 4. Open-ended questions
	Step 5. Conversational intention explained\consent asked

APPENDIX E. SAMPLE ROLE-PLAY SCENARIOS

ITA Role	Student Role
You notice that one of your students is constantly sleeping in class, you can tell that the student would get higher grades if he/she would pay more attention in class, you have called the student into your office to discuss the issue.	Your TA has called you into his/her office and you have a feeling it is about your behavior in class. You know you have fallen asleep a few times but you have a new baby that is keeping you awake at night.
You have just read the final exam from two students in the class. After reading the papers, you notice that the students' answers are so close that you suspect them of cheating. You did not catch them cheating in class but you decide to confront them about it anyway.	(2 students) You and a roommate have been taking the same class, and you spend a lot of time studying together, including sharing notes. You have been called into your TA's office for some reason.
You have one student in your class who always asks questions in class that are above the level of the other students. You like the fact that the student is interested in your field, but you feel that the digressions are taking time away from the simple explanations other students need.	You are a senior ready to graduate from your program. Your advisor has informed you that you need to take one general education class to graduate. You have taken many other classes in this department and are bored with the content of the class.

PART 3

Collaborative Practices and Partnerships across Disciplines

CHAPTER 10

Orientation for International Teaching Assistants: Integrating Drama for Communication

Dean Papajohn

❖ INTRODUCTION

> When I was first preparing to teach as an ITA [international teaching assistant] at the University of Illinois at Urbana-Champaign, one of the most important sources of support, encouragement, and information for me during those agitating moments was the Orientation for ITAs. The experience will long stay with me in terms of personal nourishment, source of confidence, and understanding of the manifold dimensions associated with the teaching process in the United States. (graduate student in library and information science)

Globalization has brought increasing numbers of international graduate students to U.S. universities to advance their own studies and to teach U.S. undergraduate students. The ITA orientation at the University of Illinois at Urbana-Champaign (UIUC) is designed to help ITAs develop as teachers as part of their graduate education as well as to enhance undergraduate education. ITAs may encounter specific cultural and linguistic challenges that can be compounded by their unfamiliarity with the language of their students and the language needed to teach effectively. The ITAs of today are tomorrow's scholars and faculty, and their views of teaching in higher education can be powerfully affected by their preparation.

❖ CONTEXT

Institutional Information

UIUC was chartered as a land-grant institution in 1867 and is the largest public university in Illinois. UIUC is located 140 miles south of Chicago in the twin cities of Urbana and Champaign. The campus encompasses 1,470 acres and more than 200 major buildings. The library system is the third largest academic library in the United States. The 38,000 students on campus (74% undergraduate) have access to approximately 850 clubs, coalitions, societies, and teams. There are approximately 1,400 ITAs at UIUC each year.

ITA Program Mandate

In the mid-1980s complaints from undergraduate students about the language skills of ITAs came to the attention of legislators. Illinois was one of 17 states instituting state-wide mandates for oral English assessment of ITAs (Monoson & Thomas, 1993). In 1987 the Illinois legislature passed Illinois Compiled Statute 110ILCS 305/ 7C (Illinois General Assembly), which states

> The Board of Trustees of the University of Illinois shall establish a program to assess the oral English language proficiency of all persons providing classroom instruction to students at each campus under the jurisdiction, governance or supervision of the Board, and shall ensure that each person who is not orally proficient in the English language shall attain such proficiency prior to providing any classroom instruction to students.

In response, the UIUC vice chancellor for academic affairs issued a policy statement regarding the appointment of nonnative-English-speaking (NNES) graduate students as teaching assistants. UIUC defines a nonnative English speaker as someone whose first language is other than English regardless of which country they originate from or reside in. Those with dialects other than U.S. or British English are also included, such as English speakers from Africa and India.

ITA Orientation

International graduate students who pass an oral English test called the Speaking Proficiency English Assessment Kit (SPEAK) and who are awarded an assistantship are required to attend the ITA orientation. The Center for Teaching Excellence (CTE) coordinates the ITA orientation, which is held each August and January during the week before classes begin (Papajohn, Alsberg, Bair, & Willenborg, 2002). The first 2 days are specifically designed for ITAs and address the relevant language and cultural skills needed for teaching in U.S. university classrooms. During the following 2 days, native-English-speaking (NES) teaching assistants and ITAs come together to focus on teaching skills and university policy related to teaching, such as capricious grading and academic integrity. On the final day, the teaching assistants present an 8-minute lesson that is videotaped and later analyzed one on one with an instructional development consultant from CTE or their department. In 2004, for example, approximately 200 new ITAs from more than 50 departments attended the August orientation and 50–60 attended in January. Although ITAs come from all over the world, approximately 25% of those at UIUC come from China, 15% from South Asia, and 10% from Korea.

◈ DESCRIPTION

ITAs may serve as lab assistants, discussion section leaders, lecturers, or graders with office hours. The ITA program at UIUC (University of Illinois, 2005) consists of four main parts: assessment, courses, monitoring, and orientation (Papajohn, 2002).

Assessment

Assessment of ITAs is directed by CTE, which utilizes the SPEAK test. The SPEAK is a semidirect test of general English speaking ability (ETS, 1996). In 2003–2004, the

SPEAK test was used to assess nearly 700 potential ITAs at UIUC. A score of 50, indicating "communication generally effective, task performed competently," was chosen as the minimum score for a teaching assistantship at UIUC (Papajohn, 1998, 2002). Students with borderline scores, with the support of their department, can opt to take the SPEAK Appeals test, which is a performance test that assesses the examinee's language in a teaching context. Approximately 45 SPEAK Appeals tests occur each year.

Courses for ITAs

ESL courses for ITAs are offered by the Division of English as an International Language. These courses provide an opportunity for those international graduate students who do not pass the SPEAK test to improve their language and communication skills. Two types of classes are offered: "ESL 504: English Pronunciation for ITAs" and "ESL 506: Communication Skills for ITAs."

Monitoring ITA Performance

ITAs at UIUC are monitored by their departments as they begin teaching on campus. Monitoring consists of observing the new ITAs while they teach and having the new ITAs collect feedback from students early in the semester. If a department needs assistance with an ITA, CTE can be contacted for additional support.

ITA Orientation Sessions

The 2-day ITA orientation is divided between large- and small-group sessions (see Table 1). The ITA orientation begins with a large-group session called "Drama Techniques for Communication in the U.S. University Classroom." In order to provide a sample of the orientation content, a detailed description of this particular session is given in the next section. After this first large-group session, ITAs rotate through small-group sessions. In "Academic Role-Plays," ITAs act out various classroom situations in pairs or watch short video clips of teacher-student interactions. They discuss cultural differences in body language, voice tone, and word choice. "Voice Skills for Communication" deals with word stress, phrase stress, pausing, and intonation. "Classroom Communication Strategies" focuses on the language appropriate for various classroom tasks (greeting or getting class started, ending class, explaining the grading system, clarifying student comments and checking understanding, inviting feedback or discussion, and collecting or assigning

TABLE 1. ITA ORIENTATION SESSIONS

Large-Group Sessions	Small-Group Sessions
• Drama Techniques for Communication in the U.S. University Classroom	• Academic Role-Plays
	• Voice Skills for Communication
• Coherence in Teaching	• Classroom Communication Strategies
• International Teaching Experience	• Cross-Cultural Classroom Issues
• Undergraduate Panel	• ITA Share Session
	• Practice Teaching

homework) as well as some undergraduate slang (*to ace, to bomb, to book, to cram, to blow off, to be psyched, to dis, brain cramp, Greek, rush, to nail someone*). "Cross-Cultural Classroom Issues" discusses aspects of culture and a process of cultural adjustment. In "ITA Share Session," seasoned ITAs share their experiences, field questions, and discuss strategies for dealing with a variety of classroom issues. One ITA mentor shared the following about his experience helping to facilitate at the ITA orientation:

> Helping ITAs understand multiple nuances associated with complex class-room situations that I had faced during my teaching experience provided other ITAs pointers toward dealing with anticipated scenarios and problematic situations. My role as an ITA Mentor was to give an opportunity to new incoming ITAs for asking questions, removing doubts, and voicing concerns about various issues perceived significant by them. (graduate student in library and information science)

Interspersed between the small-group sessions are additional large-group sessions. "Coherence in Teaching" provides suggestions on how to effectively use words, phrases, intonation, and gestures to add coherence when communicating. "International Teaching Experience" is led by an international professor who has been recognized at UIUC for effective teaching. The international professor shares cross-cultural or language challenges he or she has faced. The "Undergraduate Panel" fields questions from the new ITAs on topics such as fraternities and sororities, part-time jobs, extracurricular activities, and changing majors. In "Practice Teaching," ITAs teach a simple topic from their field and receive feedback.

ITA Orientation: Drama Techniques for Communication in the U.S. University Classroom

Drama has been considered an effective tool for ESL and ITA professional development for some time (Di Pietro, 1987; Hines, 1973; Maley & Duff, 1982; Smith, 1984; Stern, 1983; Stevens, 1989; Via, 1976). Stevens (1989) enthusiastically advocated the importance of drama for instructors:

> To consider each classroom appearance nothing less than a performance with a powerful message, a performance requiring scripting (notes and outlines) and even rehearsal—a performance tailored to the needs and learning styles of students—is to do more than draw a charming analogy. Rather, it is to design a teaching assistant training program that elevates teaching to a place of prominence within the graduate program and to communicate to the teaching assistant that teaching is an art and profession requiring painstaking work and practice. (p. 185)

The "Drama Techniques" session at the UIUC ITA orientation was designed in conjunction with faculty from the theater department. Teaching/performing analogies were developed around the themes of *scripting, rehearsal, warm-ups, staging, program, performance,* and *curtain call.* Scripting highlights the importance of lesson plans. Scripts have plots that flow and dialogues for interaction; lesson plans should have cohesive content and thoughtful questions. Teachers should be familiar enough with their lesson plan that they do not need to stare at it. A certain amount of rehearsal is important to effectively implement a lesson plan. Scripting and rehearsal prompt actors to consider how best to communicate through visual as well as auditory means; teachers should do the same. In addition to meaningful gestures and facial expressions, teachers can use diagrams, charts, and graphs to convey their ideas.

Prior to teaching, warm-ups can get the teacher's body and voice prepared for effective delivery. Because enthusiasm is an important quality for effective teaching, a tired body and voice will not communicate well. To demonstrate this point, the faculty member from the theater department facilitating the session leads the new ITAs through a number of body warm-ups, including neck stretches, arm stretches, body bends, toe touches, and jogging in place. There is also the hand and foot shake. First the right hand is shaken 10 times, followed by the left hand, right foot, and left foot. Then the right hand is shaken 9 times, cycling through hands and feet to the count of one. After this exercise, hearts are pumping and eyes are alert. These body warm-ups are followed by voice warm-ups. First everyone takes deep breaths of air. Next sound is added by slowly counting first to 10, then to 15, and finally to 20. ITAs are asked to project their voices so as to be heard across the room as they exhale and count. The vocal mechanism is warmed-up with various exercises: by stretching the mouth wide open, rounding the lips, moving the jaw by pretending to chew, and extending the tongue in all directions. Tongue twisters are introduced to work on clear articulation. The words of one tongue twister reminds the ITAs about the crucial articulators in their mouths—"the tip of the tongue, the roof of the mouth, the lips, and the teeth." Tongue twisters may be simple phrases, for example, "red leather, yellow leather." This is said slowly at first and then repeated with increased speed over and over again. Whereas this tongue twister focuses on distinctions in consonants, the next tongue twister focuses on distinctions in vowels: "unique New York." This is also said slowly at first and sped up with each repetition. There is a relaxed atmosphere even with more than 200 ITAs practicing these body and voice warm-ups. To successfully lead these types of activities, the session facilitator must establish trust with the participants.

New as well as experienced instructors often fail to consider issues of staging before teaching. Instructors should not limit their performing space to the area behind a lectern or to a narrow aisle in front of the chalkboard. The teacher can enter the audience space to help break down communication boundaries, add variety, and increase student alertness. Because audiences tend to view a stage or the front of a classroom from left to right, the strongest entrance to a class is from the left. The right portion of a stage or classroom is considered the weakest area in which to stand; front and center is the strongest. The amount of movement ITAs can make will depend in part on the classroom furniture and layout. When classroom furniture is movable, instructors should consider alternative arrangements. Even though instructors generally have limited control over lighting, ceiling lights and natural light from windows should be taken advantage of. Inadequate lighting tends to put people to sleep and overly bright light may drown out visuals from an overhead or computer projector.

Clothing is also part of staging. If ITAs intend to utilize their classroom space and move around to interact with students, comfortable clothing is important. However, comfort should not go to the extreme of being distracting to student learning. It is helpful to look around to get an idea of the standards of dress in a particular department; in this way the level of formality can be discerned. ITAs do not have to abandon their cultural norms of dress; some ITAs have found that wearing personal items from their country, like hats, scarves, or jewelry, can help them share some of their own personality and culture (Stanley & Wiley, 1998, p. 31).

At a live theater it is common for ushers to hand each patron a program guide. Although instructors do not generally print a detailed program for each class session, sharing lesson objectives can be extremely useful. The chalkboard is ideal for this purpose. The instructor can write objectives or the day's schedule on the board before the class starts. Whether or not students are on time to hear an instructor's opening comments, the information is there for all the students to see. If a student loses concentration for a few moments, the schedule or objectives are there for reference. If all items on the schedule are not covered, the instructor can give the class directions on whether students will be responsible for covering material on their own or if it will be covered in the next class period.

Two facets of performance are empathy and intermission. Empathy is the bond or connection a teacher establishes with his or her class. Empathy can be affected by the physical distance between the instructor and students. Instructors transmit empathy to their students in their tone of voice, their passion for the content and teaching of their subject, and their commitment to help their students. As a visual and physical reminder of empathy, the ITAs are asked to open their hands and rub them together. As they rub with a small circular motion they are asked to slowly separate their hands. They are instructed to concentrate on the sense or feeling the hands have for each other even as they are separated. The hands continue to separate until the spread is too wide for the hands to sense the presence of the other any more. When instructors can read whether their students follow an explanation or not, empathy is present. If the gap between the instructor and student gets too wide, then empathy is broken.

Even the most talented performers utilize intermissions. For classes more than 60 minutes, intermissions can take the form of a restroom or snack break; a change in student activity, such as from note-taking to pair work; or a commercial break for a student to announce an upcoming event on campus. Intermissions allow students to change positions, give their minds a break, and reenter the class with renewed alertness.

Every live theater performance ends with a curtain call and no class should end without closure. Bowing and applause are unlikely at the close of a class, yet instructors can ask for questions, remind students of assignments or upcoming events, recap the highlights from the lesson, or preview the next class period. Many instructors find it useful to have a standard phrase to end class, which could be informal or simple, such as "that's it for today" or "see you next time." A closing comment helps the instructor communicate to the students that the end of class has come.

Through the drama seminar, ITAs gain a fresh perspective on teaching that motivates them to want to learn more about teaching and learning. When asked what they liked best about the ITA orientation, many ITAs unequivocally mentioned the drama session. The following is a sample of their comments:

- This session develops your overall teaching personality which is an important part of teaching.
- It was useful to remind us of important nonverbal issues involved in teaching, such as enthusiasm and space occupation.

- Showed me the way what teaching should be.
- It gave tools to use in class.
- Demonstrated benefits of a lively classroom technique.
- Got me interested in the ITA assignment; it proliferated my enthusiasm for ITA.
- The professor makes me feel some valuable aspects of performance.
- It shows how to approach the class from a different perspective.
- Very useful, it can let us know how to perform in the classroom.
- Helped understand how teaching and performance is so similar.
- Learned that teaching is also one kind of performance.
- Specific techniques, active performance, useful tactics.
- Very good for me to think about getting class lively.
- Hopefully will make me a more interesting speaker.

◈ DISTINGUISHING FEATURES

The presemester ITA orientation helps new ITAs bridge the gap from student mode to instructor mode. Distinguishing features of the UIUC ITA orientation include integrated preparation, a holistic approach, active learning, and positioning ITA professional development within a comprehensive framework.

Integrated Preparation

Key features of integrated preparation include

- keeping the focus of the ITA orientation on the language and culture of the U.S. university classroom because pedagogy and policy are covered in the teaching assistant orientation designed for NES teaching assistants and ITAs

- expanding similar topics in different sessions without overlapping content

The ITA orientation has become an intentionally integrated program. Each session is connected and flows into succeeding sessions. For example, "Academic Role-Plays" follows "Drama Techniques" to provide an opportunity for ITAs to practice concepts of space and gestures while working through realistic teacher-student encounters. "Drama Techniques," "Voice Skills," and "Coherence in Teaching" all touch on the topic of voice but take it in different directions. "Drama Techniques" provides an opportunity for instruction in voice warm-ups. "Voice Skills" introduces features of intonation. "Coherence in Teaching" highlights how intonation can be used to enhance or distract from coherency. Likewise, a number of sessions touch on different aspects of cross-cultural issues. "Cross-Cultural Classroom Issues" discusses the fundamental principles of culture. The cross-cultural challenges of an individual faculty member are presented in "International Teaching Experience." ITAs can pose their cross-cultural questions to experienced ITA mentors in the "ITA Share Session" and to U.S. undergraduate students in the "Undergraduate Panel." Finally, "Practice

Teaching" allows the ITAs to apply the knowledge of culture and language in a mock teaching scenario.

Holistic Approach

Key features of a holistic approach include

- content knowledge for the mind
- use of body and voice for communication
- feedback and encouragement to motivate the spirit

The ITA orientation seeks to appeal to the mind, body, and spirit of new ITAs. The needs of the mind are addressed in content that covers cultural differences, student slang, methods of coherency, and audience awareness. The needs of the body are appealed to through voice and body warm-up activities, communication through body language, and voice skills, such as pausing, stress, and intonation. The spirit is appealed to by providing a welcoming environment to learn, encouragement through successful international faculty and teaching assistants sharing their stories, and a positive atmosphere that affirms the value of teaching.

Active Learning

Key features of active learning include

- modeling effective teaching strategies in large- and small-group settings
- engaging ITAs in active learning to help them derive the maximum possible benefit from the ITA orientation

Each facilitator at the ITA orientation seeks to model effective active learning techniques. "Practice Teaching," in which ITAs present minilessons, is the most obvious example of active learning, but the other sessions incorporate active learning as well. "Drama Techniques" involves ITAs in warm-up activities. "Academic Role-Plays" involves the ITAs in hypothetical teacher-student interactions. "Coherence in Teaching" asks participants to prioritize needs, identify cohesive devices, discuss answers with a partner, discuss as a group, and respond to a self-analysis survey. We believe that these active learning methods allow the ITAs to learn faster and deeper.

Positioning ITA Professional Development Within a Comprehensive Framework

Key features of positioning ITA professional development within a comprehensive framework include

- in-classroom observation or videotape of teaching
- one-on-one consultation with an instructional developer
- instructional workshops during the semester
- help with analyzing student feedback on teaching
- certificate programs for teaching assistants

UIUC takes a comprehensive approach to orienting new ITAs. The presemester orientation provides ITAs with basic language, culture, and teaching skills they can utilize immediately in their classes. However, new ITAs are not left on their own. The ITA program offers follow-up services. Some ITAs need continued support to develop as good instructors; other ITAs are motivated to go beyond what is expected of them and want to develop into excellent instructors.

ITAs have the opportunity to be videotaped or observed in class while teaching. The videotape is reviewed with a teaching consultant from CTE or with a faculty member from the ITA's department. Instructional workshops on such topics as gathering student feedback and test construction are offered during each semester. An ITA can receive help from CTE or from his or her department in interpreting student feedback and developing a plan to debrief with his or her students. CTE also offers the Graduate Teacher Certificate (GTC) and the Advanced Graduate Teacher Certificate (AGTC) programs to NES teaching assistants as well as ITAs who are interested in documenting teaching development and excellence in teaching effectiveness. The GTC documents teaching development activities like the orientations, instructional workshops, and reflective essays on student feedback and videotaped teaching. The AGTC documents excellence in teaching through the creation of a teaching portfolio and experience in various teaching competencies, including classroom teaching experience, continuing education, teaching other teaching assistants, mentoring, community engagement, the scholarship of teaching and learning, and instructional technology.

All ITAs at UIUC are required to have a minimal amount of instructional preparation, and all ITAs have access to further opportunities to develop as teachers. Although these services are not considered part of the orientation, the orientation is positioned as a foundational element from which ITAs can take advantage of additional instructional development opportunities.

◈ PRACTICAL IDEAS

The concept of partnerships provides a framework for considering practical ideas for ITA programs. Potential partnerships include administration, departments, experienced ITAs, undergraduate students, and publishers and other institutions.

Foster Partnerships With University Administration

Practical ideas for administrative partnerships include

- financial support for staff and resources
- thoughtful policy formation and consistent policy implementation that garners respect from the campus

Partnerships with upper-level administration are vital for the ongoing success of ITA programs. Successful ITA programs depend on skilled personnel and steady financial resources for smooth-running, comprehensive programming. Coordinators, facilitators, and support staff are all needed for an ITA orientation. Providing housing for ITAs who lack accommodations helps keep newly arrived ITAs focused on the professional development. Providing meals at the orientation so ITAs do not have to worry about finding a place to eat lunch helps to schedule the orientation efficiently and allows ITAs to develop relationships with each other.

Administrative partnerships are indispensable in garnering the respect of the ITAs and the academic departments that appoint them. If the campus administration is lax in its support of ITA programming, departments will take this as an opportunity to bypass oral English and orientation requirements. On the other hand, if the campus administration is visible and strong in its support of the ITA program, departments are more likely to participate. With all the competing interests an ITA faces at the beginning of the semester, including looking for housing, registering for classes, attending departmental meetings, and conducting research, the orientation can only reach new ITAs if the administration requires them to attend. One strength of the UIUC ITA Program is the support it receives from the Office of the Vice Chancellor for Academic Affairs.

Develop Partnerships With Departments

Practical ideas for departmental partnerships include

- scheduling departmental meetings so they do not conflict with ITA professional development
- inviting faculty and students from departments to help facilitate professional development sessions
- encouraging faculty to help ITAs develop their teaching skills

Partnerships with academic departments are necessary for a couple of reasons. First, it takes partnership to accomplish the basics of scheduling oral English tests and orientations that do not conflict with other departmental meetings and professional development. Second, and more significantly, partnerships with departments can be a way to get the culture and the discourse of the departments more fully integrated into ITA professional development. Partnerships with departments can take numerous forms. Faculty and students from departments can be invited to facilitate at ITA orientation sessions. To illustrate such a partnership, this chapter explains in detail how a faculty member from the theater department shares about teaching from his departmental perspective. An international faculty member and graduate students who serve as ITA mentors bring their departmental viewpoints to the "International Teaching Experience," "Academic Role-Plays," and "ITA Share Sessions." Undergraduate students from different departments also share their perceptions during the "Undergraduate Panel."

Faculty can show support by encouraging international graduate students to work on improving their oral English and teaching skills. Faculty from departments could also participate in oral English performance tests, as is done at the UIUC SPEAK Appeals test. Faculty can also support ITAs by mentoring them as instructors, which could include meeting to talk about teaching on a weekly basis or observing the ITA's teaching and providing feedback through discussion. This type of mentoring is part of the AGTC program offered to NES teaching assistants and ITAs. Departments could also support ITA professional development by encouraging and supporting experienced NES teaching assistants and ITAs to help prepare new ITAs, which is the focus of the next subsection.

Engage Experienced ITAs as Mentors

Practical ideas for partnerships with experienced ITAs include

- showing respect for the contribution of ITAs by inviting experienced ITAs to facilitate

- authenticating professional development with experienced ITA facilitators because they have faced the types of challenges that the new ITAs will soon face

- providing a safe context for new ITAs to share teaching concerns without fear of exposing their weaknesses to their departments

Experienced ITAs serve as mentors at the UIUC ITA orientation. The following are some of their reflections on their experiences as mentors:

> I imagine ITA candidates must have felt more comfortable talking with ITA mentors as I had been. An ITA from Turkey asked about the grading system at UIUC. She said that only a few students in a given class in Turkey get A's. As if that were a universal rule, she thought that she would have to give perhaps only one or two students A's in her class at UIUC. The ITA mentors informed her that was certainly not the case. (graduate student in communications research)

> Many ITAs are concerned about their English. With my Japanese accent, I share my experiences of difficult or problematic situations, hoping my accent and experiences give the ITAs some confidence and sense of being prepared in various situations. (graduate student in educational psychology)

The ITA mentors know what it is like to teach in a second language and culture on the UIUC campus. They can share stories and answer questions based on their experiences with undergraduate students. ITA mentors serve as a nonthreatening source to which new ITAs can pose questions because they are not so closely associated with the university administration. In addition to sharing experiences and answering questions, ITA mentors can provide feedback on lesson plans, teaching skills, and simulated role-plays. UIUC has effectively used ITA mentors during orientation week, but ITA mentors could also be appointed to work alongside new ITAs for a full semester.

Include Undergraduate Students in the ITA Professional Development Program

Practical ideas for partnerships with undergraduate students include

- convening a panel of undergraduate students who share about their lives as U.S. college students

- providing feedback to new ITAs on brief practice teaching sessions

Most ITAs are eager to know more about U.S. undergraduate students. Images from television and movies often mislead ITAs; therefore, opportunities for new ITAs to interact with undergraduate students are extremely useful. Undergraduate students serve on a panel at the UIUC orientation. This provides an excellent forum for undergraduates to explain how they think about school and spend their time, as well as respond to questions from the ITAs. Undergraduate students also provide feedback on oral English ability as part of the UIUC SPEAK Appeals panel.

Conduct Research, Publish, and Network
With Colleagues Through Professional Associations

Practical ideas for partnerships with publishers and other institutions include

- researching and publishing studies on the assessment and professional development of ITAs

- connecting with colleagues from other institutions through professional associations

While ITAs benefit from campus-specific professional development, ITA developers can benefit from sharing information and ideas with other institutions, through publications, conferences, and one-on-one interactions. The number of ITAs is not as large as other audiences ESL publishers often target, but ITAs are a permanent part of many U.S. university campuses, with a steady turnover. The advanced level of English that most ITAs possess is not well suited to general ESL texts. Materials that take into account ITA-specific contexts are preferable. UIUC faculty have published materials targeting pronunciation (Hahn & Dickerson, 1999a, 1999b) and communication strategies and fluency (Papajohn, 2005). Research articles on ITA issues have found homes in a number of journals (Briggs, 1997), and the ITA Interest Section of TESOL has an active membership in which ITA developers can find congenial colleagues.

❖ CONCLUSION

In the future, ITA orientation and professional development will remain critical for UIUC and other campuses as globalization continues and increasing attention is directed toward both the quality of undergraduate education and preparing future faculty. ITA programs need to fit the academic and political contexts in which they are situated in order to meet the needs of ITAs, academic units, and the education of undergraduate students. The UIUC ITA program offers comprehensive services beginning with assessment and ESL courses and extending to orientations and ongoing professional development. A presemester ITA orientation provides instructional development in a timely fashion to a large number of ITAs. One future challenge is to find locally a sufficient number of facilitators qualified to address the language and culture needs of ITAs at an orientation where enrollment continues to grow. Materials for ESL professionals in the area of ITA professional development could be designed. The characteristics that help make the UIUC ITA orientation successful include integrated preparation, a holistic approach, active learning, and positioning ITA professional development within a comprehensive framework. At the orientation ITAs discover that they can learn from faculty outside their department, such as those from the theater department. An opportunity exists to identify methods from other departments that can be integrated into the orientation to create an ever-increasing interdisciplinary, professional development experience. Strategic partnerships with administration, departments, experienced ITAs, undergraduate students, and publishers and other institutions provide opportunities for the campus to influence the ITA program and for the ITA program to influence the campus.

◈ ACKNOWLEDGMENTS

I would like to thank a number of people for their contributions to this chapter: Bharat Mehra, Jin Park, and Yukari Takahashi for their insights into the perspectives of ITAs and ITA mentors; Nancy Hovasse and James Zager for their dynamic facilitation of the "Drama Techniques" session; and my colleagues at UIUC who faithfully and cheerfully participate in the ITA orientations year after year.

◈ CONTRIBUTOR

Dean Papajohn is a specialist in education in the Center for Teaching Excellence and a teaching associate in the Division of English as an International Language at the University of Illinois, Urbana-Champaign. He has worked with ITAs for more than 12 years.

CHAPTER 11

Addressing the Cultural and Linguistic Needs of Students

Allison N. Petro

◈ INTRODUCTION

The International Teaching Assistant (ITA) Program at the University of Rhode Island (URI) began in 1992 out of a concern that international graduate students were arriving on campus in growing numbers, but their English language skills were often too weak to ensure their success as teaching assistants. Initially, the program was limited to a 3-week summer intensive program. It soon became clear, however, that this was not enough, especially for students who arrived on campus with low English language proficiency. Gradually, the program moved away from the summer program and toward courses offered during the semester, which allowed us to address the multiple needs of students. It also provided them with access to other campus resources that could supplement ITA development (the language lab, writing center, and various tutoring services).

In contrast to the typical pattern of ITA program development, URI already had a well-established teaching assistant development program in place before the ITA program was created. Since the 1980s, the university has offered a week-long, presemester workshop for teaching assistants in the sciences, mathematics, and engineering that is departmentally based. Even before the ITA program was created, ITAs took these workshops alongside native-English-speaking (NES) teaching assistants, benefiting from the practical advice offered by experienced teaching assistants and supervising professors. In many departments, teaching assistants' professional development sessions continue during the academic year, including departmental meetings with supervising professors as well as the option to work with instructional consultants on teaching skills. With such an effective teaching assistant development program in place, why would we need an ITA program?

◈ CONTEXT

Although the existing teaching assistant development program offers many resources for developing pedagogical skills, it does not address the specific linguistic and cultural needs of ITAs. From the outset, the focus of the ITA program at URI has been on language and culture. Because of the existence of a solid teaching assistant development program, it has been less critical to focus on classroom pedagogy and more time has been available for issues of language, culture, and cross-cultural communication.

From the start, the question has been how to address the various needs of students, given the small number of ITAs on campus and the limited resources available. Originally, approximately 25–30 ITAs were enrolled in professional development courses per year, so offering the summer program and the fall course was enough. When the summer program was discontinued, the fall course became too full and it became necessary to add a spring course on a regular basis. With only one ITA course offered each semester, the challenge has been how to address the multiple needs of students in our courses.

Another limitation of the ITA program initially was its structure; it had been created as a series of courses taught by adjunct faculty members. The program itself had no director and staff changes were frequent, so it became difficult to maintain continuity in program policy and curriculum, and communication with departments was limited. Initially, there was also no funding for assessment, so the Speaking Proficiency English Assessment Kit (SPEAK) test was not used and teaching evaluations were performed by the ITA instructors themselves, limiting the validity of the assessment.

Over time, we sought to overcome these limitations by developing consistent program policy and curriculum and communicating with faculty and staff in key departments. Because ITA professional development was not required by the university but only recommended, we frequently needed to remind departments about the necessity of SPEAK testing and to encourage them to have incoming ITAs enroll in professional development courses. Eventually, the ITA program coordinator was given administrative time equivalent to one course per semester to communicate with departments about program policies and student progress. In 2002, the ITA program became the partial responsibility of a full-time faculty member, giving it continuity for the first time.

The ITA program at URI is smaller and more focused than most programs, but these limitations allowed us to develop unique solutions in the areas of collaboration and curriculum. Limited staff resources forced us to find creative ways to utilize existing resources on campus. For example, we expanded on the professional development program for all teaching assistants that already existed on campus by focusing our curriculum on issues that are unique to ITAs.

The first ITA summer program at URI was initiated by ESL faculty to address the English language needs of international graduate students. Within a year, the Board of Governors for Higher Education in Rhode Island (1993) adopted a mandate that all teaching faculty be "orally proficient in the English language" in order "to deliver classroom instruction" (p. 10.0). Under this mandate, the University of Rhode Island was required "to assess, and where necessary, improve the oral English language proficiency of all newly hired teaching personnel" (p. 10.0). From 1993 on, the ITA courses were designed to meet the requirements of this state mandate and to ensure that ITAs become orally proficient for classroom instruction.

Incoming ITAs typically have not only solid preparation in their scientific or technical specialties gained through undergraduate study in their native countries but also Test of English as a Foreign Language (TOEFL) scores above 550, which demonstrate proficiency in English. When they take the SPEAK test, however, their scores are more typically in the range of 35–45, indicating limited oral proficiency. In general, their prior English language development tended to build their reading, writing, and grammar skills, with few opportunities for oral communication with native English speakers. A needs assessment conducted at URI in 1995 found several important areas of need. In the area of language, ITAs tended to have little experience with the English language as it is actually spoken. They need intensive work in recognizing and producing the basic sounds of U.S. English. They need an introduction to the patterns of reduction and linking that are used in informal spoken English. They need regular practice in intensive listening to strengthen their ability to recognize and understand natural, spoken English. Finally, they need to give oral reports to develop their basic presentation skills and build their confidence in expressing the complexities of their field in English. Many resources are available to ITA instructors for addressing these linguistic needs, including a variety of pronunciation and ITA textbooks and videos.

In addition to these language needs, however, our needs assessment identified cultural needs. ITAs on the URI campus often live and work with other graduate students from their native country and have little or no contact with native English speakers. In some departments, the majority of their professors may also be nonnative English speakers. This isolation leaves them with no one to ask about the meaning of English phrases or details of U.S. culture. ITAs need the chance to speak to native English speakers, preferably undergraduates, on a regular basis. They need the opportunity to learn about and reflect on the differences between their native cultures and U.S. culture, especially differences in education. Ideally, they also need a chance to understand the values system that underlies U.S. culture, so they can develop an understanding of the goals and objectives of the U.S. education system (Petro, 2000). This area of ITA curriculum is less developed, although existing resources from other fields can be adapted to ITA development.

Some ITAs receive tutoring free of charge from several on-campus programs, either during the ITA course or afterward. For overall oral fluency, ITAs can be offered an undergraduate tutor, someone who has demonstrated an interest in other languages and cultures and a willingness to learn about cross-cultural adjustment issues. ITAs meet with these tutors for several hours a week during a given semester, and they focus on whatever needs and goals they choose together. The director of English Language Studies supervises these tutoring sessions, offering advice or resources to tutors as needed.

For problems with pronunciation, ITAs can be referred to tutors at the Speech and Hearing Center, which sponsors pronunciation sessions for nonnative English speakers. The tutors are preservice speech therapists who are working on their master's degrees and are satisfying part of their practicum requirement by working with nonnative English speakers. The tutoring sessions typically meet 2 hours per week and focus on segmentals as well as suprasegmentals. The director of the Speech and Hearing Center supervises these tutoring sessions.

To develop written fluency, ITAs can be referred to the Writing Center, where some of the tutors have specialized ESL preparation. Writing tutors work with students, in one-on-one or small-group sessions, on the particular writing projects that students bring with them. Sessions may focus on brainstorming, paragraphing, sharpening thesis statements, documenting sources, enhancing clarity, using appropriate evidence, or practicing and internalizing specific grammatical concepts.

All of these tutoring programs supplement the ITA courses, providing ITAs with tutoring targeted to their individual needs.

◈ DESCRIPTION

Courses

ITA development courses at URI are offered through the English Language Studies Program, which is housed in the Department of English and funded by the dean of arts and sciences. Currently two courses are available—ELS 612 in the fall and ELS 512 in the spring (see Appendix A for sample syllabi). Both courses meet twice a week for a total of 3 hours per week for 15 weeks, or 45 contact hours. These courses are for credit and carry a letter grade that appears on a student's transcript. (However, that grade does not get averaged into a student's GPA and these courses do not count toward degree requirements in their graduate program.) ITA courses can be repeated until the oral proficiency requirement has been reached. Class size is generally limited to 15.

The curriculum for both courses is designed around the specific needs of ITAs—to improve their language, teaching, and intercultural communication skills. In theory, the curriculum is designed sequentially, with ELS 512 focusing more on building oral fluency and ELS 612 more on developing advanced skills to prepare for teaching. In practice, however, ITAs may be required by their department to take either of the courses at any time, which results in students with varying levels of fluency being enrolled in both courses. Given that students have different needs and are at different levels, the curriculum is designed to combine core requirements like pronunciation practice with assignments that allow students the flexibility to choose their topic.

ELS 612 is a content-based language course that focuses on cross-cultural differences in education. Topics include education in the United States, U.S. students and teachers, cross-cultural differences in education, issues for international students, culture shock and cultural adaptation, and effective teaching in U.S. universities. The major assignment is an interview with a U.S. undergraduate (see Appendix B), which requires ITAs to draw conclusions about differences between their educational experiences and those of the student interviewed. Students also complete regular language lab assignments on pronunciation and several microteaching presentations.

ELS 512 is a content-based language course that focuses on U.S. culture. Topics include traditional U.S. values, the frontier, U.S. business, education in the United States, and U.S. universities. Students complete several short writing assignments, including reflective essays related to traditional U.S. values and aspects of U.S. culture. Similar to ELS 612, there are also language lab assignments and microteaching presentations.

Summer Intensive Program

When it was offered, the summer intensive course provided a similar number of contact hours as the courses later did, but compressed into 14 days of study instead of 15 weeks. Classes met 3 hours every morning for 3 weeks to discuss issues of pedagogy and culture, with 6–8 afternoon sessions on pronunciation. Materials included the ITA textbook *Communicate: Strategies for International Teaching Assistants* (Smith, Meyers, & Burkhalter, 1992), as well as pronunciation materials from textbooks such as *Accurate English* (Dauer, 1993) and *Well Said* (Grant, 2001). Courses were not graded and there was no fee to enroll.

In 1999, the ITA program coordinator concluded that the summer course was not meeting the most pressing needs of ITAs and it was canceled. For students with solid fluency, the intensive nature of the summer course allowed them to get a quick introduction to the expectations of the U.S. classroom and to be ready for the fall semester. However, for students with limited fluency (35–40 on the SPEAK test) the summer program did not effectively build their fluency because the fast pace was overwhelming. There was no time between sessions for reflective homework assignments and, because of the timing of the summer program during the first 3 weeks of August, campus resources such as the language lab and tutoring services were unavailable. It was also difficult to find undergraduates willing to participate in discussion sessions or to evaluate microteaching presentations. Finally, some departments were unwilling to require incoming ITAs to arrive a full month early to participate in both ITA development and teaching assistant development before the start of the fall semester. By changing the timing and format of the courses, we were able to address the ITAs' needs more effectively.

Assignments

The following assignments have been used in our program:

Discussion Sessions

In these sessions, ITAs meet in small groups with undergraduate assistants or course instructors to discuss cultural issues. Topics include cross-cultural communication, U.S. students and teachers, university life in the United States, and traditional U.S. values. The instructor provides a list of questions to guide the discussions.

Microteaching Assignments

For the microteaching assignments, the ITAs choose cultural topics. These presentations provide a useful addition to assignments that focus on field-specific topics, especially early in the semester when students are looking for what they have in common with their classmates who may come from vastly different academic disciplines.

Reflective Essays

The reflective essays allow students to reflect on cross-cultural or educational issues. These short writing assignments can serve a variety of goals, from giving ITAs more practice in academic writing to allowing them to explore cross-cultural differences in a deeper way. Instructors have a range of options for offering feedback as well, depending on the goals of the course (Petro, 1999).

Long-Term Projects

During the long-term projects, ITAs pursue a variety of activities on a focused topic. In one example, ITAs compile a series of questions, interview an undergraduate, and then prepare both oral and written reports of their findings (see Appendix B). In another, they read Martin Luther King's "I Have a Dream" speech, write an analysis of the speech, and then watch a video of the speech and discuss the rhetorical elements Dr. King uses (see Appendix C). In the Mirroring Project, students choose a scene from an English-language film, create a script of the scene, study the verbal and nonverbal patterns of the actors, and perform the scene in class, mirroring the actor's performance (Monk & Meyers, 2004; see Appendix D). Such projects allow students to develop their skills in speaking, listening, reading, and writing by focusing on a long-term assignment.

◈ DISTINGUISHING FEATURES

Integration of Affective Factors

Many studies have pointed to the critical role of affective factors in the language acquisition process, especially for adult learners (Arnold, 1999; Peirce, 1995; Schumann, 1978). The key difference between adults who effectively acquire a second language and those who do not often depends on affective factors such as motivation, identity, needs, and goals. ITAs have clear reasons for wanting to improve their English language skills. It is important to harness their natural interest and motivation by explicitly stating how class activities relate to their overall needs and goals as international graduate students.

The integration of affective factors in our course assignments has been one of the distinguishing features of our program. In reflective writing assignments, we ask students to consider what they already know and what they want to learn. Reflective essays also offer them the chance to consider issues of cultural and pedagogical self-identity—what they consider an ideal teacher and what steps they could take to approach that ideal. In self-evaluations and peer evaluations, we offer them the chance to evaluate their own teaching and that of others (e.g., by observing classmates, videos of other teaching assistants) to determine what contributes to effective teaching, what role models they have, and what areas they want to prioritize for improvement. In the Mirroring Project, the students choose the actor, scene, and verbal/nonverbal patterns they want to mirror. Then they perform the scene in front of their classmates, which motivates them to master the material (see Appendix D). Affective factors are the driving force in our curriculum design. By providing multiple sources of input, a variety of assignments, and a choice of topics, we allow students with different learning preferences and different goals to find what inspires and motivates them.

Involvement of Undergraduates

Undergraduates are a regular part of our professional development courses, providing an opportunity for communication between ITAs and their target audience. Initially, undergraduates were hired in the summer program to evaluate microteaching assignments. Since 1998, they have worked in the academic-year courses, participating in classroom discussion sessions as well as evaluating microteaching presentations (Petro, 2001). These undergraduates are selected based on their cross-cultural experience and their ability to work with nonnative English speakers. (They have typically completed a course in intercultural or ethnic studies.)

The ITA course instructor is primarily responsible for preparing undergraduates for their roles as facilitators of classroom discussions and evaluators of microteaching assignments. The instructor meets briefly with them as a group before each class. They lead small-group discussions on cultural topics based on a recommended list of questions, and they evaluate microteaching presentations. Their written evaluations of microteaching become part of the feedback to the ITAs but are not used to calculate grades or determine readiness for teaching.

Focus on Intercultural Communication

Although pronunciation and pedagogy are part of the curriculum, culture becomes the central theme that weaves through the entire semester. The goal is to build the intercultural competence of ITAs—maintaining their own cultural identity while gaining the ability to live and work comfortably in a U.S. environment. They not only become aware of cultural differences but also develop deeper levels of intercultural sensitivity, such as understanding and empathy for these differences (Bennett, 1998).

Focusing the curriculum on intercultural issues requires a shift from instructors. When we require not only linguistic but also intercultural competence from students, we need to become more explicit about our role as intercultural mediators. In order to be effective, we have to develop our own awareness, skills, and knowledge of cultural differences and learn from the field of intercultural communication (Fantini, 1999).

This unique cultural emphasis is possible at URI because of the faculty's backgrounds. Faculty members have extensive backgrounds in intercultural communication, having studied several foreign languages, traveled extensively, and taught English in other countries. Some of the undergraduates we work with have also studied languages, traveled or lived elsewhere, or come from immigrant families. These backgrounds allow faculty, undergraduates, and ITAs to work together —in an environment of cultural tolerance—to consider cultural differences and offer strategies for cultural adaptation.

Use of Video

Most ITA programs use video to record microteaching assignments and review them one on one with students, outside of class. At URI also, video use has an integral role in class sessions, largely in response to requests from ITAs for more concrete examples. A carefully selected video can be used to preview almost any topic in ITA development, from pronunciation to pedagogy to cross-cultural differences.

To focus on body language, we use video segments of teaching assistants' instruction in various classroom settings. We turn off the sound and look at the body language of the teacher or students. Is the nonverbal communication effective? What is he or she conveying without words? Do the students seem engaged or not? How can we tell? To begin a discussion of teaching styles, we show several segments and talk about contrasting teaching personalities or teaching styles. There are numerous personality styles among effective teachers—what are the differences and is there anything they have in common? (ITAs are encouraged to find a mentor or a role model who has a teaching personality they admire.)

To highlight U.S. culture, we sometimes choose segments from classic movies. To introduce the topic of the frontier, we might show a scene from *The Magnificent Seven* (Mirisch & Sturges, 1960); for U.S. business, *Working Girl* (Wick & Nichols, 1988); and for competition and sports, *Jerry McGuire* (Crowe, 1996). The films offer concrete examples and introduce themes that we can explore further in our discussion of traditional U.S. values.

Each semester, we consider the ingredients of good teaching before we discuss what the experts say. Early in the course, we create an imaginary scenario—that they have graduated and become faculty members and now they are being asked by their department to evaluate the teaching skills of a potential instructor. What categories will they consider in order to decide if a video of the applicant indicates good teaching or not? They work on a list of criteria in groups and then a complete list is compiled, which becomes our evaluation form.

We then watch video segments of several teaching assistants and decide which one we would hire, based on our criteria. We use a video produced by Iowa State University that includes actual segments of teaching assistants' instruction in the classroom (Douglas & Myers, 1990). An added bonus of this video is that all of the teaching assistants in the video received departmental teaching awards, so there is a variety of effective teaching styles. Best of all, it includes examples of NES teaching assistants and ITAs. So far, our classes have nearly always selected an international student as their top candidate. From this exercise, they learn that language skills alone do not make a good teacher and that effective teaching skills can create a positive learning experience for students even when the teacher is not a native English speaker.

◈ PRACTICAL IDEAS

Collaborate With Departments

ITA instructors need to work with professors and graduate school directors as closely as possible in order to understand the contexts in which ITAs teach. Most important, we need to be aware of the great differences in academic discourse across the disciplines and not attempt to generalize about good teaching based on our own experience, especially if we have studied and taught exclusively in the humanities. The experts on teaching chemistry, electrical engineering, or pharmacy are the faculty in those departments, and we need to learn from them. Ideally, the materials, assignments, and advice offered in ITA development programs should be flexible enough to be relevant to most disciplines. When information or advice is not broadly applicable, ITA instructors should highlight potential differences.

Involve Undergraduates

Undergraduates are the target audience for ITAs. Involve them in ITA development courses—as conversation partners, discussion participants, cultural resources, and microteaching evaluators (Sarkisian & Maurer, 1998). The more ITAs know about the day-to-day realities of their students, the better they will be able to teach them. Assignments that require ITAs to interview undergraduates or to have a series of conversations about daily life inevitably yield great results, especially when they discover misconceptions they had about U.S. students (Bagchi, 2003; Cen, 2003). An unexpected bonus is that U.S. undergraduates can develop their own skills in intercultural communication from working with ITAs (Ronesi, 2001).

Expand the Intercultural Curriculum

The typical ITA course meets for only 40–45 hours a semester, so how is it possible to expand the curriculum to incorporate more of a focus on intercultural communication? By having multiple goals for each assignment. When a microteaching assignment focuses on asking questions, make the content cultural. When the focus is on organization or rhetoric, make the subject U.S. culture (see Appendix C for Martin Luther King Project). When the assignment involves reflective writing, make the topic cross-cultural differences. When the goal is learning more about undergraduates, make the discussion revolve around educational differences (see Appendix B for Interview Project). It is possible to have culture be the central theme of the ITA course, weaving it through the language and teaching tasks (see Appendix A for sample syllabi).

Offer Courses for Credit

Credit-bearing courses offer an incentive. Instructors can motivate ITAs by grading each assignment, rewarding attendance, and encouraging additional work by offering extra credit. Extensive comments on graded assignments can give ITAs useful feedback about their progress. Ideally the grades should be reported to their department and appear on their transcripts, but not be factored into their GPA. ITA instructors should be able to give useful feedback to students without jeopardizing the ITAs' graduate careers, and ITAs should be able to take risks without worrying about their GPAs.

Include Incentives

Provide ITAs with positive feedback whenever appropriate. They are used to being the best in their native countries—let them know when they do top-quality work in your ITA courses. Examples include a certificate of excellence for the highest grade in the class, gold stars for the highest-scoring quiz, and best presentation or most improved awards for the top microteaching presentations, as selected by evaluators. Encourage ITAs to think about how to provide similar incentives for their own students, and help them explore the range of possibilities.

Network With Other ITA Programs

Through e-mail and national conferences, ITA instructors can connect with colleagues, learn about other programs, and receive good ideas. Regional networks are a local option. ITA instructors at a dozen universities in our region created the New England ITA Network in 1999, and our group has met every semester since then. Over time, we have developed a network of colleagues to turn to for advice, support, and encouragement (Jarvis & Petro, 2000). Topics for our one-day conferences include curriculum, technology, or assessment, allowing us to explore critical issues in the field.

❖ CONCLUSION

It is possible to build a solid ITA program, even on a small scale. No matter how big or small the program is, however, we inevitably face some problems that are common to most ITA programs and others that are unique to our individual campuses. To address common problems, ITA instructors should network and learn from one another. To solve problems unique to our own context, we need the flexibility to create reasonable policies, the freedom to design innovative curriculum, and the opportunity to coordinate with departments and other campus resources. Given the right circumstances, most of us can rise to the multiple challenges involved in preparing ITAs and, in the process, improve the educational environment on campus.

❖ ACKNOWLEDGMENTS

My thanks to Dean Winnie Brownell for supporting the ITA program from the start, to Richard Blakely for having the vision to create the summer program, and to Lynne Ronesi for being a true colleague for so many years.

❖ CONTRIBUTOR

Allison N. Petro worked as ITA program coordinator at the University of Rhode Island from 1995 to 2005. She has taught ESL and EFL courses in the United States and other countries, including a Fulbright lectureship in Russia, and has served the TESOL ITA Interest Section as chair, secretary, member-at-large, and newsletter editor. She is currently an assistant professor of English at the Community College of Rhode Island.

❖ APPENDIX A: SAMPLE SYLLABI

Fall Semester

ELS 612—Advanced Communication Skills for ITA

Course Expectations:

This course will focus on the skills you need to be successful in your graduate studies. You will build your fluency in U.S. English by developing your ability to listen carefully and speak clearly. You will develop your presentation skills by giving oral reports. You will improve your academic skills by writing clear and concise summaries of your observations. Finally, you will enhance your cross-cultural awareness by reflecting on differences between the United States and your country, especially differences in educational systems.

Textbooks:

- Meyers, C., & Holt, S. (2001). *Pronunciation for success: Student workbook* (2nd ed.). Burnsville, MN: Aspen Productions.
- Course packet

Grading Policy:

Language Lab	20%
Pronunciation Quizzes	20%
2 Presentations	20%
Oral Report	20%
Written Report	20%

Schedule:

Week 1:	Introduction to the course
Week 2:	Pronunciation basics
	Background of education in the United States
Week 3:	Enunciation—Consonants
	U.S. students/U.S. teachers
Week 4:	Enunciation—Vowels
	Discussion—University education in the United States
Week 5:	1st Presentation—Topic of general interest
Week 6:	Video—"*Cold Water*" (Ogami, 1987)
	Discussion—Cross-cultural communication
Week 7:	Syllables & word endings
	Create a teaching evaluation form
Week 8:	Stress in words
	"Effective teaching" in U.S. universities
Week 9:	Stress in sentences
	Nonverbal communication
Week 10:	2nd presentation—Cross-cultural differences
Week 11:	Reductions and linking in U.S. speech
	Handling questions
Week 12:	Individual conferences
	*Holiday—Thanksgiving
Week 13:	Oral report #1—Interview reports
Week 14:	Pronunciation tutorials
	Last class, evaluations/Written report due

Spring Semester
ELS 512—Oral Communication Skills for ITA

Course Expectations:

This course will focus on the oral communication skills you need to be successful in your graduate studies. You will build your fluency in English by developing your speaking and listening skills. You will develop your presentation skills by giving oral reports. Finally, you will enhance your cross-cultural awareness by reflecting on differences between the United States and your country.

Textbooks:

- Grant, L. (2001). *Well Said: Pronunciation for Clear Communication* (2nd ed.). Boston: Heinle & Heinle.

- Course packet with excerpts from Datesman, M. K., Crandall, J., & Kearny, E. N. (2004). *The American Ways: An Introduction to American Culture* (3rd ed.). White Plains, NY: Longman.

Grading Policy:

Language Lab	20%
Pronunciation Quizzes	20%
Reflective Essays	20%
Oral Reports	20%
Final Presentation	20%

Schedule:

Week 1: Introduction to the course

Week 2: Introduction to the textbook
Discussion—Martin Luther King, Jr.

Week 3: Vowels
Traditional U.S. values

Week 4: Review vowels
The Frontier Heritage

Week 5: Stress in words
What is good teaching?

Week 6: *Holiday—Washington's birthday
Teaching round-robin

Week 7: Oral Report #1—Topics in U.S. culture

Week 8: Stress in sentences
U.S. business

Week 9: SPRING BREAK

Week 10: Review of stress & rhythm
Education in the United States

Week 11: Oral Report #2—Topic from your field

Week 12: Consonants
Discussion—University education

Week 13: Voiced vs. voiceless consonants, endings
intonation

Week 14: Final presentations

Week 15: Last day of class—Conclusion & evaluations

◈ APPENDIX B: ELS 612—INTERVIEW PROJECT

1. Develop a series of questions.

2. Interview a URI undergraduate.

3. Prepare an oral and written report of your findings.

4. Compare and Contrast:
Your experience as a student vs. the experience of the U.S. student.
The different experiences of two U.S. students.
Cross-cultural differences between students in the U.S. and your country.

APPENDIX C: ELS 512— MARTIN LUTHER KING, JR. PROJECT

1. Read Dr. King's speech "I Have a Dream."

2. Write an essay:
   Who is the audience for this speech?
   What are the main themes?
   What U.S. values does Dr. King focus on?
   What is your reaction?

3. Prepare to discuss the speech in class:
   What is the introduction?
   What are the main ideas in the body?
   What is the conclusion?
   Is the organization effective?

APPENDIX D: MIRRORING PROJECT

1. Choose a scene from an English-language movie:
   Choose your movie, character, and scene.
   Explain the verbal/nonverbal patterns you most want to practice.
   Your instructor must approve the choice of movie and scene.

2. Write a script and mark it:
   Listen carefully to the scene, and write down every word.
   Bring the script to class, typed, double-spaced, with each actor's lines.
   Mark the script for stress, thought groups, intonation.

3. Analyze the verbal/nonverbal patterns:
   Bring a copy of your film to class, plus your script.
   Watch the scene, analyze the verbal/nonverbal patterns.

4. Present the scene in class:
   Present your mirroring assignment in class.
   Bring a 2nd copy of the script to class (if there is a 2nd actor).

5. Reflect in writing (Optional):
   Evaluate the Mirroring Assignment in a reflective essay (optional topic).

Questions adapted from Monk, M., & Meyers, C. (2004, December). Documenting prosodic acquisition using the mirrorinSg project. As We Speak . . . The Newsletter of TESOL's Speech, Pronunciation, and Listening Interest Section, 2(1). Retrieved August 14, 2005, from http://www.tesol.org//s_tesol/ article.asp?vid=176& DID=3169&sid=1&cid=744&iid=3164&nid=3162

CHAPTER 12

Creating Partnerships: International Teaching Assistant Links in a Campus-Wide Chain— The Carnegie Mellon Experience

Peggy Allen Heidish

◈ INTRODUCTION

The idea to create a language support center at Carnegie Mellon University developed in 1983 when the number of nonnative-English-speaking (NNES) students at the university—graduate and undergraduate—reached a critical mass. The number of international students in graduate programs had increased to such a level that this population was affecting those programs, and faculty and students alike were forced to confront a variety of communication issues. A great majority of the 341 international graduate students (20% of the total graduate population) at the time worked as teaching assistants or members of research teams—contexts in which any language deficiencies soon became apparent. Faculty reported that many of their teaching assistants and research assistants lacked sufficient fluency in English to handle the job, and increasing numbers of undergraduate students complained to the administration that they were unable to understand many of their international teaching assistants (ITAs). To compound these issues, the university had no support services for international students and nonnative English speakers—there was no ESL program or international student office. If students needed language development, they had to go to ESL programs at other universities in Pittsburgh or hire tutors on their own.

Two years elapsed before funding became available to open what was then called the ESL Center. From the beginning, the center was designed to take into account the challenges presented by the nature of the university and its particular international student body:

- Graduate programs at Carnegie Mellon are highly competitive, with heavy emphasis on interdisciplinary research and major demands on students' time.

- Unlike those at some other universities, our graduate students are unable to take a reduced course load during the first year in order to take ESL classes.

- Graduate students at Carnegie Mellon are highly motivated, have strong academic backgrounds, and are used to being at the top of their classes in their own countries.

- International students arrive at Carnegie Mellon with widely divergent levels of language ability and enter diverse programs that require different skill sets in terms of language and cultural understanding.

The students' diverse language and cultural needs indicated that no single ESL course could work for this group; instead, the university created an ESL program based primarily on small-group instruction and individual tutoring help.

◈ CONTEXT

Under the center's first director, Dr. Thomas Huckin, the program was designed as an English for specific purposes (ESP) program using Huckin's principle of "professionally oriented ESL" (Huckin & Olsen, 1984, p. 289). According to Huckin, professionally oriented ESL is designed for students who are preparing for professional careers, and must focus on "features of general English and general communication skills" (p. 289). He states, "It [professionally oriented ESL] can be used to organize a formal class . . . bringing together students from a cluster of related disciplines . . . and giving them training in communicating across those disciplines. Or it can be used for one-on-one tutoring" (p. 289). The program was tailor-made to Carnegie Mellon's needs, and was inexpensive, innovative, and theory-based in line with the "best-supported, most widely agreed upon principles of second language acquisition theory" (Crandall, 1988, p. 2).

The program was further influenced by the Wyoming/National Association of Foreign Student Advisors (NAFSA) Institute on Foreign Teaching Assistant Training, held at the University of Wyoming in 1987. Conference participants joined one of three working groups to investigate areas related to the implementation of ITA professional development programs: academic and pedagogical issues, cross-cultural communication issues, and testing issues (Constantinides, 1986, 1987). Much of the work done at the conference laid the groundwork for ITA development and testing programs around the country and gave our center the advantage of experimenting with and adapting what were then some of the most innovative ideas for ITA development. These ideas included the use of teaching simulation as a crucial part of ITA testing, a better understanding of how ITA development differs from traditional ESL programs, and a commitment to ensuring that our program adequately prepared international graduate students to succeed in their individual programs and within the structure of Carnegie Mellon.

In the mid-1990s, the ESL Center's name was changed to the Intercultural Communication Center (ICC) to better reflect the breadth and scope of our mission as it had evolved. Eighteen years after its inception, the ICC consists of a full-time director, four instructors, administrative staff, and approximately 5–6 undergraduate and graduate tutors. As with all university-level academic support services at Carnegie Mellon, the ICC has a small core staff supplemented by support from the academic units. We are a support service for students and faculty, housed under the associate provost for education and funded by the central university administration on a 12-month basis. We work closely with other university units, including the Eberly Center for Teaching Excellence (both to coordinate our ITA development with the broader teaching assistant support for native English speakers and to offer assistance to NNES faculty members) and the Office of International Education (for

International Student Orientation each August and for general issues related to international students). The international student population has increased by 317% since 1986. There are now 1,444 international graduate students (34% of the total graduate population); of that number, roughly 95% are nonnative English speakers.

Carnegie Mellon is a private, coeducational research university located in Pittsburgh, Pennsylvania, with all 50 states and more than 87 countries represented in our student population. The university consistently ranks among the top national universities in the *U.S. News and World Report* ratings. Several of our individual programs are ranked very highly; for instance, *U.S. News and World Report* ("America's Best Graduate Schools," 2005) ranked our doctoral program in computer science first in the nation and rated our computer engineering, cognitive psychology, and two management programs in the top four. In addition, the *Wall Street Journal* (Alsop, 2005) ranked our business school in the top 3 both nationally and internationally. Because of its high ranking in many fields, Carnegie Mellon attracts many stellar students from around the world. The university is also renowned for its rigorous curriculum at the undergraduate as well as graduate levels, and lack of English proficiency can make learning at Carnegie Mellon a formidable task for nonnative English speakers.

For international students, serving as a teaching assistant often proves to be even more challenging than dealing with graduate studies. Fifty-three percent of our doctoral students and 24% of our master's students are international, and many are expected to serve as teaching assistants. In addition to meeting advisor and departmental expectations for serving as teaching assistants, international students must abide by university policy and Pennsylvania law regarding fluency. Since 1987, university policy has required that all NNES teaching assistants pass a language test before being allowed to work as teaching assistants. (It should be noted that native language—not citizenship—is the determining factor.) In 1990, a Pennsylvania law called English Fluency in Higher Education went into effect, requiring all NNES teaching assistants in the state to pass a fluency test before teaching undergraduates. The university faces a $10,000 fine for each uncertified teacher. Carnegie Mellon policy additionally requires that all nonnative English speakers pass a language test before teaching graduates or undergraduates. We also require that ITAs who supervise laboratories have as much English proficiency as do ITAs who lecture.

Furthermore, because Carnegie Mellon does not have a central graduate school, each academic department or program makes its own decisions regarding admission procedures and standards, degree requirements, and minimum scores for standardized tests such as the Test of English as a Foreign Language (TOEFL) or the Graduate Record Examination (GRE). This decentralized structure gives the center much more responsibility to help, advise, and guide departments as they make decisions and policies for their international students, but also gives us tremendous freedom and opportunity to innovate and to test new ideas as conditions change.

◈ DESCRIPTION

Given the large number of nonnative English speakers and the strict guidelines that must be followed for allowing these students to serve as teaching assistants, our center runs an ITA development program whose goals are to test NNES teaching assistants for language and cultural proficiency and to give remedial help to those who lack sufficient skills in either area. We see ourselves as a full-service program designed to develop academic fluency for all nonnative English speakers in degree programs. Our mission statement reads, in part, that the goal of the ICC is to equip international students with the skills they need to succeed in their academic programs and to equip ITAs and faculty with the skills they need to provide effective instruction in the U.S. classroom (see Appendix A for an overview of our program).

Graduate students are expected to take on more and more tasks that require not only high-level proficiency in English but also strong cultural knowledge. These tasks include participating in seminars, working in multidisciplinary research teams, meeting directly with project sponsors, giving presentations at international conferences, and working as teaching assistants. By developing advanced fluency, international graduate students can develop the skills needed to succeed as teaching assistants, the fluency to function in the previously mentioned situations, and eventually rise to their full potential as professionals after graduation.

The students in our program are highly motivated graduate students from all departments, but the majority are from science and engineering. Because of the competitive nature of Carnegie Mellon's admissions process, most of these students are accustomed to being at the top of their classes in their native countries. Many departments at the university require TOEFL scores of at least 600, so many of the students have had years of English study in their countries. However, because the TOEFL was often the only measure used for language proficiency, some students arrive at Carnegie Mellon not only lacking the oral language skills needed to pass the ITA test, but also possessing a level of proficiency that makes it difficult for them to work in research groups, participate in their classes, communicate with faculty and staff, or become integrated into the academic community.

The ICC currently serves approximately 415 students per semester during the academic year and 156 during the summer. It is difficult to quantify the amount of classroom work we offer to students because our center provides a variety of teaching modalities, including short workshops, longer credit classes, and individual tutoring hours. One way we can capture this figure is by calculating contact hours, that is, the number of students multiplied by the hours of ICC work they attended. During the 2004–2005 academic year, for example, we provided 7,805 contact hours of professional development.

Our program has been responsible for ITA testing since 1986. Since that time, we have given 3,210 ITA tests to 2,431 students (reflecting the fact that students can take the test repeatedly until they pass). Currently, students from Asia account for 69% of those tested, with the greatest numbers coming from China (23%), India (23%), and Korea (6%). Of the remaining students tested, 21% are European, 10% are Latin American, and less than 1% are African.

The ICC currently has four full-time instructors, not including the director, all of whom handle a wide variety of teaching responsibilities. Given the nature of our center, where professional development is highly individualized and classes are continually created or revised to better meet the needs of our students, our instructors need to be flexible, innovative, and not dependent on a strict curriculum. In addition to having a strong background in ESL, our instructors must understand the nature of the graduate community and the demands (both linguistic and cultural) placed on graduate students at Carnegie Mellon. Ideally, they have a background in other types of teaching situations such as native-English-speaking

(NES) undergraduate classes or public speaking courses, and (it is hoped) language teaching abroad.

Our instructors also need to have experience with all aspects of our program, particularly with ITA testing. In fact, we find that having instructors serve as ITA test raters each semester serves as a type of professional development because it constantly helps us recalibrate our sense of what skills successful NNES teaching assistants really need. Therefore, instructors are expected to

- teach credit and noncredit classes throughout the year

- meet individually with students for feedback and advising about how students should continue developing academic fluency pronunciation, cultural understanding, and teaching skills

- screen and evaluate students in both the initial placement interview and the ITA test

- develop new classes and new materials

- supervise undergraduate tutors

In addition to shaping the professional development of our instructors, the ICC also prepares undergraduate students to provide tutoring sessions in which ITAs can practice teaching to an audience.

The ITA test, required since 1990 by Pennsylvania law, evaluates the language proficiency of nonnative English speakers who want to work as teaching assistants. The test is a teaching simulation (described in more detail in the following paragraphs) that determines if the student has the language and communication skills needed to teach effectively in the U.S. classroom. As a follow-up to the test, students are required to return for an individual appointment in which they receive the results of their test and detailed feedback about their performance and the specific skills that need improvement.

When we first began testing in the late 1980s, students were allowed to choose a topic and prepare a presentation in advance. However, we discovered that this method had a critical flaw: we were often testing the students' ability to memorize rather than their actual teaching fluency. Also, given that one of the most common complaints about ITAs was their inability to respond to unexpected questions or concerns in labs and recitation classes, it seemed important to find a way to assess their ability to talk about their field without preparation.

In our current testing procedure, the student meets with a panel of four instructor-raters. We talk informally before moving to the teaching simulation. The test topics are not prefabricated; instead, we find a topic with which the student is familiar and that can be explained to people outside of the student's field. For example, during the initial informal conversation, a student may mention that he or she is working on a project developing materials for data storage systems. We could then ask him or her to explain the properties of materials that can make them useful for data storage systems.

To ensure that students understand what they are being asked to do in the test, an ICC staff member always gives the following verbal instructions:

> This is not a test of your knowledge; so if we give you a topic you are not comfortable with, tell us. We can find another topic and this will not affect

your score. What we are interested in is how you use English to explain this topic to us. Remember that we do not have background in your field.

The teaching simulation lasts between 5 and 10 minutes. After the student leaves, the instructor-raters individually fill out their rating forms (see Appendix B for the test scoring guide and Appendix C for the test results) and then deliberate as a group until they reach consensus about the student's final score. A number of sources have been useful to us in defining the goals for our testing and in setting up our testing procedure (Briggs, 1994; Hoekje & Williams, 1992, 1994; Smith, Meyers, & Burkhalter, 1992).

We offer ITA testing three times each year: November, near the end of the fall semester; April, near the end of the spring semester; and August, during the International Student Orientation. In the fall and spring semesters, ITA testing becomes the full-time focus of our center for nearly 3 weeks. We offer test appointments from 9:30 am to 5:00 pm each day and generally test 240 students each year.

Our ITA training program offers instruction and support in a variety of formats (see the Sample Semester Schedule in Appendix D and Course Overview in Appendix E), and makes use of a number of materials designed for ITA training (Sarkisian, 2000; Smith, Meyers, & Burkalter, 1992; *Teaching in America: A Guide for International Faculty*, 1993; Wennerstrom, 1989). The program is designed to allow full-time international graduate students to take the specific mix of workshops, tutoring sessions, and self-paced appointments that give them the maximum amount of training in a minimum amount of time. Because the demographics, language fluency levels, and work assignments of our population change from year to year, we are continually reassessing our workshops to address those trends. In addition, we routinely pilot one or two new workshops each year.

◈ DISTINGUISHING FEATURES

An Individualized Approach

Our language preparation program takes an individualized approach in which we spend quite a bit of time working one on one with the students and the individual academic departments. Working in this way helps create productive partnerships with both of these groups.

Partnerships With Graduate Departments

Because the university's decentralized graduate program structure allows each department to set its own requirements for graduate student admission, it has proven crucial for us to establish and maintain close working relationships with the graduate programs in the various departments. Our steps for doing so are described in the next section.

Explaining Advanced Fluency and ITA Testing

The first step in creating partnerships with the graduate departments is to make sure that faculty and staff in those departments understand what we mean by *advanced fluency* and *ITA testing*. For example, they might assume that an international student is fluent enough to teach because that student could make small talk at a departmental party or could discuss research problems with the advisors. We realized that the people working most directly with NNES graduate students need to understand the complexities of evaluating advanced fluency, and that fluency in one context or with one person (e.g., an advisor who already knows the context and the terminology) does not necessarily carry over into the teaching situation. Therefore, we felt that it was important—and well worth the time—to make it part of our mission to help faculty and staff become more educated about language assessment in general and about ITA testing in particular. To that end, we developed the following two initiatives.

Developing a Definition of Robust Academic Fluency

We named the type of fluency needed for success in graduate school and developed a definition of that fluency so that the students and their faculty advisors could envision the level of fluency the students would need to develop. We called this level of fluency *robust academic fluency*, and defined it as follows:

> To be fully functional and successful in the Carnegie Mellon academic environment, both graduate and undergraduate students who are nonnative speakers of English need to develop robust academic fluency that will enable them to
>
> - put knowledge into words so that they can participate as equals in class discussions or research groups, talk to advisors or research funders, or interact with students
>
> - talk to a variety of audiences about their field
>
> - use technical and nontechnical language easily
>
> - know the language of their field
>
> - reword terms and concepts
>
> - define key terms clearly and simply
>
> - give examples that illustrate technical and theoretical concepts
>
> - coherently connect concepts and ideas through appropriate use of transitional language
>
> - participate in small talk about their field and general academic topics
>
> - master material presented in English in either spoken or written form
>
> - write in the expected style for U.S. academic papers
>
> - interact with administrators and staff
>
> - understand English as it is spoken in the U.S. academy including the underlying meanings and connotations
>
> - respond to unexpected questions and comments (Intercultural Communication Center, 2005)

Explaining the ITA Test to Faculty

In the early days of our testing, we had some problems with faculty members who not only became upset when their students failed the ITA test ("I talk with him everyday and I can understand him, so why didn't he pass the test?") but also blamed our test rather than the students' lack of fluency. To address this, we had meetings with faculty, either individually or with groups in departmental meetings, to explain the ITA test and to teach them, at a basic level, how the test is rated. Additionally, we showed videotapes of actual ITA tests to the faculty. The results have been amazing. If the testing procedure is presented in this way and the right questions are asked, an untrained rater (in this case, the faculty) can fairly accurately rate the speakers. In several cases, faculty who had been upset about the ratings their students received came to understand the process much better and supported the test results and our recommendations about specific remedial work for those students.

Students as Active Participants in Their Language Development

As previously mentioned, our ITA development program is a highly individualized program. When students enter our program, they take either a placement interview (to place them into the appropriate ICC work) or the ITA test and then receive an evaluation of their spoken language ability and cultural understanding.

As students progress through our program, they continue to get individualized feedback and evaluation from instructors and tutors. We typically spend an hour with each student watching videotapes of their practice lessons or prepared speeches, and discussing language issues that need improvement (e.g., grammar usage, pronunciation, awareness of learner or presentation) and cross-cultural differences that may be interfering with a student's ability to communicate effectively in the U.S. classroom culture (e.g., a student from a culture in which academic discourse is required to be abstract and highly theoretical may find that he or she is unable to give simple examples because of his or her cultural background rather than because of a lack of fluency). The need for training on this wide set of skills has been identified by a number of experts in the field of ITA training (Madden & Myers, 1994; Plakans, 1997; Rubin, 1992). We have come to believe that these meetings are an extremely worthwhile investment of the instructor's time, and build appointment times into the structure of each course.

ITA Test Information Session

Throughout the years we often noticed that some students—even highly fluent speakers—did poorly on the ITA test, primarily because they did not seem to understand what was expected of them. For example, when asked to teach a topic from their field, they might instead answer as if it were a question asked by their advisor. They did not take on the role of the teacher, did not see us as learners, and saw the ITA test as a test of their knowledge rather than as a test of their ability to communicate their knowledge to students in English. In addition, sometimes students became angry or upset if they got a poor score because they did not know how or what was being rated.

We therefore started offering a 2-hour information session called, "ITA Information Session: What You Need to Know Before Taking the ITA Test." In the session, we use a format similar to the one used for faculty preparation (see Explaining the ITA Test to Faculty, p. 172): We explain the rationale for the test, show students detailed copies of our rating form and what we are looking for in each category, review the scoring, and give tips on how to best approach the test. We watch videos of actual tests and ask the students to rate these. Once again, students almost always rate the speakers the way we did. Many students worry that they can never achieve native fluency in English (and they are right), so when I show an example of a teaching assistant who scored in the highest category, I choose a speaker who clearly has nonnative features to his or her language but is also highly communicative and skilled as a teacher.

Finally, we also provide written materials to help students understand the process more thoroughly.

◈ PRACTICAL IDEAS

Our experience at Carnegie Mellon has demonstrated four important principles related to the success of an ITA professional development program.

Connect the ITA Professional Development Program With Other Units in the University, Academic Departments, and Faculty

Forming partnerships strengthens the ITA program. By building relationships with the academic departments, for example, the language preparation program creates partners who will reinforce language development on campus, encourage their students to attend language preparation, and have more realistic expectations about their students' abilities to pass the ITA test. Similarly, by knowing more about the academic departments, the ITA professional development instructors can be in a position both to offer help when it is requested and to proactively step in to make recommendations to the departments and other university planning offices.

Integrate the Program Into the Larger, More Comprehensive Language Development Program

The preparation that helps students develop the language and cultural skills needed to be successful teaching assistants can also help them succeed in graduate programs, as researchers, and eventually, in their professional lives.

Develop Relationships With the Students Themselves

When students understand the communication patterns expected in the U.S. academy, have a realistic understanding of their own language strengths and weaknesses, and can link ITA fluency to success in their future careers, they are better able, and much more willing, to take an active role in their language development. Maintaining close relationships with the students can keep language instructors aware of the fact that there are many needs and approaches to helping students develop academic fluency. Such relationships foster the sense of community that has become an essential element of the modern U.S. university.

Adapt the Program to the Culture of Your Institution

The ICC program at Carnegie Mellon arose out of an immediate need to deal with a large number of students who lacked the appropriate language and cultural skills to successfully function as members of the academic community. Meeting this need has fostered a program that is flexible and open to changing demands and has broadened the perspective of a number of different academic programs that might not seem affected by communication studies or the remedial needs of conventional ESL preparation.

◈ CONCLUSION

It appears that the number of international students, both graduate and undergraduate, will continue to increase at Carnegie Mellon. Not only will more and more of our students be required to work as teaching assistants, due to financial reasons as well as the requirement of their graduate programs, but an increasing number will need to work in interdisciplinary research teams. As we look to the future, we envision that the ICC will move in the following directions:

- Develop more professional development programs that allow our increasingly busy students to work on language skills in a way that fits their schedules. For example, we hope to create a stronger and more defined program for self-paced work (using videos, tapes, and software on a drop-in basis) and to increase the number of drop-in workshop sessions that students can attend when they have the time and without needing to preregister. We also want to continue to increase the number of individual tutoring sessions.

- Expand ITA development and testing to undergraduates. An increasing number of departments have begun to hire undergraduate teaching assistants, so we will need to test more students. We will also need to redesign some of our ITA development materials, given that undergraduates have different backgrounds and types of teaching experience than do graduates.

- Work more closely with Carnegie Mellon's teaching center, the Eberly Center for Teaching Excellence, to offer more support for faculty, including language and cultural preparation for international and NNES faculty as well as workshops on cross-cultural issues for NES faculty. Although faculty are not required to pass the ITA test before being allowed to teach, there have been cases in which NNES faculty were removed from teaching responsibilities by the department chair due to student complaints about the faculty member's command of English.

A new awareness of internationalism has arisen in many U.S. universities—not just in language development but also in the social sciences, liberal arts, and even in the sciences. To create successful ITA development programs, partnerships must be established and maintained among students, faculty, and staff. Through a partnership model, universities can accommodate and adapt to the continually changing academy and find ways to effectively respond to the academic and professional needs of international and NES students alike.

◈ CONTRIBUTOR

Peggy Allen Heidish is director of the Intercultural Communication Center at Carnegie Mellon University, where she is responsible for ITA development and testing, tutor training, and faculty outreach. She has created and taught many classes for ITA development, advanced academic fluency for international students, and workshops to increase international awareness on campus, including "Teaching and Learning Across Cultures" and "Adapting to the Culture of the U.S. Classroom: A Workshop for International Faculty." She has been teaching ESL since 1976 and has worked with ITAs at Carnegie Mellon since 1985.

◈ APPENDIX A: OVERVIEW OF ITA TRAINING AT CARNEGIE MELLON

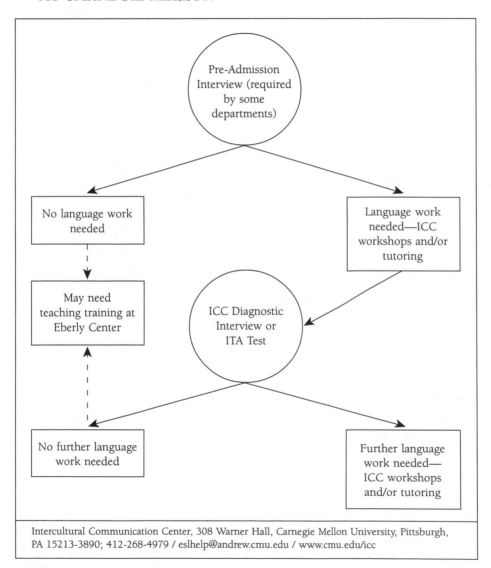

Intercultural Communication Center, 308 Warner Hall, Carnegie Mellon University, Pittsburgh, PA 15213-3890; 412-268-4979 / eslhelp@andrew.cmu.edu / www.cmu.edu/icc

◈ APPENDIX B: ITA TEST SCORING GUIDE

Intercultural Communication Center   Carnegie Mellon

ITA Test Scoring Guide

Testing is in accordance with Carnegie Mellon policy and the PA certification requirement. Final scores are based on pronunciation, grammar, fluency, listening, and overall comprehensibility. Students get feedback on teaching skills and cultural understanding, but these skills do not determine final score.

Full Pass

PASS for all teaching assistant assignments; can teach undergraduate and graduate classes, studios and labs:

Category 1: Fluent enough in English to become a teaching assistant without further language training (however, may need training in teaching skills).

Ongoing training

Category 2: Fluent enough in English to become a teaching assistant but must attend ongoing language training concurrent with any teaching assignment. Some language problems interfere with comprehensibility but may not seriously hinder the ability to communicate in the classroom (note: Category 2 students do not need to strive to become Category 1).

Restricted Pass

PASS for the restricted teaching assistant assignments listed below:

Category 3: Fluent enough in English to work as 1) a teaching assistant for graduate classes, 2) a tutor for one-on-one undergraduate sessions such as office hours or individual tutoring, or 3) an instructor assistant for undergraduate labs or studios (if supervised by an instructor who is present in the lab or studio, and not responsible for safety instructions or for giving presentations to the class). Must attend the prescribed language work concurrent with a TEACHING ASSISTANT assignment. Can negotiate meaning in one-on-one conversations, but lacks the fluency to present material clearly in the classroom, lab, or studio. Continued language training needed for academic success.

Grading

PASS for grading assignments

Category 4: Not fluent enough to become a teaching assistant, but may grade. Language often interferes with clear communication. Lacks ability to negotiate meaning, even in one-on-one interactions; language deficiencies may affect success in graduate work. Must work regularly on language skills to succeed in graduate work.

Not ready

Not ready to TA

Category 5: Not fluent enough in English to do either teaching or grading. Students in this category have great difficulty communicating and need to work very seriously on language skills to be able to succeed in their academic work.

Category	1	2	3	4	5
Concurrent language training required		✓	✓		
Undergraduate classes/labs	✓	✓			
Graduate classes/labs	✓	✓	✓		
Individual Tutoring/Office Hours	✓	✓	✓		
Grading	✓	✓	✓	✓	

Intercultural Communication Center, 308 Warner Hall, Carnegie Mellon University, Pittsburgh, PA 15213-3890; 412-268-4979 / eslhelp@andrew.cmu.edu / www.cmu.edu/icc

❖ APPENDIX C: ITA TEST RESULTS

Intercultural Communication Center   Carnegie Mellon

International Teaching Assistant (ITA)
Test Results

Name _____   ITA Test Category _____
                                  see category descriptions on back

Department _____   Date of Test _____

Diagnosis   *Comments*

Pronunciation   [ ] strength   [ ] weakness   _____

Grammar   [ ] strength   [ ] weakness   _____

Fluency   [ ] strength   [ ] weakness   _____

Listening   [ ] strength   [ ] weakness   _____

Understanding of
U.S. Classroom   [ ] strength   [ ] weakness   _____

Teaching Skills   [ ] strength   [ ] weakness   _____

Other   [ ] strength   [ ] weakness   _____

Requirements

Students should attend the following classes and/or workshops:

_____

_____

_____

If the student fulfills the above requirements, he/she should be prepared to re-take the ITA Test in _____.

Distribution: ICC, Department

◈ APPENDIX D: SAMPLE SEMESTER SCHEDULE
Services for Students
Fall 2004

Credit Mini-Courses

> Language & Culture for Teaching

Noncredit Workshops

> Stress & Intonation
> Presentation Skills I
> Presentation Skills II
> Advanced Fluency Challenges
> Speaking & Listening
> Advanced Grammar Monitoring
> Public Speaking Clinic
> Job Interviewing Skills

ITA Seminars

> Conversational Styles
> Elevator Talk
> Pronunciation for Advanced Speakers
> Teaching & Learning in the Multicultural Classroom

Individual Appointments

> Self-Paced Videos
> Writing Clinic

Information Sessions

> Becoming a Better Language Learner
> ITA Test Information

ICC Practice Sessions

> Pronunciation Targets
> Fluency Targets

ITA Tests

Intercultural Communication Center, 308 Warner Hall, Carnegie Mellon University, Pittsburgh, PA 15213-3890; 412-268-4979 / eslhelp@andrew.cmu.edu / www.cmu.edu/icc

❧ APPENDIX E: COURSE OVERVIEW

Intercultural Communication Center   Carnegie Mellon

Fall 2004: Language and Culture for Teaching (99–452)

Course Objective:

The goal of this course is to help you develop the skills needed to succeed as a TEACHING ASSISTANT. To do that you must, first of all, develop the fluency to put your knowledge of your field into clear and simple English. In addition, you must understand the culture of the U.S. classroom and know how "teaching" and "learning" are defined in the U.S. academy. Finally, you need to develop a **robust teaching fluency**.

Class sessions (90 minutes):

Identifying your starting point

- Introduction: What Skills do ITAs Need to Develop?
- Videotaping (prepare short presentations from your fields; follow up: individual appointments with instructor)

Taking the "noise" out of your signal

- English Stress & Intonation Patterns
- Stress & Intonation Patterns (cont.)

Understanding your audience

- An Inside Look at the U.S. Educational System

Building "robustness"

- Building Robust Fluency: Redundancy, Rewording and Restating
- Redundancy, Rewording and Restating (cont.)
- Teaching by Example
- Defining Concepts Simply and Concisely

Interacting effectively with students

- Integrating & Synthesizing Redundancy, Examples, and Definitions
- Handling Student Questions
- Putting Students to Work

Putting it all together

- Impromptu Talks
- Final Videotaping (see description above)

Materials used

- Smith, J., Meyers, C., & Burkhalter, A. (1992). *Communicate: Strategies for International Teaching Assistants.* Englewood Cliffs, NJ: Regents/Prentice Hall.

- *Teaching in America: A Guide for International Faculty* [Video]. (1993). Cambridge, MA: Harvard University, Derek Bok Center for Teaching and Learning.

- Wennerstrom, A. (1989). *Techniques for Teachers: A Guide for Non-Native Speakers of English*. Ann Arbor: University of Michigan Press.

Intercultural Communication Center, 308 Warner Hall, Carnegie Mellon University, Pittsburgh, PA 15213-3890; 412-268-4979 / eslhelp@andrew.cmu.edu / www.cmu.edu/icc

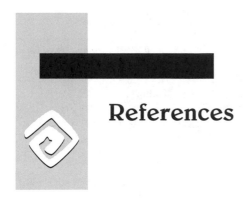

References

Abel, D. (2002, February 25). A failure to communicate? *Boston Sunday Globe,* p. C5.

Adler, N. (2002). Stereotypes. In *International dimensions of organizational behavior* (pp. 81–83). Boston: Thomson Learning.

Ahluwalia, S. (Producer), Barker, K., & Ross, C. (Directors/Advisors). (2001). *Respect on the line* [Video]. (Available from the University of Connecticut, University Center for Instructional Media and Technology, 249 Glenbrook Road, Storrs, CT 06269-2001)

Alsop, A. (2005, September 21). Back on top. *The Wall Street Journal,* p. R1. Retrieved December 6, 2005, from http://online.wsj.com/public/article/SB112688234637942950.html

Althen, G. (1988). *American ways: A guide for foreigners in the United States.* Yarmouth, ME: Intercultural Press.

Ambrose, S. (1991). From graduate student to faculty member: Teaching Ph.D. candidates to teach. In J. D. Nyquist, R. D. Abbott, D. H. Wulff, & J. Sprague (Eds.), *Preparing the professoriate of tomorrow to teach* (pp. 157–167). Dubuque, IA: Kendall/Hunt.

American Association for the Advancement of Science (AAAS). (2001). *Designs for science literacy: Project 2061.* Washington, DC: Author.

American Council for the Teaching of Foreign Languages (ACTFL). (2002). *Program standards for the preparation of foreign language teachers.* Yonkers, NY: Author. Available from http://www.actfl.org/i4a/pages/index.cfm?pageid=3384

America's best graduate schools 2006. (2005). *U.S. News & World Report, USNews.com.* Retrieved December 1, 2005, from http://www.usnews.com/usnews/edu/grad/rankings/phdsci/brief/com_brief.php

Angelo, T., & Cross, K. P. (1993a). *Classroom assessment techniques* (2nd ed.). San Francisco: Jossey-Bass.

Angelo, T., & Cross, K. P. (1993b). Lessons and insights from six years of use. In *Classroom assessment techniques* (2nd ed.; pp. 370–377). San Francisco: Jossey-Bass.

Ard, J. (1989). Grounding an ITA curriculum: Theoretical and practical concerns. *English for Specific Purposes, 8,* 125–138.

Arnold, J. (Ed.). (1999). *Affect in language learning.* New York: Cambridge University Press.

Austin, E. (2002). Preparing the next generation of faculty. *The Journal of Higher Education, 73*(1), 94–122.

Bachman, L., & Palmer, A. (1996). *Language testing in practice.* Oxford, England: Oxford University Press.

Bagchi, A. (2003). *Reaching out: The Buddy Program at Michigan State University.* Retrieved June 30, 2004, from http://tap.msu.edu/PDF/aloka.pdf

Bailey, K. M. (1984). The "foreign TA problem." In K. M. Bailey, F. Pialorsi, & J. Zukowski-

Faust (Eds.), *Foreign teaching assistants in U.S. universities* (pp. 3–15). Washington, DC: NAFSA: Association of International Educators.

Bailey, K. M., & Nunan, D. (Eds.). (1995). *Voices from the language classroom.* New York: Cambridge University Press.

Bailey, K. M., Pialorsi, F., & Zukowski-Faust, J. (Eds.). (1984). *Foreign teaching assistants in U.S. universities.* Washington, DC: NAFSA: Association of International Educators.

Bakhtin, M. M. (1986). *Speech genres and other late essays.* Austin: University of Texas Press.

Bauer, G. (1991). Instructional communication concerns of international (non-native English speaking) teaching assistants: A qualitative analysis. In J. D. Nyquist, R. D. Abbott, D. H. Wulff, & J. Sprague (Eds.), *Preparing the professoriate of tomorrow to teach* (pp. 420–426). Dubuque, IA: Kendall/Hunt.

Beatty, K. (2003). *Teaching and researching computer-assisted language learning.* London: Pearson.

Bennett, M. (1998). Overcoming the golden rule: Sympathy and empathy. In M. Bennett (Ed.), *Basic concepts in intercultural communication* (pp. 191–214). Yarmouth, ME: Intercultural Press.

Benson, P. (2001). *Autonomy in language learning.* London: Pearson.

Board of Governors for Higher Education, State of Rhode Island and Providence Plantations. (1993). *Oral English proficiency policy for instructional personnel.* Retrieved August 14, 2005, from http://www.ribghe.org/oralenglishproficient.pdf

Borjas, G. (2005). Do foreign students crowd out native students from graduate programs? In R. G. Ehrenberg & P. E. Stephan (Eds.), *Science and the university.* Madison: University of Wisconsin Press. Retrieved July 18, 2005, from http://ksghome.harvard.edu /~GBorjas/publications_for_download.html

Borjas, G. (2000, May). Foreign-born teaching assistants and the academic performance of undergraduates. *American Economic Review, 90,* 355–359. Retrieved August, 10, 2005, from http://ksghome.harvard.edu/~GBorjas/publications_for_download.html

Bransford, J. D., Brown, A. L., & Cocking, R. R. (2000). *How people learn: Brain, mind, experience, and school.* Washington, DC: National Academies Press.

Briggs, S. (1994). Using performance assessment methods to screen ITAs. In C. G. Madden & C. L. Myers (Eds.), *Discourse and performance of international teaching assistants* (pp. 63–80). Alexandria, VA: TESOL.

Briggs, S., Clark, V., Madden, C., Beal, R., Hyon, S., Alridge, P., et al. (1997). *The international teaching assistant: An annotated critical bibliography.* Ann Arbor, MI: English Language Institute.

Brindley, G. (1995). Competency-based assessment in second language programs: Some issues and questions. In G. Brindley (Ed.), *Language assessment in action* (pp. 145–164). Sydney, New South Wales, Australia: National Centre for English Language Teaching and Research.

Brinton, D. M., Snow, M. A., & Wesche, M. B. (1989). *Content-based second language instruction.* New York: Harper and Row.

Brookfield, S. (1995). *Becoming a critically reflective teacher.* San Francisco: Jossey-Bass.

Brown, D. (2004). *Language assessment: Principles and classroom practices.* White Plains, NY: Pearson.

Brown, J. (2000, March/April). Growing up digital: How the web changes work, education, and ways people learn. *Change, 32*(2), 11–20.

Burns, A. (1999). *Collaborative action research for English language teachers.* Cambridge, England: Cambridge University Press.

Cardillo, M. (2002, February 21). You know you are at UConn when . . . [Letter to the editor]. *Daily Campus,* p. 4.

Carrell, P., Sarwick, S., & Plakans, B. (1987). Innovative ITA screening techniques. In N. V. N. Chism (Ed.), *Institutional responsibilities and responses in the employment and education of teaching assistants: Readings from a national conference* (pp. 351–354). Columbus: Ohio State University, Center for Teaching Excellence.

Carson, B. (1999). Bad news in the service of good teaching: Students remember ineffective professors. *Journal on Excellence in College Teaching, 10*(1), 91–105.

Carter, K. (1990). Teachers' knowledge and learning to teach. In W. Houston, M. Haberman, & J. Sikula (Eds.), *Handbook of research on teacher education* (pp. 291–310). New York: Macmillan.

Casanave, C. P., & Schecter, S. R. (Eds.). (1997). *On becoming a language educator: Personal essays on professional development.* Mahwah, NJ: Lawrence Erlbaum.

Cen, Z. (2003). *Findings and understandings: My experience in the Buddy Program.* Retrieved June 17, 2004, from http://www.tap.msu.edu/PDF/zhiwei.pdf

Chickering, A., & Gamson, G. (1987). Seven principles for good practice in undergraduate education. *AAHE Bulletin, 39,* 5–10.

Classroom assessment of teaching and learning. (1998). *CIDR Teaching and Learning Bulletin, 1*(2). Retrieved August 14, 2005, from http://depts.washington.edu/cidrweb /TLBulletins/1(2)ClassroomAssessment.html

Classroom observation. (1998). *CIDR Teaching and Learning Bulletin, 1*(4). Retrieved August 14, 2005, from http://depts.washington.edu/cidrweb/TLBulletins/1(4)Classroom Observation.html

Clayton, M. (2000, September 5). Foreign teaching assistants' first test: The accent. *Christian Science Monitor.* Available from http://www.csmonitorservices.com/csmonitor /archivesearch.jhtml?A-EntryImage

Cole, G., Rawley, L., & Carkin, S. (1985). *Report on the Pilot Instructional Program: Workshop for foreign teaching assistants held at Utah State University.* Unpublished report.

College freshman survival guide [Video]. (1992). McLean, VA: Information Video.

Coming and going—Intercultural transitions for college students [Video]. (2003). Northfield, MN: Carleton College.

Constantinides, J. (Ed.). (1986). *Wyoming Institute on Foreign TA Training working papers: Vol. I.* Laramie, WY: NAFSA Institute on Foreign TA Training.

Constantinides, J. (Ed.). (1987). *Wyoming Institute on Foreign TA Training working papers: Vol. II.* Laramie, WY: NAFSA Institute on Foreign TA Training.

Crandall, J. (1988). *Report on the ESL program* [Internal report]. Pittsburgh, PA: Carnegie Mellon University.

Crandall, J. (1993). Content-centered learning in the United States. *Annual Review of Applied Linguistics, 13,* 111–126.

Crandall, J., & Kaufman, D. (2002). *Content-based instruction in higher education settings.* Alexandria, VA: TESOL.

Crowe, C. (Producer/Director). (1996). *Jerry Maguire* [Motion picture]. United States: Columbia/Tristar.

Crystal, D. (1995). *The Cambridge encyclopedia of the English language.* New York: Cambridge University Press.

Crystal, D. (1997). *English as a global language.* New York: Cambridge University Press.

Darling-Hammond, L. (2001). Forward. In L. Darling Hammond (Ed.), *Studies of excellence in teacher education* (pp. v–xi). Washington, DC: American Association of Colleges for Teacher Education.

Darling-Hammond, L., & Bransford, J. (Eds.). (2005). *Preparing teachers for a changing world.* San Francisco: Jossey-Bass.

Datesman, M. K., Crandall, J., & Kearny, E. N. (2004). *The American ways: An introduction to American culture* (3rd ed.). White Plains, NY: Longman.

Dauer, R. (1993). *Accurate English: A complete course in pronunciation.* Englewood Cliffs, NJ: Prentice Hall Regents.

Di Pietro, R. J. (1987). *Strategic interaction: Learning languages through scenarios.* New York: Cambridge University Press.

Dinerman, M., Feldman, P., & Ello, L. (1999). Preparing practitioners for the professorate. *Journal of Social Work, 18,* 23–32.

Discourse within the disciplines. (1999). Retrieved August 23, 2005, from http://www.iei .uiuc.edu/TESOL/index.html

Donald, J. (2002). *Learning to think: Disciplinary perspectives.* San Francisco: Jossey-Bass.

Dorsey, G. (2000, April 2). A language barrier visits top classes on campus. *Boston Sunday Globe,* p. A13.

Douglas, D., & Myers, C. (1990). *Teaching assistant communication strategies* [Video and instructor's manual]. Ames: Iowa State University.

Dunn, T., & Constantinides, J. (1991). Standardized test scores and placement of international teaching assistants. In J. D. Nyquist, R. D. Abbott, D. H. Wulff, & J. Sprague (Eds.), *Preparing the professoriate of tomorrow to teach* (pp. 413–419). Dubuque, IA: Kendall/Hunt.

Dyck, I., & Forwell, S. J. (1997). Occupational therapy students' first year fieldwork experiences: Discovering the complexity of culture. *Canadian Journal of Occupational Therapy, 64,* 185–196.

Edge, J. (1996). Cross-cultural paradoxes in a profession of values. *TESOL Quarterly, 30,* 9–30.

Edge, J. (2002). *Continuing cooperative development: A discourse framework for individuals as colleagues.* Ann Arbor: University of Michigan Press.

Educational Testing Service (ETS). (1996). *The SPEAK rater training kit.* Princeton, NJ: Author.

Evans, L. (2002). What is teacher development? *Oxford Review of Education, 28,* 123–137.

Fantini, A. (1999). Comparisons: Towards the development of intercultural competence. In J. K. Phillips (Ed.), *Foreign language standards: Linking research, theories, and practices* (pp. 165–218). Lincolnwood, IL: National Textbook Company.

Fishman, J. A., Cooper, R. L., & Conrad, A. W. (1977). *The spread of English: The sociology of English as an additional language.* Rowley, MA: Newbury House.

Fitzgerald, B. (2003, March 28). BU and prospective TAs hook up in virtual interviews. *B.U. Bridge, 1,* 4.

Ford, J., Gappa, L., Wendorff, J., & Wright, D. (1991). Model of an ITA institute. In J. D. Nyquist, R. D. Abbott, D. H. Wulff, & J. Sprague (Eds.), *Preparing the professoriate of tomorrow to teach* (pp. 341–439). Dubuque, IA: Kendall/Hunt.

Fox, M. A., & Hockerman, N. (2003). *Evaluating and improving undergraduate teaching in science, technology, engineering, and mathematics.* Washington, DC: National Academies Press.

Freeman, D. (1996). "To take them at their word": Language data in the study of teachers' knowledge. *Harvard Educational Review, 66,* 732–761.

Freeman, D., & Johnson, K. E. (Eds.). (1998). Research and practice in English language teacher education [Special issue]. *TESOL Quarterly, 32*(3).

Freeman, D., & Richards, J. C. (1996). *Teacher learning in language teaching.* New York: Cambridge University Press.

Gallego, J. C., Goodwin, J., & Turner, J. (1991). ITA oral assessment: The examinee's perspective. In J. D. Nyquist, R. D. Abbott, D. H. Wulff, & J. Sprague (Eds.), *Preparing the professoriate of tomorrow to teach* (pp. 404–412). Dubuque, IA: Kendall/Hunt.

Gebhard, G., & Oprandy, R. (1999). *Language teaching awareness: A guide to exploring beliefs and practices.* New York: Cambridge University Press.

Goffman, E. (1974). *Frame analysis: An essay on the organization of experience.* New York: Harper & Row.

Goode, T. (2001, Fall/Winter). The role of self-assessment in achieving cultural competence. *The Cultural Competence Exchange, 4,* 9.

Goodlad, J. (1990). *Teachers for our nation's schools.* San Francisco: Jossey-Bass.

Goodwin, M. (2000, September 20). TAs should speak English. [Letter to the Editor]. *Daily Campus,* p. 4.

Gorsuch, G. J. (2003). The educational cultures of international teaching assistants and U.S. universities. *TESL-EJ, 7*(3), 1–17. Retrieved June 6, 2005, from http://writing .berkeley.edu/TESL-EJ/ej27/a1.html

Gorsuch, G., Stevens, K., & Brouillette, S. (2003). Collaborative curriculum design for an international teaching assistant workshop. *The Journal of Graduate Teaching Assistant Development, 9*(2), 57–68.

Grant, L. (2001). *Well said: Pronunciation for clear communication* (2nd ed.). Boston: Heinle & Heinle.

Graves, K. (Ed.). (1996). *Teachers as course developers.* New York: Cambridge University Press.

Greene, N., & Shehan, C. (2001). *Evaluation of the Academic Spoken English Program at UF.* Unpublished report, University of Florida at Gainesville, University Center for Excellence in Teaching.

Gumperz, J. J. (1982). *Discourse strategies.* Cambridge, England: Cambridge University Press.

Gumperz, J. J., Jupp, T. C., & Roberts, C. (1979). *Crosstalk* [Video]. London, England: National Center for Industrial Language Training.

Hahn, L., & Dickerson, W. (1999a). *Speechcraft: Discourse pronunciation for advanced learners.* Ann Arbor: University of Michigan Press.

Hahn, L., & Dickerson, W. (1999b). *Speechcraft: Workbook for international TA discourse.* Ann Arbor: University of Michigan Press.

Hahn, L., & Hall, T. (1991). The engineering TA as communication. In J. D. Nyquist, R. D. Abbott, D. H. Wulff, & J. Sprague (Eds.), *Preparing the professoriate of tomorrow to teach* (pp. 191–197). Dubuque, IA: Kendall/Hunt.

Hall, J. K. (2002). *Teaching and researching language and culture.* London: Pearson.

Halleck, G. B., & Moder, C. L. (1995). Testing language and teaching skills of international teaching assistants: The limits of compensatory strategies. *TESOL Quarterly, 29,* 733–758.

Hansen, E. (1998, November). Essential demographics of today's college students. *AAHE Bulletin, 51*(3), 3–5.

Hemmert, A., & O'Connell, G. (1998). *Communicating on campus.* San Francisco: Alta Book Center.

Hiiemae, K., Lambert, L., & Hayes, D. (1991). How to establish and run a comprehensive teaching assistant training program. In J. D. Nyquist, R. D. Abbott, D. H. Wulff, & J. Sprague (Eds.), *Preparing the professoriate of tomorrow to teach* (pp. 123–134). Dubuque, IA: Kendall/Hunt.

Hines, M. (1973). *Skits in English as a second language.* New York: Regents.

Hinofotis, F., Bailey, K., & Stern, S. (1981). Assessing the oral proficiency of prospective foreign teaching assistants: Instrument development. In A. Palmer, P. Groot, & G. Trosper (Eds.), *The construct validation of tests of communicative competence* (pp. 106–126). Washington, DC: TESOL.

Hoekje, B., & Williams, J. (1992). Communicative competence and the dilemma of international teaching assistant education. *TESOL Quarterly, 26,* 243–269.

Hoekje, B., & Williams, J. (1994). Communicative competence as a theoretical framework for ITA education. In C. G. Madden & C. L. Myers (Eds.), *Discourse and performance of international teaching assistants* (pp. 11–26). Alexandria, VA: TESOL.

Huckin, T., & Olsen, L. (1984). The need for professionally oriented ESL instruction in the United States. *TESOL Quarterly, 18,* 273–292.

Hutchinson, T., & Waters, A. (1987). *English for specific purposes: A learning-centred approach.* Cambridge, England: Cambridge University Press.

Illinois General Assembly. (1987). *Higher education, Illinois compiled statue (110ILCS 305/ 7C). University of Illinois Act.* Retrieved on October 21, 2005, from http://www.ilga.gov /legislation/ilcs/ilcs3.asp?ActID=1086&ChapAct=110%26nbsp%3BILCS%26%nbsp %3B305%2F&ChapterID=18&ChapterName=HIGHER+EDUCATION&ActNames= University+of+Illinois+Act%2E

Institute of International Education (IIE) Open Doors. (2004). *Open Doors 2004 data tables: International students in U.S. institutes of higher education.* Retrieved June 6, 2005, from http://opendoors.iienetwork.org/?p=49929

Intercultural Communication Center. (2005). *Robust academic fluency.* Carnegie Mellon University. Retrieved October 20, 2005, from http://www.cmu.edu/icc/languagetraining /robust.shtml

International Teaching Assistant (ITA) Program at the University of Utah. (2005). Salt Lake City: University of Utah, The Graduate School. Retrieved on October 21, 2005, from http://www.utah.edu/ita/

International Teaching Assistant (ITA) Training Program. (1998). *International teaching assistant training at Texas Tech University.* Available from http://www.ttu.edu/ita/

Interstate New Teacher Assessment and Support Consortium (INTASC), Science Standards Drafting Committee. (1992). *Model standards in science for beginning teacher licensing and development: A resource for state dialogue.* Washington, DC: Author.

Interstate New Teacher Assessment and Support Consortium (INTASC), Science Standards Drafting Committee. (2002). *Model standards in science for beginning teacher licensing and development: A resource for state dialogue.* Washington, DC: Author.

Jarvis, C., & Petro, A. (2000). Creating a regional network of ITA programs. *TESOL Matters, 10*(3). Retrieved August 14, 2005, from http://www.tesol.org/s_tesol/sec_ document.asp?CID=195&DID=618

Jenkins, S., & Parra, I. (2003). Multiple layers of meaning in an oral proficiency test: The complementary roles of nonverbal, paralinguistic, and verbal behaviors in assessment decisions. *The Modern Language Journal, 87,* 90–107.

Johnson, D. W., & Johnson, R. T. (1984). *Circles of learning: Cooperation in the classroom.* Alexandria, VA: Association for Supervision and Curriculum Development.

Johnson, J. (1998). *Statistical profiles of international doctoral recipients in science and engineering: Plans to stay in the United States.* Arlington, VA: National Science Foundation.

Johnson, K. E. (1992). The relationship between teachers' beliefs and practices during literacy instruction for non-native speakers of English. *Journal of Reading Behavior 24,* 83–108.

Johnson, K. E. (1999). *Understanding language teaching: Reason in action.* Boston: Heinle & Heinle.

Johnson, K. E. (2000). Innovations in TESOL teacher education: A quiet revolution. In K. E. Johnson (Ed.), *Teacher education* (pp. 1–7). Alexandria, VA: TESOL.

Kachru, B. (1985). Standards, codification, and sociolinguistic realism: The English language in the outer circle. In R. Quirk & H. Widdowson (Eds.), *English in the world: Teaching and learning the language and literature* (pp. 11–30). Cambridge, England: Cambridge University Press.

Kachru, B. (Ed.). (1992). *The other tongue* (2nd ed.). Urbana: University of Illinois Press.

Kachru, Y. (2001). Discourse competence in world Englishes. In A. Thumboo (Ed.), *The three circles of English* (pp. 341–355). Singapore: UnitPress.

Kaufman, D. (2000). Developing professionals: Interwoven visions and partnerships. In K. E. Johnson (Ed.), *Teacher education* (pp. 51–69). Alexandria, VA: TESOL.

Kaufman, D. (2004). Issues in constructivist pedagogy for L2 learning and teaching. *Annual Review of Applied Linguistics, 24,* 303–319.

Kaufman, D., & Brooks, J. G. (1996). Interdisciplinary collaboration in teacher education: A constructivist approach. *TESOL Quarterly, 30,* 231–251.

Kaufman, D., & Brownworth, B. (2002, April). *Partnering pre-service teachers in ITA professional development.* Paper presented at the 36th Annual TESOL Convention, Salt Lake City, UT.

Kaufman, D., & Crandall, J. (2005). *Case studies in content-based instruction in primary and secondary settings.* Alexandria, VA: TESOL.

Kearsley, G. (2001). *Explorations in learning and instruction: The theory into practice database.* Retrieved June 8, 2005, from http://www.gwu.edu/~tip/index.html

Kelley, C., & Meyers, J. E. (1992). *Cross-cultural adaptability inventory (CCAI).* Minneapolis, MN: NCS Pearson.

Kessler, C. (Ed.). (1992). *Cooperative language learning.* Englewood Cliffs, NJ: Prentice Hall Regents.

Kirkpatrick, A. (Ed.). (2002). *Englishes in Asia: Communication, identity, power and education.* Melbourne, Victoria, Australia: Language Australia.

Lackstrom, J. E. (2002). [Notes on USU FTA/ITA workshop]. Unpublished raw data.

Landa, L. N. (1976). *Instructional regulation and control: Cybernetics, algorythmization and heuristics in education.* Englewood Cliffs, NJ: Educational Technology.

Landa, L. N. (1993). Landamatics ten years later [Interview]. *Educational Technology, 33,* 7–18.

Lawrence, M., & Jacobson, W. (2003). A framework for international teaching assistant program changes: Responding to the call for accountability. In W. Davis, J. Smith, & R. Smith (Eds.), *Ready to teach: Graduate teaching assistants prepare for today and for tomorrow* (pp. 177–182). Stillwater, OK: New Forums Press.

Lee, V. (1999). The influence of disciplinary differences on consultations with faculty. *To Improve the Academy, 18,* 278–290.

Lewis, K. (1997). Training focused on postgraduate teaching assistants: The North American model. In *National Teaching and Learning Forum.* Retrieved August 14, 2005, from http://www.ntlf.com/html/lib/bib/lewis.htm

Liao, X. (2001, January/February). What influenced teachers' adoption of the communicative approach in China? *TESOL Matters, 11*(1), 6.

Luckmann, J. (2000). *Transcultural communication in health care.* Albany, NY: Thomson Learning.

MacDonald, R. (1998). What is cultural competency? *British Journal of Occupational Therapy, 61,* 325–328.

Madden, C., & Myers, C. (Eds.). (1994). *Discourse and performance of international teaching assistants.* Alexandria, VA: TESOL.

Maley, A., & Duff, A. (1982). *Drama techniques in language learning: A resource book of communicative activities for language teachers.* New York: Cambridge University Press.

Mangan, K. (2002, May 10). Panic, depression, and settling for second-choice jobs. *The Chronicle of Higher Education,* p. A43.

Martin, J., Nakayama, T., & Flores, L. (1998). *Readings in cultural contexts.* Mountain View, CA: Mayfield.

McArthur, T. (1998). *The English languages.* New York: Cambridge University Press.

McArthur, T. (2002). *The Oxford guide to world English.* Oxford, England: Oxford University Press.

McBride, T., Miller, R., & Nief, R. (n.d.). *Mindset list.* Beloit, WI: Beloit College. Retrieved August 14, 2005, from http://www.beloit.edu/~pubaff/mindset/

McClosky, M. (2003, January/February). EFL standards frameworks in China and Egypt. *TESOL Matters, 13*(1), 3.

McKeachie, W. J. (2002). Vitality and growth throughout your teaching career. In *Teaching tips: Strategies, research, and theory for college and university teachers* (11th ed.; pp. 326–330). Boston: Houghton Mifflin.

McNamara, T. (1996). *Measuring second language performance.* London: Longman.

Meyers, C., & Holt, S. (2001). *Pronunciation for success: Student workbook* (2nd ed.). Burnsville, MN: Aspen Productions.

Miller, J. E., Groccia, J. G., & Miller, M. S. (2001). *Student-assisted teaching: A guide to faculty-student teamwork.* Bolton, MA: Anker.

Miller, M. S. (1996). Creating cross-cultural roommate relationships between American and foreign undergraduates (Doctoral dissertation, University of Kentucky, 1996). *Dissertation Abstracts International, 57-06, Section A,* 2387.

Mirisch, W. (Producer), & Sturges, J. (Director). (1960). *The magnificent seven* [Motion picture]. United States, MGM/UA Video.

Missouri Census Data Center. (2000). *Census 2000: Data products, information, and activities.* Retrieved June 7, 2005, from http://mcdc2.missouri.edu/index.shtml

Mohan, B. A. (1986). *Language and content.* Reading, MA: Addison Wesley.

Mohan, B., Leung, C., & Davison, C. (2001). *English as a second language in the mainstream.* Essex, England: Pearson.

Monk, M., & Meyers, C. (2004, December). Documenting prosodic acquisition using the mirroring project. *As We Speak . . . The Newsletter of TESOL's Speech, Pronunciation, and Listening Interest Section, 2*(1). Retrieved August 14, 2005, from http://www.tesol.org//s_tesol/article.asp?vid=176&DID=3169&sid=1&cid=744&iid=3164&nid=3162

Monoson, P. K., & Thomas, C. F. (1993). Oral English proficiency policies for faculty in U.S. higher education. *The Review of Higher Education, 16,* 127–140.

Mueller, C. (1997). Landamatics: Learning theory of Lev Landa. In *Cyberslang: The ultimate instant online encyclopedia.* Retrieved June 8, 2005, from http://tecfa.unige.ch/staf/staf9698/mullerc/3/landa.html

Murphy, J., & Byrd, P. (2001). *Understanding the courses we teach: Local perspectives on English language teaching.* Ann Arbor: University of Michigan Press.

Murrell, P. C. (2001). *The community teacher: A new framework for effective urban teaching.* New York: Teachers College Press.

Myers, I. B. (1977). *Myers-Briggs type indicator.* Mountain View, CA: Consulting Psychologists Press.

National Board for Professional Teaching Standards (NBPTS). (2001). *Toward high and rigorous standards for the teaching profession* (3rd ed.). Washington, DC: Author.

National Council for Accreditation of Teacher Education (NCATE). (2001). *Professional standards for the accreditation of schools, colleges, and departments of education.* Washington, DC: Author.

National Council of Teachers of Mathematics (NCTM). (2000). *Principles and standards for school mathematics.* Reston, VA: Author.

National Science Foundation. (2000). *Science and engineering indicators 2000.* Arlington, VA: Author. Retrieved August 24, 2005, from http://www.nsf.gov/sbe/srs/seind00/start.htm

Nunan, D. (1988). *The learner-centred curriculum.* Cambridge, England: Cambridge University Press.

Nunan, D. (1992). *Research methods in language learning.* Cambridge, England: Cambridge University Press.

Nunan, D., & Lamb, C. (1996). *The self-directed teacher: Managing the learning process.* Cambridge, England: Cambridge University Press.

Nyquist, J. D., Manning, L., Wulff, D. H., Austin, A. E., Sprague, J., Fraser, P. K., et al. (1999). On the road to becoming a professor: The graduate student experience. *Change, 31*(3), 18–27.

Nyquist, J. D., & Wulff, D. H. (1996). *Working effectively with graduate assistants.* Thousand Oaks, CA: Sage.

Ogami, N. (Producer/Director). (1987). *Cold water* [Video and instructional guide]. (Available from Intercultural Press, P. O. Box 700, Yarmouth, ME)

Pakir, A. (2001). English as a cross-cultural lingua franca: Multiforms, multimedia, multidisciplines. In A. Thumboo (Ed.), *The three circles of English* (pp. 77–90). Singapore: UnitPress.

Papajohn, D. (1998). Reviewing the standard setting for the new Test of Spoken English. *The Journal of Graduate Teaching Assistant Development, 6*(1), 45–52.

Papajohn, D. (2000, June/July). ITA discourse within the disciplines. *TESOL Matters 10*(2). Retrieved June 6, 2005, from http://www.tesol.org/s_tesol/sec_document.asp?TRACKID =&CID=195&DID=609

Papajohn, D. (2002). The standard setting process for the new Test of Spoken English: A university case study. In W. Davis, J. Smith, & R. Smith (Eds.), *Ready to teach: Graduate teaching assistants prepare for today and for tomorrow* (pp. 167–176). Stillwater, OK: New Forums Press.

Papajohn, D. (2005). *Toward speaking excellence: The Michigan guide to maximizing your performance on the TSE test and SPEAK test* (2nd ed.). Ann Arbor: University of Michigan Press.

Papajohn, D., Alsberg, J., Bair, B., & Willenborg, B. (2002). An ESP program for international teaching assistants. In T. Orr (Ed.), *English for specific purposes* (pp. 89–101). Alexandria, VA: TESOL.

Park, P. (2001, October). Managing the scientific multitudes. *The Scientist–The News Journal of the Life Scientist, 15*(19), 31.

Peirce, B. N. (1995). Social identity, investment, and language learning. *TESOL Quarterly, 29,* 9–31.

Pennington, M. (1995). The teacher change cycle. *TESOL Quarterly, 29,* 705–732.

Pennycook, A. (1994). *The cultural politics of English as an international language.* London: Longman.

Perkins, D. N., Schwartz, J. L., West, M. M., & Wiske, M. S. (Eds.). (1995). *Software goes to school: Teaching for understanding with new technologies.* New York: Oxford University Press.

Petro, A. (1999). On culture: Cross-cultural journal assignments. *International Teaching Assistants, 4,* 8–9.

Petro, A. (2000, February/March). Bridging the cultural gap. *TESOL Matters, 10*(1). Retrieved August 14, 2005, from http://www.tesol.org/s_tesol/sec_document.asp?CID =195&DID=599

Petro, A. (2001, November). Undergraduates in ITA programs. *International Teaching Assistants Newsletter, 6*(2), 3–4. Retrieved August 14, 2005, from http://ita-is.org /Newsletters/news0111_petro.html

Pickering, L. (2001). The role of tone choice in improving ITA communication in the classroom. *TESOL Quarterly, 35,* 233–255.

Pickering, L., & Wiltshire, C. (2000). Pitch accent in Indian-English teaching discourse. *World Englishes 19,* 173–183.

Plakans, B. (1997). Undergraduates' experiences with and attitudes towards international teaching assistants. *TESOL Quarterly, 31,* 95–119.

Powell, M. (1996). *Presenting in English.* Hove, England: Language Teaching.

Prabhu, N. S. (1996). Concept and conduct in language pedagogy. In G. Cook & B. Seidlhofer (Eds.), *Principle and practice in applied linguistics: Studies in honor of H. G. Widdowson* (pp. 57–71). Oxford, England: Oxford University Press.

Purnell, L. D., & Paulanka, B. J. (1998). *Transcultural health care: A culturally competent approach.* Philadelphia: F. A. Davis.

Putnam, R., & Borko, H. (2000). What do new views of knowledge and thinking have to say about research on teacher learning? *Educational Researcher, 29*(1), 4–15.

Respect on the line [Video]. (2001). Storrs: University of Connecticut, Center for Instructional Media and Technology.

Richard-Amato, P. A. (2003). *Making it happen: From interactive to participatory language teaching theory and practice* (3rd ed.). White Plains, NY: Pearson.

Rivers, D. (2002). *The seven challenges: A workbook and reader about communicating more cooperatively.* Retrieved October 21, 2005, from http://www.newconversations.net /downloadwkbk.html

Role of the graduate teaching assistant [Video]. (1995). Seattle: University of Washington, Center for Instructional Development and Research.

Ronesi, L. (2001). Training undergraduates to support ESL classmates: The English Language Fellows Program. *TESOL Journal, 10*(2/3), 23–27.

Rubin, D. L. (1992). Non-language factors affecting undergraduates' judgments of nonnative English speaking teaching assistants. *Research in Higher Education, 33,* 511–531.

Sakamoto, N., & Naotsuka, R. (1982). Conversational ballgames. In *Polite fictions: Why Japanese and Americans seem rude to each other* (pp. 80–86). Tokyo, Japan: Kinseido.

Sarkisian, E. (2000). *Teaching American students: A guide for international faculty and teaching assistants in colleges and universities.* Cambridge, MA: Harvard University, Derek Bok Center for Teaching and Learning.

Sarkisian, E., & Maurer, V. (1998). International teaching assistant development and beyond: Out of the program and into the classroom. In M. Marincovich, J. Prostko, & F. Scott (Eds.), *The professional development of graduate teaching assistants* (pp. 163–180). Bolton, MA: Anker.

Schumann, J. H. (1978). The acculturation model for second language acquisition. In R. Gingras (Ed.), *Second language acquisition and foreign language teaching* (pp. 27–50). Arlington, VA: Center for Applied Linguistics.

Seidlhofer, B. (2004). Research perspectives on teaching English as a lingua franca. *Annual Review of Applied Linguistics, 24,* 209–239.

Shaw, P. (1994). Discourse competence in a framework for ITA development. In C. G. Madden & C. L. Myers (Eds.), *Discourse and performance of international teaching assistants* (pp. 27–51). Alexandria, VA: TESOL.

Shaw, P., & Garate, E. (1984). Linguistic competence, communicative needs, and university pedagogy: Toward a framework for TA training. In K. Bailey, F. Pialorsi, & J. Zukowski-Faust (Eds.), *Foreign language teaching assistants in U.S. universities* (pp. 22–40). Washington, DC: NAFSA: Association of International Educators.

Sheridan, J. (1991). A proactive approach to graduate teaching assistants in the research university: One graduate dean's perspective. In J. D. Nyquist, R. D. Abbott, D. H. Wulff, & J. Sprague (Eds.), *Preparing the professoriate of tomorrow to teach* (pp. 24–28). Dubuque, IA: Kendall/Hunt.

Shohamy, E. (2001). *The power of tests: A critical perspective on the uses of language tests.* Essex, England: Pearson.

Shores, C. (2003, March 4). Do not chastise those TAs that are not fluent in English. [Letter to the Editor]. *Daily Campus,* p. 4.

Short, D. (1993). Assessing integrated language and content instruction. *TESOL Quarterly, 27,* 627–656.

Shulman, L. S. (1986). Those who understand: Knowledge growth in teaching. *Educational Researcher, 15*(2), 4–14.

Shulman, L. S. (1987). Knowledge and teaching: Foundations of the new reform. *Harvard Educational Review, 57,* 1–22.

Sinclair, J. M., & Coulthard, M. (1975). *Towards an analysis of discourse: The English used by teachers and pupils.* London: Oxford University Press.

Smith, J. (1994). Enhancing curricula for teaching assistant development. In C. G. Madden & C. L. Myers (Eds.), *Discourse and performance of international teaching assistants* (pp. 52–80). Alexandria, VA: TESOL.

Smith, J., Meyers, C., & Burkhalter, A. (1992). *Communicate: Strategies for international teaching assistants.* Englewood Cliffs, NJ: Regents/Prentice Hall.

Smith, S. M. (1984). *The theater arts and the teaching of second languages.* Reading, MA: Addison Wesley.

Snow, M. A., & Brinton, D. M. (Eds.). (1997). *The content-based classroom: Perspectives on integrating language and content.* White Plains, NY: Longman.

Sridhar, K., & Sridhar, S. N. (1986). Bridging the paradigm gap: Second language acquisition theory and indigenized varieties of English. *World Englishes, 5,* 3–14.

Stake, R. E. (1995). *The art of case study research.* Thousand Oaks, CA: Sage.

Stanley, C. A., & Wiley, J. A. (1998). *A teaching handbook for international TAs at the Ohio State University.* Columbus: Ohio State University, Faculty and TA Development.

Stern, S. (1983). Why drama works: A psycholinguistic perspective. In J. W. Oller & P. Richard-Amato (Eds.), *Methods that work* (pp. 207–225). Rowley, MA: Newbury House.

Stevens, S. G. (1989). A "dramatic" approach to improving the intelligibility of ITAs. *English for Specific Purposes, 8,* 181–194.

Stevick, E. (1976). *Memory meaning and method.* Boston: Heinle & Heinle.

Stewart, E., & Bennett, M. (1991). *American cultural patterns: A cross cultural perspective.* Yarmouth, ME: Intercultural Press.

Stigler, J. W., & Hiebert, J. (1999). *The teaching gap: Best ideas from the world's teachers for improving education in the classroom.* New York: Free Press.

Stoller, F. (2004). Content-based instruction: Perspectives on curriculum planning. *Annual Review of Applied Linguistics, 24,* 261–283.

Storr, R. (1953). *The beginning of graduate education in America.* Chicago: University of Chicago Press.

Teaching in America: A guide for international faculty [Video]. (1993). Cambridge, MA: Harvard University, Derek Bok Center for Teaching and Learning.

TESOL. (2001). *Forward plan.* Alexandria, VA: Author.

TESOL. (2002). *TESOL/NCATE standards for accreditation of initial programs in P–12 ESL education.* Alexandria, VA: Author.

Texas Tech Department of Institutional Research. (2003). *Faculty count by ethnic group: Fall 2003.* Retrieved June 6, 2005, from http://www.irs.ttu.edu/NEWFACTBOOK/2003/Faculty/ETHNIC.htm

Texas Tech Department of Institutional Research. (2004). *Factbook: Enrolled and admitted.* Retrieved October 24, 2005, from http://www.irs.ttu.edu/NEWFACTBOOK/2004/Applied/NEWINDEX.htm

Texas Tech University. (2005). *Operating procedure 32.19: Non-native English speaking faculty and teaching assistants.* Lubbock, TX: Author.

Thiagarajan, S., & Steinwachs, B. (1990). *Barnga: A simulation game on cultural clashes.* Yarmouth, ME: Intercultural Press.

Thomas, C., & Monoson, P. (1991). Issues related to state-mandated English language proficiency requirements. In J. D. Nyquist, R. D. Abbott, D. H. Wulff, & J. Sprague (Eds.), *Preparing the professoriate of tomorrow to teach* (pp. 382–392). Dubuque, IA: Kendall/Hunt.

Thumboo, E. (Ed.). (2001). *The three circles of English.* Singapore: Unit Press.

Tyler, A. (1995). The co-construction of cross-cultural miscommunication: Conflicts in perception. *Studies in Second Language Acquisition, 17,* 129–152.

Tyler, A., & Bro, J. (1993). Discourse processing effort and perceptions of comprehensibility in nonnative discourse. *Studies in Second Language Acquisition, 15,* 507–522.

University of Florida Academic Spoken English (ASE). (2000). *English needs questionnaire.* Retrieved November 4, 2005, from http://ase.ufl.edu/EnglishNeedsQuest.html

University of Florida Graduate School. (2005). *Teaching at the University of Florida.*

Retrieved November 4, 2005, from http://www.teachingcenter.ufl.edu/ta_development .html

University of Florida Graduate School. (2005). *University of Florida Graduate Catalogue.* Retrieved November 4, 2005, from http://gradschool.rgp.ufl.edu/personnel/catalog.html

University of Illinois. (2005). *Services for international graduate teaching assistants (ITAs).* Retrieved on October, 21, 2005, from http://www.cte.uiuc.edu/Did/ITAs/index.htm

University of Missouri–Columbia (UMC) Division of Enrollment Management. (2005a). *Enrollment summary (fall 2004).* Columbia, MO: Curators of the University of Missouri, Division of Enrollment Management. Retrieved November 3, 2005, from http://registrar .missouri.edu/Statistics-Student_Information_and_Reporting/Fall_2004/index.htm

University of Missouri–Columbia (UMC) Division of Enrollment Management. (2005b). *Enrollment summary (fall 2004): International student enrollment.* Columbia, MO: Curators of the University of Missouri, Division of Enrollment Management. Retrieved November 3, 2005, from http://registrar.missouri.edu/Statistics-Student_Information _and_Reporting/Fall_2004/international_student_enrollment.htm

University of Missouri–Columbia (UMC) Division of Enrollment Management. (2005c). *Enrollment summary (fall 2004): Campus enrollment.* Columbia, MO: Curators of the University of Missouri, Division of Enrollment Management. Retrieved November 3, 2005, from http://registrar.missouri.edu/Statistics-Student_Information_and_Reporting /Fall_2004/campus_enrollment.htm

University of Missouri–Columbia (UMC) Division of Enrollment Management. (2005d). *Table 5: Fall enrollments by level, 1983–2004.* Columbia, MO: Curators of the University of Missouri, Division of Enrollment Management. Retrieved November 3, 2005, from http://registrar.missouri.edu/Statistics-Student_Information_and_Reporting/resources /04Enroll/page13.html

University of North Carolina at Chapel Hill, Center for Teaching and Learning. (1997). *Diversity in the college classroom.* Retrieved August 14, 2005, from http://www.unc.edu /depts/ctl/tfitoc.html

University of Washington study of undergraduate learning (UW SOUL). (2001). Retrieved August 14, 2005, from http://www.washington.edu/oea/soul.htm

Via, R. A. (1976). *English in three acts.* Honolulu: University Press of Hawaii.

Weimer, M., Svinicki, M., & Bauer, G. (1989). Designing programs to prepare TAs to teach. In J. D. Nyquist, R. D. Abbott, & D. H. Wulff (Eds.), *Teaching assistant training in the 1990s* (pp. 57–70). San Francisco: Jossey-Bass.

Wells, S. A. (1993). *Developing multicultural competency: An education and resource manual for educators and practitioners.* Rockville, MD: The American Occupational Therapy Association.

Wennerstrom, A. (1989). *Techniques for teachers: A guide for nonnative speakers of English.* Ann Arbor: University of Michigan Press.

What students want [Video]. (1993). Cambridge, MA: Harvard University, Derek Bok Center for Teaching and Learning.

Wick, D. (Producer), & Nichols, M. (Director). (1998). *Working girl* [Motion picture]. United States, Twentieth Century Fox.

Wilson, A. (1993). The promise of situated cognition. In S. Merriam (Ed.), *An update on adult learning theory* (pp. 71–79). San Francisco: Jossey-Bass.

Wulff, D., Nyquist, J. D., & Abbott, R. (1991). Developing a TA training program that reflects the culture of an institution: TA training at the University of Washington. In J. D. Nyquist, R. D. Abbott, D. H. Wulff, & J. Sprague (Eds.), *Preparing the professoriate of tomorrow to teach* (pp. 113–122). Dubuque, IA: Kendall/Hunt.

Yin, R. K. (1994). *Case study research: Design and methods* (2nd ed.). Thousand Oaks, CA: Sage.

Young, R., & He, A. W. (Eds.). (1998). *Talking and testing: Discourse approaches to the assessment of oral proficiency.* Philadelphia: John Benjamins.

Zamel, V., & Spack, R. (Eds.). (2002). *Enriching ESOL pedagogy: Readings and activities for engagement, reflection, and inquiry.* Mahwah, NJ: Lawrence Erlbaum.

Zeichner, K., & Gore, J. (1990). Teacher socialization. In W. Houston, M. Haberman, & J. Sikula (Eds.), *Handbook of research on teacher education* (pp. 329–348). New York: Macmillan.

Zhou, Y. (2001). *Landamatics.* Retrieved December 1, 2005, from http://64.233.161.104 /search?q=cache:yqMsWMtR3MkJ:www.personal.psu.edu/users

Zukowski-Faust, J. (1984). Problems and strategies: An extended training program for foreign teaching assistants. In K. Bailey, F. Pialorsi, & J. Zukowski-Faust (Eds.), *Foreign language teaching assistants in U.S. universities* (pp. 76–86). Washington, DC: NAFSA: Association of International Educators.

Index

Note: Page numbers followed by letters *f* and *t* refer to figures and tables, respectively.

A

Abel, D., 84
Abbott, R., 73
Academic fluency, robust, 171
Accent modification course, 98–99
Accurate English (Dauer), 154
Active learning, 144
Adler, N., 87
Administrative partnerships, 145–146
Affective factors, in language acquisition, 156
Ahluwalia, S., 98, 100, 101
Alsberg, J., 138
Alsop, A. 167
Althen, G., 87
Ambrose, S., 73
American Association for the Advancement of Science (AAAS), 5
American Council for the Teaching of Foreign Languages (ACTFL), 5
Angelo, T., 46, 100
Ard, J., 9
Arnold, J., 156
Assessment. *See also* Screening procedures
  evaluation forms for
    for interview, 91*t*
    for microteaching, 134
    for peer review, 133
    for presentation, 75*t,* 78–80
  of microteaching, 74–76, 75*t,* 87
  multiple forms of, 21–22
  quantitative and qualitative analyses in, 77*t*

  as recommendation material, 88–89
  of teaching skills
    argument against, 72–73
    argument for, 72
    discrimination in, 72–73
    issues concerning, 71–72
  troubleshooting observations, 101
Austin, A. E., 45
Austin, E., 45
Authentic voice, 128

B

Bachman, L., 72, 76
Bagchi, A., 158
Bailey, K., 69, 71, 72
Bailey, K. M., 2, 6
Bair, B., 138
Bakhtin, M. M., 9
Barker, K., 98, 100, 101
Bauer, G., 72, 73
Beatty, K., 11
Bennett, M., 87
Benson, P., 5
Blackboard use, 76, 142
Borjas, G., 1, 9, 84
Borko, H., 41
Boston University, ITA program
  in academic-year, 88–89
  background of, 83–84
  orientation program in
    assessment in, 86–87
    content of, 87–88
    schedule of, 85*t*
  teaching requirements for ITAs in, 89
Bransford, J. D., 5, 11, 44
Breaks and intermissions, 142